Best Science and Technology Reference Books for Young People

Best Science and Technology Reference Books for Young People

by H. Robert Malinowsky

ORYX PRESS
1991

The rare Arabian Oryx is believed to have inspired the myth of the unicorn. This desert antelope became virtually extinct in the early 1960s. At that time several groups of international conservationists arranged to have 9 animals sent to the Phoenix Zoo to be the nucleus of a captive breeding herd. Today the Oryx population is nearly 800, and over 400 have been returned to reserves in the Middle East.

Copyright © 1991 by The Oryx Press
4041 North Central at Indian School Road
Phoenix, Arizona 85012-3397

Published simultaneously in Canada

Printed and Bound in the United States of America

The paper used in this publication meets the minimum requirements of American National Standard for Information Science—Permanence of Paper for Printed Library Materials, ANSI Z39.48, 1984.

Library of Congress Cataloging-in-Publication Data

Malinowsky, H. Robert (Harold Robert), 1933–
  Best science and technology reference books for young people / by H. Robert Malinowsky.
     p. cm.
  Includes bibliographical references and index.
  Summary: Guide lists reference books in physical, applied, and natural sciences and technology for readers from elementary school age to young adults. Includes prices, where reviewed, annotations, and subject terms.
  ISBN 0-89774-580-9 (alk. paper)
  1. Science—Juvenile literature—Bibliography. 2. Technology-
-Juvenile literature—Bibliography. 3. Children's literature-
-Bibliography. 4. Bibliography—Best books—Science.
5. Bibliography—Best books—Technology. 6. Reference books-
-Bibliography. [1. Science—Bibliography. 2. Technology-
-Bibliography. 3. Reference books—Bibliography. 4. Bibliography-
-Best books.] I. Title.
Z7401.M277 1991
[Q163]   90-48595
016.5—dc20   CIP

CONTENTS

PREFACE

Best Science and Technology Reference Books for Young People is a guide to 669 science and technology reference books for children and young people (third grade through high school), including preteens, teens, adolescents, and young adults, and for those individuals responsible for purchasing these books in libraries. It includes some older, well-established titles that may be out of print, older books still in print, newer editions, and newer books that have not been completely tested by time. The criteria for inclusion of a title were flexible. The choices were made by applying my knowledge of the subjects and the books themselves to the reviews in *Science and Technology Annual Reference Review (STARR)*, and to reviews included in *Reference Books Bulletin* and in *American Reference Books Annual (ARBA)*. Other guides to science and technology literature were also scanned to identify a core list of titles. The original list has been reviewed, refined, revised, and updated to ensure that a good cross-section has been selected. After the list was compiled, each title was searched for complete bibliographical data, including price and where reviewed; annotations were written; and subject terms identified. Books that covered broad subjects or areas were chosen over those that were narrowly defined, especially in the area of field guides. Attempts to set a reasonable price ceiling were difficult; some excellent reference books are limited by their high cost to the few libraries able to afford them. Nevertheless, they were included, especially if they were very favorably reviewed. Some difficult choices had to be made in areas where there were large numbers of books published, such as botany, zoology, and geology.

USING THIS BOOK

This is a multi-purpose book. It can guide a student who scans the necessary chapters or searches the indexes to find a book that will serve the needed purpose. After identifying a particular book or books, the student can check the library to see if the selected title(s) are available. Teachers and librarians can use the book as a collections development guide or an assessment guide. Holdings of a particular library can be noted in the book so that patrons using the book will know what is available. For newer books, *Best Science and*

Technology Reference Books for Young People provides those who are responsible for buying books with necessary ordering information, including reviews. It is ideally suited for school and public libraries, but could also be useful in college or university libraries that support education departments at their institutions.

Also included in this book are other guides to the literature which will be of additional help in selecting books that are not specifically reference works. Obviously, no one library will have all the listed books, so many titles have been included that basically cover the same topic. No indication is given as to which of the books listed on a particular topic is best. The fact that a book is listed here indicates its acceptability. If, for instance, a library has two out of six dictionaries on a particular subject, it is not necessary to acquire the other four unless funds are available and some of the other titles are newer.

BIBLIOGRAPHICAL ENTRIES

The entries for the books contained in this guide are arranged by broad subjects into 12 chapters: **General Science, Astronomy, Mathematics/Computer Science, Physics, Chemistry, Earth Sciences, General Biology, Botany, Zoology, Technology/Engineering, Energy/ Environment/Ecology,** and **Medical Sciences.** Within each chapter the books are further arranged by the following types of publications: **Atlas—Medical, Atlas—Science, Bibliography, Biographical Source, Catalog, Dictionary, Directory, Encyclopedia, Field Book, Glossary, Guide, Guide to the Literature, Handbook, History, How-to-do-it Book, Index, Manual, Table, Textbook, Yearbook/Annual/Almanac.** Finally, the books are arranged alphabetically by title within each type of publication.

Each title has some or all of the following information: 1) Title (and subtitle, if appropriate); 2) Edition; 3) Author(s), Editor(s), and Compiler(s); 4) City and State or Country of Publication; 5) Name of Publisher (and parent company if appropriate); 6) Year of Publication (if it is a new printing the copyright date is given in parentheses); 7) Collation Information (including indication of pages, volumes, il- lustrations, tables, charts, maps, glossaries, and indexes); 8) ISBN or ISSN (*pbk* is added to ISBNs of paperbacks; some older books may not have an ISBN); 9) Price (The price indicated is the latest price found at the time of editing, but this may not be the current price. Consult *Books in Print* or contact the publisher for latest price. Also, discounts are not considered. If the book is out of print, it is so indicated. Keep in mind that books go out of print on a regular basis and even though a price is given the book may now be out of print. If both hard copy and paperback are available, prices are given for both with *pbk* added to the paperback price); 10) Series Statement; 11) Annotation (annotations are purposely brief, with an indication of the book's coverage and any special features that it may have); 12) Grade Level indicating which grades the book is appropriate for, including 3-5 (elementary school), 6-8 (middle school), 9-12 (high school and young adult), or whether the book is suitable as a teacher's/librarian's resource; and 13) Sources of Book Reviews (the letter codes used for these sources are listed below in the section "Sources of Reviews"); some books do not have book review sources listed. (See below.)

SOURCES OF REVIEWS

As part of the bibliographical citation, codes for sources of reviews are indicated. These codes are identified below and give the full name of the reviewing source and its address. Only selected sources are cited; in some cases, many other sources are available. To locate other sources, consult the *Book Review Index* (a bimonthly publication with cumulations in April, August, and December, and an annual cumulation, published by Gale Research, Inc.). In addition to this source, one can search indexing and abstracting journals, such as the *Science Citation Index*, for specific reviews. Also, there are instances where, at the time of editing this volume, a review for a new edition was not available. In these cases, reviews for previous editions have been cited if available.

These sources for reviews have been included as an aid to selectors who need to have a published review of a book before it is purchased. The number of reviews a book receives is an indication of how well publicized the book was, and could be equated in some cases to how good the book is. Some books, especially older and very new titles, do not have reviews. This does not mean that the book is unacceptable. Sometimes review copies of books never reach the reviewing sources. Following is a list of reviewing sources arranged by the code that identifies that source in the citations.

Reviewing Sources

ALib—*American Libraries*
American Library Association
50 E. Huron St.
Chicago, IL 60611

**ARBA—*American Reference
    Books Annual***
Libraries Unlimited, Inc.
P.O. Box 3988
Englewood, CO 80155-3988

**ASBYP—*Appraisal: Science
    Books for Young People***
605 Commonwealth Ave.
Boston, MA 02215

BL—*Booklist*
American Library Association
50 E. Huron St.
Chicago, IL 60611

BRpt—*Book Report*
5701 N. High St., Ste. 1
Worthington, OH 43085

BW—*Book World*
Washington Post
1150 15th St. N.W.
Washington, DC 20071

BWatch—*Bookwatch*
166 Miramar Ave.
San Francisco, CA 94112

CBRS—*Children's Book Review
Service*
220 Berkeley Place
Brooklyn, NY 11217

CCB-B—*Center for Children's
Books, Bulletin*
University of Chicago Press
Journals Division
P.O. Box 37005
Chicago, IL 60637

Choice—*Choice*
100 Riverview Center
Middletown, CT 06457

CSM—*Christian Science
Monitor*
P.O. Box 11202
Des Moines, IA 50340-1202

CurR—*Curriculum Review*
407 S. Dearborn
Chicago, IL 60605

Kliatt—*Kliatt Young Adult
Paperback Book Guide*
425 Watertown St.
Newton, MA 02158

KR—*Kirkus Reviews*
Kirkus Service, Inc.
200 Park Ave. S.
New York, NY 10003

LJ—*Library Journal*
P.O. Box 1977
Marion, OH 43305-1977

NewTechBks—*New Technical
Books*
New York Public Library
5th Ave. & 42nd St.
New York, NY 10018

PW—*Publishers Weekly*
P.O. Box 1979
Marion, OH 43302

RefBkR—*Reference Book Review*
P.O. Box 190954
Dallas, TX 75219

R&RBkN—*Reference & Research
Book News*
5600 N.E. Hassalo St.
Portland, OR 97213

RSR—*Reference Services Review*
Pierian Press
P.O. Box 1808
Ann Arbor, MI 48106

SA—*Scientific American*
415 Madison Ave.
New York, NY 10017

SB—*Science Books & Films*
P.O. Box 3000, Dept. SBF
Denville, NJ 07834

SchLib—*School Librarian*
School Library Association
Liden Library, Barrington Close
Liden, Swindon SN3 6HF
England

SciTech—*SciTech Book News*
5600 N.E. Hassalo St.
Portland, OR 97213

SerR—*Serials Review*
Pierian Press
P.O. Box 1808
Ann Arbor, MI 48106

SLJ—*School Library Journal*
P.O. Box 1978
Marion, OH 43305-1978

SLMQ—*School Library Media Quarterly*
American Library Association
50 E. Huron St.
Chicago, IL 60611

S&T—*Sky & Telescope*
Sky Publishing Corp.
P.O. Box 9111
Belmont, MA 02178-9111

STARR—*Science and Technology Annual Reference Review*
Oryx Press
4041 N. Central
Phoenix, AZ 85012-3397

VOYA—*Voice of Youth Advocates*
Scarecrow Press, Inc.
52 Liberty St.
P.O. Box 4167
Metuchen, NJ 08840

WCRB—*West Coast Review of Books*
Rapport Publishing Co., Inc.
5265 Fountain Ave.
Upper Terrace
Hollywood, CA 90029

WLB—*Wilson Library Bulletin*
H.W. Wilson Co.
950 University Ave.
Bronx, NY 10452

INDEXES

The first of the four indexes is the Title Index covering all titles, distinctive subtitles, previous titles of older editions, and series titles. The second is the Name Index, which includes all authors, editors, compilers, and corporate bodies identified in the bibliographical entries or in the body of the annotation. The third is the Subject Index, which includes both very general and specific terms. Most synonymous terms have their own entries; cross-references are not used. The final index lists books by grade level groups: Grades 3-5 (elementary), Grades 6-8 (middle school), Grades 9-12 (high school and young adult), and Teacher's/Librarian's Resources.

ACKNOWLEDGMENTS

I would like to thank the many individuals at Oryx Press for their patience in preparing this book, especially John Wagner. What had originally appeared to be an easy task developed into a lengthier job in order to produce a useful book for young people. Needless to say, some titles may have been overlooked and some titles included may be questioned. If that is the case I would appreciate written suggestions so that future editions can be made even more complete. I would like to thank the University of Illinois at Chicago Library for its encouragement to publish and for giving me the time to work on this book. Finally, I would like to thank Charles Crumet for his patience during the time I spent huddled over the terminal inputting all the data, neglecting some of the day-to-day living activities.

GENERAL SCIENCE

The term "science" encompasses a large body of knowledge that is characterized by its ability to make precise statements that can be tested and proven. It can be divided into "exact science," which includes such disciplines as physics, chemistry, mathematics, and part of astronomy, and "descriptive science," which includes geology, biology, astronomy, medical science, and agriculture. Of course, some aspects of all descriptive sciences are exact, so that the two distinctions become somewhat clouded. The phrase "physical science" separates such disciplines as physics, chemistry, and astronomy from engineering or technology, which are "applied sciences."

Physical science includes the following disciplines and all of their subfields: *astronomy, biology, chemistry, geology, meteorology, mineralogy,* and *physics.* Mathematics is usually included in the physical sciences even though it is really the language that permits communication in the physical, applied, and medical sciences. Agriculture is both a physical and applied science, but is more applied.

Reference works in general science include any materials that cover two or more of the subfields of science. They may even cover applied science. Almost every type of reference work is represented. For access to the journal literature, two Wilson indexes have been included. The first, *General Science Index,* covers just the physical sciences and indexes materials that are commonly found in public and large school libraries. *Applied Science and Technology Index* is primarily an applied science index, but its coverage of physics, chemistry, and geology makes it an appropriate title to be included in this chapter. For reviews of books in science and technology, the most used source is *Science Books and Films.*

Encyclopedias and dictionaries are many, varied, and sometimes expensive. For those who can afford it, the *McGraw-Hill Encyclopedia of Science and Technology* is well established and includes a yearbook as well as numerous spin-offs in special subject disciplines. The *McGraw-Hill Dictionary of Scientific and Technical Terms* is also recommended. The smaller, less-expensive encyclopedias and dictionaries included in this chapter are fairly up-to-date and are revised on a regular basis. For general science purposes, a title four or five years old will be adequate, leaving the subject disciplines to have the more current materials. *Chambers Science and Technology Dictionary* is very good. The *Dictionary of the Physical Sciences, The Encyclopedic Dictionary of Science,* and the *Young People's Science Dictionary* are also recommended. For encyclopedias, consider *Illustrated Ency-*

clopedia of Science and Invention: How It Works, The New Illustrated Science and Invention Encyclopedia, and volumes one and two of the *Oxford Illustrated Encyclopedia*. Facts on File has a 25-volume set called *The World of Science*, which is also very good.

Science fairs are of interest to students and teachers and the *Science Fair Project Index* is intended to help in locating ideas. The National Science Resource Center publishes *Science for Children: Resources for Teachers*, an excellent resource guide for teachers, as well as *Teaching Science to Children: A Resourcebook* and *The Best Science Books & A-V Materials for Children: An Annotated List of Science and Mathematical Books, Films, Filmstrips, and Videocassettes*. Two chronologies, which can serve as histories, are recommended—*Breakthroughs: A Chronology of Great Achievements in Science and Mathematics, 1200-1930* and *Milestones in Science and Technology: The Ready Reference Guide to Discoveries, Inventions, and Facts.*

Bibliographies

1. The Best Science Books & A-V Materials for Children: An Annotated List of Science and Mathematics Books, Films, Filmstrips, and Videocassettes
Susan M. O'Connell; Valerie J. Montenegro; Kathryn Wolff.
Washington, DC: Association for the Advancement of Science; 1988.
335p., index. $20.00. 0-87168-316-4.
This bibliography contains close to 1,200 books and audiovisual materials that are either "recommended" or "highly recommended." It is arranged in classified order with complete bibliographic information and the original review from *Science Books & Films*. *Grade Level:* Grades 3–5. Grades 6–8. Teacher's/Librarian's Resource.

2. Discovering Nature with Young People: An Annotated Bibliography and Selection Guide.
Carolyn M. Johnson, comp. Westport, CT: Greenwood Press; 1987.
495p., index. $49.95. 0-313-23823-5.
Over 2,400 entries are grouped into five major parts: written works for young people, audiovisual items for young people, items for educators and parents, selection sources, and activity supplies and aids. Included are fiction and nonfiction works on animals, plants, earth science, astronomy, wilderness areas and national parks, biographies of persons with backgrounds in these fields, and works relating to the enjoyment and appreciation of nature. *Grade Level:* Grades 3–5. Grades 6–8. Teacher's/Librarian's Resource.
ALib, May 88, p.407; BRpt, September 88, p.50; R&RBkN, June 88, p.30; STARR, 89, n.56.

3. The Museum of Science and Industry Basic List of Children's Science Books 1973-1984.
Bernice Richter; Duane Wenzel, comps. Chicago, IL: American Library Association; 1985. 154p., index. $9.75pbk. 0-8389-3294-0.
This is a descriptive and evaluative list of children's books in the areas of science. The titles are arranged alphabetically within broad subject categories and include full bibliographical citation, annotation, evaluation, and references to citations in selected reviewing sources. There are annual updates. *Grade Level:* Grades 3-5. Grades 6-8. Teacher's/ Librarian's Resource.
ARBA, 86, n.1415, 89, n.1346; BL, 15 March 86, p.1071.

4. Science Books and Films.
Washington, DC: American Association for the Advancement of Science; 1965-. v. 1- , index. Quarterly. $20.00 per year. 0098-342X.
This is a selective reviewing publication of books for children in the areas of science. It also includes films. The reviews can be critical and indicate level of audience. *Grade Level:* Grades 3-5. Grades 6-8. Grades 9-12. Teacher's/Librarian's Resource.

5. Science Books for Children: Selections from *Booklist*, 1976-1983.
Denise Murcko Wilms, ed. Chicago, IL: American Library Association; 1985. 183p., index. $15.00pbk. 0-8389-3312-2pbk.
This is an alphabetically arranged, main entry list of books that have been reviewed in *Booklist*. Full bibliographic information is given, along with age or grade level, and an annotation. *Booklist*, which stresses school materials, is one of the major reviewing publications for books at all levels. *Grade Level:* Grades 3-5. Grades 6-8. Grades 9-12. Teacher's/Librarian's Resource.
ARBA, 86, n.1416; SLJ, December 85, p.16.

6. Teaching Science to Children: A Resourcebook.
Mary D. Iatridis. New York, NY: Garland; 1986. 110p., index. $28.00. 0-8240-8747-X.
The four chapters of this annotated bibliography cover science textbooks for elementary schools, science activity books, general science books, and science books for special education. Many of the materials are adult in content but still are recommended for use in schools. *Grade Level:* Grades 3-5. Grades 6-8. Teacher's/Librarian's Resource.
ARBA, 87, n.327; BL, 15 January 87, p.770.

Biographical Sources

7. Asimov's Biographical Encyclopedia of Science and Technology: The Lives and Achievements of 1,510 Great Scientists from Ancient Times to the Present Chronologically Arranged.
2nd revised. Isaac Asimov. New York, NY: Doubleday; 1982. 941p., illus., index. $29.95. 0-385-17771-2.

This biographical source contains over 1,510 entries, chronologically arranged. Each biography stresses the achievements of the individual. The table of contents lists the biographees alphabetically; the index covers only subjects and persons mentioned in the text. *Grade Level:* Grades 6–8. Grades 9–12.
ARBA, 84, n.1243; BL, 1 September 84, p.31; KR, 1 January 72, p.64; LJ, July 82, p.1314; LJ, 1 March 83, p.449; SB, January 83, p. 149; SLJ, May 83, p.25.

8. Biographical Dictionary of Scientists.
David Abbott, ed. New York, NY: Harper and Row; 1983–1985. 6v., illus., index. $28.00 per volume. 0-911745-80-7, v.1; 0-911745-82-3, v.2; 0-911745-81-5, v.3; 0-911745-79-3, v.4; 0-87226-009-7, v.5; 0-87226-008-9, v.6.
This is a well-written biographical source for scientists and engineers. The six volumes cover astronomers, biologists, chemists, engineers and inventors, mathematicians, and physicists. Over 200 biographies are included in each volume, arranged alphabetically by name. *Grade Level:* Grades 9–12.
ARBA, 86, n.1418–1421, 87, n.1378–1379; BL, 1 June 85, p. 1380; Choice, February 85, p. 791, September 86, p.78, July 86, p.1651; LJ, 15 March 85, p.52; SB, May 85, p.295, September 85, p.31, September 86, p.72, January 86, p.147; SciTech, May 86, p.5.

9. A Biographical Dictionary of Scientists.
3rd. Trevor I. Williams, ed. New York, NY: Halsted Press; 1982. 704p. $29.95. 0-470-27326-7.
This dictionary covers deceased scientists, technologists, inventors, and explorers from ancient times to the present in the fields of agriculture, astronomy, biochemistry, botany, chemistry, geology, mathematics, medicine, physics, technology, and all branches of engineering. Bibliographical references are provided at the end of each biographical sketch. *Grade Level:* Grades 9–12.
ARBA, 76, n.1330; Choice, June 75, p.516; LJ, Spring 69, p.47; SB, September 69, p.106; WLB, October 76, p.126.

10. Scientists and Inventors.
Anthony Feldman; Peter Ford. New York, NY: Facts on File; 1986. 352p., illus. (part in color), index. $24.95. 0-87196-410-4.
This small biographical encyclopedia contains over 150 scientists and inventors. The entries are arranged chronologically and each one covers a two-page spread that includes a portrait, a picture or diagram of the scientific principle or the equipment or product discovered or invented, and, in some cases, a photograph of a contemporary application of the invention. *Grade Level:* Grades 9–12.
ARBA, 80, n.1325; BL, 15 February 80, p.804; BL, 1 July 80, p.1631; LJ, 1 November 79, p.2362; SB, May 80, p.256; WLB, January 80, p.331.

11. Who's Who in Nobel Prize Winners.
2nd. Bernard S. Schlessinger; June H. Schlessinger. Phoenix, AZ: Oryx Press; 1991. 256p., index. $39.50. 0-89774-599-X.
The 593 entries are arranged chronologically, and then by prize category. Each entry contains information on the type of prize and year it was awarded; birth and death dates; names of parents, spouses, and children; nationality; religion; education; career highlights; selected publications; selected references; and brief commentary on why the person won the prize. *Grade Level:* Grades 9–12.
ARBA, 88, n.33.

Dictionaries

12. Chambers Science and Technology Dictionary.
New. Peter M.B. Walker, ed. New York, NY: Cambridge University Press; 1988. 1,008p. $39.50. 1-85296-150-3.
Over 45,000 entries in this comprehensive dictionary cover all areas of science and technology, including chemistry, engineering, botany, zoology, medical science, physics, architecture, behavioral science, computing, building, mathematics, biology, paper making, electronics, telecommunications, textiles, and printing. *Grade Level:* Grades 9–12.
ARBA, 89, n.1348; LJ, 1 November 88, p.90; STARR, 90, n.323.

13. Concise Dictionary of Science.
Robin Kerrod. New York, NY: Arco; 1985. 253p., illus. $11.95. 0-668-06514-1.
This general science dictionary for school children contains over 3,000 entries in the fields of physics, chemistry, geology, astronomy, and technology. It is well-written, understandable, and accurate. *Grade Level:* Grades 6–8. Grades 9–12.
ARBA, 86, n.1428; Choice, March 86, p.1038; LJ, 15 February 86, p.173; LJ, 1 March 86, p.50.

14. Concise Science Dictionary.
New York, NY: Oxford University Press; 1984. 758p., illus. $22.50. 0-19-211593-6.
This is a good general dictionary of some 7,000 terms in the fields of physics, chemistry, biology, earth sciences, astronomy, mathematics, and computing. The terms are concise, accurate, and easy to understand. *Grade Level:* Grades 9–12.
ALib, March 85, p.195; ARBA, 86, n.1425; Choice, May 85, p.1303; SL, Summer 85, p.229.

15. Dictionary of Physical Sciences.
John Daintith, ed. New York, NY: Pica Press; 1977. 333p., illus. $9.95. 0-87663-723-3.
This is a general dictionary of terms in physics, chemistry, and astronomy as well as electronics, computer science, and mathematics. Definitions are concise but accurate. *Grade Level:* Grades 9–12.

ARBA, 78, n.1207; BL, 1 November 77, p.490; Choice, December 77, p.1338; LJ, August 77, p.1625; SB, December 77, p.137.

16. A Dictionary of Scientific Units: Including Dimensionless Numbers and Scales.
5th. H.G. Jerrard; D.B. McNeill. New York, NY: Chapman and Hall/ Methuen; 1986. 222p., index. $39.95, $19.95pbk. Science Paperbacks, no. 210. 0-412-28090-6, 0-412-28100-7pbk.

This well-established dictionary contains 850 entries covering scientific units in all areas of science pertaining to measurement both past and current. Appendices include a table of fundamental physical constants, conversion tables, and details of standardization committees and associations. *Grade Level:* Grades 9–12.

ARBA, 87, n.1722; SB, May 87, p.302.

17. Dictionary of the Physical Sciences: Terms, Formulas, Data, Tables.
Cesare Emiliani. New York, NY: Oxford University Press; 1987. 365p. $35.00. 0-19-503651-4.

This good, readable general dictionary of physical science covers earth sciences, physics, chemistry, and astronomy. The definitions are concise, accurate, and understandable for the layperson. *Grade Level:* Grades 9–12.

ARBA, 88, n.1728; Choice, December 87, p.598; SB, January 88, p.143; SciTech, October 87, p.5.

18. The Encyclopedic Dictionary of Science.
Candida Hunt; Monica Byles, eds. New York, NY: Facts on File; 1988. 256p., illus. (part in color), maps. $29.95. 0-8160-2021-3.

This general science dictionary covers physics, chemistry, environmental science, biology, and medicine. It also contains some brief biographical information. *Grade Level:* Grades 6–8. Grades 9–12.

ARBA, 89, n.1350; BL, 1 May 89, p.1514; SB, May 89, p.287; STARR, 90, n.325.

19. The Facts on File Dictionary of Science.
6th. E.B. Uvarov; Alan Isaacs. New York, NY: Facts on File; 1986. 468p., illus. $21.95. 0-8160-1386-1.

Published earlier as the *Penguin Dictionary of Science*, this dictionary includes almost 7,000 entries in the fields of physics, chemistry, mathematics, and astronomy, with some additional terms from interdisciplinary sciences. The definitions are clear and concise. *Grade Level:* Grades 6–8. Grades 9–12.

ARBA, 87, n.1386; BL 1 January 87, p.769; R&RBkN, Summer 86, p.18; SB, January 87, p.168.

20. Hammond Barnhart Dictionary of Science.
Robert K. Barnhart; Sol Steinmetz. Maplewood, NJ: Hammond; 1986. 740p., illus. $24.95. 0-8437-1689-4.

This dictionary of over 16,000 entries covers the physical and biological sciences. The definitions are concise and accurate and include pronunciation, parts of speech, field of study where the term is used, word origin, and associated terms. *Grade Level:* Grades 9–12.
ASBYP, Spring 87, p.11; BRpt, May 87, p.48; Choice, March 87, p.1030; LJ, 1 March 87, p.35.

21. Longman Illustrated Science Dictionary: All Fields of Scientific Language Explained and Illustrated.
Arthur Godman. New York, NY: Longman; 1982 (c1981). 255p., color illus., index. $7.95. 0-582-55645-7.
This dictionary of about 1,500 basic scientific terms is divided into three main groups—physics, chemistry, and biology. All other subjects are found within these three groups and include meteorology, astronomy, geology, health, and hygiene. Since it is not alphabetically arranged there is an index. *Grade Level:* Grades 6–8. Grades 9–12.
ARBA, 84, n.1230; Choice, April 82, p.1046; LJ, 15 May 82, p.982, 1 March 83, p.449.

22. McGraw-Hill Dictionary of Science and Engineering.
Sybil P. Parker, ed. New York, NY: McGraw-Hill; 1984. 942p. $32.50. 0-07-045483-3.
This is a dictionary of 36,000 terms from some 100 scientific and engineering disciplines. The definitions are concise, readable, and accurate. The terms have been taken from the *McGraw-Hill Dictionary of Scientific and Technical Terms.* *Grade Level:* Grades 9–12.
ARBA, 85, n.1332; BL, 15 January 85, p. 703; Choice, November 84, p.405; LJ, 1 March 85, p.42; SB, March 85, p.196; SciTech, October 84, p.1; WLB, September 84, p.67.

23. McGraw-Hill Dictionary of Scientific and Technical Terms.
4th. Sybil P. Parker, ed. New York, NY: McGraw-Hill; 1989. 2,088p., illus. $70.00. 0-07-045270-9.
This is a well-established science and technology dictionary of over 100,100 terms and 117,500 definitions. Definition are usually from three to eight lines long and use language from the specialty of the word or phrase being defined. They are clear, concise, and technical enough for the researcher but not too technical for the layperson. *Grade Level:* Grades 9–12.
STARR, 90, n.326.

24. Penguin Dictionary of Science.
6th. E.B. Uvarov; Alan Isaacs, eds. New York, NY: Penguin; 1986. 544p., illus., tables. $7.95. 0-14-051156-3.
This is an alphabetical, word-by-word listing of over 5,000 entries in the fields of astronomy, biology, biochemistry, cosmology, mathematics, physics, and space science. The definitions are concise. *Grade Level:* Grades 9–12.
BL, 15 November 73, p.298; Choice, May 73, p.434; SR, 25, November 72, p.75.

25. Scientific Words: Their Structure and Meaning.
Walter Edgar Flood. Westport, CT: Greenwood Press; 1974 (c1960).
220p. $22.50. 0-8371-7541-0.
This useful reference work is an alphabetical listing of word-elements (roots, prefixes, and suffixes) that enter into the formation of scientific terms, with a definition of each element and an illustration of how that element is used in a word. *Grade Level:* Grades 9–12.

26. What's What: A Visual Glossary of the Physical World.
Reginald Bragonier, Jr.; David Fisher. New York, NY: Ballantine Books; 1982 (c1981). 565p., illus., index. $9.95. 0-345-30302-4.
This dictionary of general information about the physical world is well-written, concise, and intended for school and public library use. *Grade Level:* Grades 6–8. Grades 9–12.
ARBA, 83, n.58; BL, 1 April 82, p.988; Choice, March 82, p.888; LJ, 1 February 82, p.248, 15 May 82, p.958; WLB, February 82, p.477.

27. Young People's Science Dictionary.
Chicago, IL: Children's Press; 1985. 2v., color illus. $11.95.
0-516-00274-0.
This dictionary provides clear, concise definitions for basic scientific terms and concepts. Following the main text is information on the planets, Greek alphabet, mammals of the world, plants and their uses, and scientists. *Grade Level:* Grades 6–8. Grades 9–12.
CSM, 10 June 65, p.11.

Encyclopedias

28. Asimov's Chronology of Science and Discovery.
Isaac Asimov. New York, NY: Harper & Row, Publishers; 1989.
707p., tables, charts, index. $29.95. 0-06-015612-0.
This Asimov book covers the history of science from its beginning to 1988, arranged chronologically. It is well-written in layperson's terms and includes both a subject and name index. *Grade Level:* Grades 6–8. Grades 9–12.
BL, 15 October 89, p.410; LJ, 1 October 89, p.113.

29. Concise Encyclopedia of the Sciences.
John David Yule, ed. New York, NY: Van Nostrand Reinhold; 1982 (c1978). 590p., illus. $19.95. 0-442-29208-2.
This is the American edition of the British book *Phaidon Concise Encyclopedia of Science and Technology.* The book is intended to be a compact and easy-to-use dictionary of the most commonly used words in science and technology. There are biographical sketches for about 1,000 persons prominent in science. *Grade Level:* Grades 9–12.
BL, 15 October 81, p.328; LJ, 1 April 81, p.783; SB, January 83, p.127.

30. Illustrated Encyclopedia of Science and Invention: How It Works.
Donald Clarke, ed. New York, NY: Marshall Cavendish; 1987. 20v.,
color illus., index. $300.00. 0-8630-7491-X.

This good general encyclopedia of applied science and technology for
school children emphasizes machines or discoveries that are around us
every day. Biographies are included. The entries are arranged alphabetically from the first volume to the last. The excellent illustrations are an outstanding feature. *Grade Level:* Grades 6–8. Grades
9–12.

LJ, 1 February 78, p.374; 1 April 78, p.723; PW, 17 October 77, p.74.

31. Illustrated Fact Book of Science.
Michael W. Dempsey, ed. New York, NY: Arco; 1983. 232p., illus.
(part in color), index. $9.95. 0-668-05729-7.

This book was originally published as the *Rainbow Fact Book of
Science* and contains over 35 sections describing the various areas of
science. The information is brief but gives a good indication of what
science covers. *Grade Level:* Grades 6–8. Grades 9–12.

ARBA, 85, n.1337.

32. Let's Discover Library.
2nd. Milwaukee, WI: Raintree; 1986. 16v., color illus., bibliog., index.
$313.00, $229.50 to schools. 0-8172-2575-7.

This is a thematically arranged children's encyclopedia of science and
social science covering animals, the earth and sea, ancient peoples,
prehistoric times, customs, occupations, the human body, sports and
entertainment, machines, transportation, and outer space. The text is
well-written and illustrated and each volume has a glossary, further
reading, questions to think about, projects, and an index. Volume 16
of the set is a master index. *Grade Level:* Grades 3–5. Grades 6–8.

ARBA, 87, n.55; BL, 15 February 87, p.881.

33. The Marshall Cavendish Library of Science Projects.
Steve Parker; Peter Lafferty. Freeport, NY: Marshall Cavendish;
1988–1989. 2 sets of 6v. each, color illus. $68.95 per set of 6v.
0-86307-624-6, set 1; 1-85435-175-3, set 2.

These two sets cover several science projects that can be done in
elementary and secondary schools. They include very good instructions
and have excellent illustrations. The 1988 set covers: "Water";
"Plants"; "Mechanics"; "Light"; "Earth"; and the "Human Body." The
1989 set covers: "Electricity and Magnetism"; "Weather"; "Heat";
"Fossils"; "Astronomy"; and "Communications." *Grade Level:* Grades
3–5. Grades 6–8. Grades 9–12. Teacher's/Librarian's Resource.

STARR, 89, n.89, 226, 227, 281, 404, 405.

34. McGraw-Hill Concise Encyclopedia of Science and Technology.
2nd. Sybil P. Parker, ed. New York, NY: McGraw-Hill; 1989.
2,222p., illus. (part in color), tables, charts, index. $110.00.
0-07-045512-0.

Although somewhat expensive, this excellent one-volume science encyclopedia has been created by extracting "the essential text from each article in the parent work while retaining the same proportionality between subjects," with the parent work being the *McGraw-Hill Encyclopedia of Science and Technology*. *Grade Level:* Grades 9–12.
CBR, May 89, p.22; STARR, 90, n.334.

35. McGraw-Hill Encyclopedia of Science and Technology.
6th. New York, NY: McGraw-Hill; 1987. 20v., illus. (part in color), index. $1,600.00, $1,440.00 to institutions. 0-07-079292-5.
Although expensive for most school libraries, this is the best of the general science and technology multi-volume encyclopedias. All major articles are signed. Most long articles begin with a definition of the subject, followed by a detailed discussion of certain aspects of a given topic and a brief bibliography. It is supplemented by the *McGraw-Hill Yearbook of Science and Technology* and numerous one-volume subject spin-offs. *Grade Level:* Grades 9–12.
BL, 15 September 87, p.118; LJ, August 87, p.116; RSR, Fall 84, p.9; WLB, September 87, p.94.

36. The New Illustrated Science and Invention Encyclopedia.
New York, NY: Marshall Cavendish; 1988. 27v., illus. (part in color), maps, index. $399.95. 0-86307-491-X.
This is a good general science and technology encyclopedia with numerous colored illustrations and diagrams. The text is very appropriate for school libraries. It was previously called *Growing Up with Science: The Illustrated Encyclopedia of Invention*. Of particular use is the thematic index which includes scientific milestones and a glossary. *Grade Level:* Grades 3–5. Grades 6–8.

37. Oxford Illustrated Encyclopedia: Volume 1—The Physical World; Volume 2—The Natural World.
Vivian Fuchs; Malcolm Coe, eds. New York, NY: Oxford University Press; 1985. 2v., illus. (part in color). $35.00 per volume.
0-19-869129-7, v.1; 0-19-869134-3, v.2.
These are the two science volumes of the eight-volume set of the *Oxford Illustrated Encyclopedia*. Each volume is alphabetically arranged. The articles are brief but accurate and supplemented with many illustrations and photographs. Biographical entries are included. *Grade Level:* Grades 9–12.
ARBA, 86, n.58-59; BL, 15 June 86, p.1520; Choice, February 86, p.852; LJ, 1 March 86, p.88; SchLib, March 86.

38. Science and Technology Illustrated: The World Around Us.
Chicago, IL: Encyclopaedia Britannica; 1984. 28v., color illus., index. $289.00. 0-85229-425-5.
There are some 1,240 alphabetically arranged articles in this general science encyclopedia for children. The articles are well-written and accurate. There are no biographies of scientists and inventors. Since the book is intended to give an overview, it does not include many

specific articles on individual animals. *Grade Level:* Grades 6–8. Grades 9–12.
ARBA, 86, n.1429; BL, 15 November 85, p.474.

39. Science Universe Series: An Illustrated Encyclopedia.
New York, NY: Arco; 1984. 8v., illus. (part in color), index. $79.60.
0-668-06175-8.
This is a very good topical encyclopedia for schools, with each volume covering a particular aspect of science and technology: "Exploring Space and Atoms"; "Language and Communication"; "Sight, Light, and Color"; "Energy, Forces, and Resources"; "Machines, Power and Transportation"; "Measuring and Computing"; "Earth, Sea, and Sky"; and "Patterns of Life on Earth." The book is well-written and contains excellent illustrations. The British edition is called *Cambridge Science Series. Grade Level:* Grades 6–8. Grades 9–12.
ARBA, 86, n.1430; BL, July 85, p.1536.

40. Van Nostrand's Scientific Encyclopedia.
7th. Douglas M. Considine, ed. New York, NY: Van Nostrand
Reinhold; 1989. 2v., illus., bibliog., index. $175.00. 0-442-21750-1.
Although this encyclopedia is now somewhat expensive for school libraries, it is still considered a reliable, authoritative, and comprehensive reference tool. Its emphasis is on the physical sciences, including animal life, biosciences, chemistry, earth and atmospheric sciences, energy sources and power technology, mathematics and information sciences, materials and engineering sciences, medicine, anatomy and physiology, physics, plant sciences, and space and planetary sciences. *Grade Level:* Grades 9–12.
BL, 1 May 89, p.1526; SB, May 89, p.287; STARR, 90, n.335.

41. The World Book Encyclopedia of Science.
New. Chicago, IL: World Book; 1989. 8v., color illus., maps, glossary, tables, charts, index. $120.00. 0-7166-3212-8.
Each of the eight volumes of this general science encyclopedia covers a different area of science: Volume 1, "The Heavens"; Volume 2, "Physics Today"; Volume 3, "Chemistry Today"; Volume 4, "The Planet Earth"; Volume 5, "The Plant World"; Volume 6, "The Animal World"; Volume 7, "The Human Body"; and Volume 8, "Men and Women of Science," which also includes a comprehensive index. Within each volume the information is arranged topically rather than alphabetically. The text is well-written, not too technical, and supplemented with good illustrations. *Grade Level:* Grades 6–8. Grades 9–12.
BL, 1 December 86, p.555.

42. The World of Science.
New York, NY: Facts on File; 1984–86. 25v., illus. (part in color), index. $9.95 per volume.
This beautifully illustrated encyclopedia is intended for school children. Each well-written volume is meant to stand alone and can be purchased separately. Each volume is arranged by topic and has its own index. There is no overall index. The 27 volumes cover all areas

of science and technology; each volume is authored separately. *Grade Level:* Grades 6–8. Grades 9–12.
ARBA, 86, n.1440.

43. Young People's Science Encyclopedia.
National College of Education, ed. Chicago, IL: Children's Press; 1985. 20v., color illus., index. $265.35. 0-516-00100-0.
This excellent general science encyclopedia for schools contains nearly 4,000 alphabetically arranged entries with emphasis on the plant and animal kingdoms. The text is well-written and intended to stimulate the reader. Some 200 suggested experiments and projects are included. *Grade Level:* Grades 6–8.
BL, April 72, p.633; CuR, February 86, p.78; SB, May 71, p.18..

Guides

44. Bioscientific Terminology: Words from Latin and Greek Stems.
Donald M. Ayers. Tucson, AZ: University of Arizona Press; 1972. 325p., bibliog. $6.95. 0-8165-0305-2.
The first part of this book covers bioscientific words derived from Greek and the second with those from Latin. It is not a dictionary of Greek and Latin prefixes and suffixes but rather a textbook presentation on how to form scientific terms. Hundreds of examples are given with definitions. *Grade Level:* Grades 9–12.
ARBA, 73, n.1410; Choice, December 72, p.1277; SB, December 72, p.211.

45. More Science for You: 112 Illustrated Experiments.
Bob Brown. Blue Ridge Summit, PA: TAB; 1988. 124p., illus. $12.95, $7.70pbk. 0-8306-9125-1, 0-8306-3125-9pbk.
A small book of scientific experiments for school-aged children. Explanations are concise and clear with good illustrations. An excellent book for science fair project ideas. *Grade Level:* Grades 3–5. Grades 6–8. Grades 9–12. Teacher's/Librarian's Resource.
SB, May 89, p.298; STARR, 90, n.336; VOYA, April 89, p.52.

46. Quick Scientific Terminology.
Kenneth Jon Rose. New York, NY: Wiley; 1988. 267p., illus., index. $12.95pbk. 0-471-85763-7pbk.
This is a guide or textbook that instructs the user in how scientific terminology is developed in the various scientific disciplines. There are numerous examples and tests to see how well the material is learned. *Grade Level:* Grades 9–12.
SB, May 89, p.287; STARR, 90, n.337.

Guides to the Literature

47. Core List of Books and Journals in Science and Technology.
Russell H. Powell; James R. Powell, Jr, eds. Phoenix, AZ: Oryx Press; 1987. 144p., index. $38.50. 0-89774-275-3.

The purpose of this book is to "bring together prime choices of English-language books and journals in the areas of contemporary science and technology." It covers agriculture, astronomy, biology, chemistry, computer science, engineering, geology, mathematics, and physics with only those books that have been published in the 1980s. *Grade Level:* Grades 9–12. Teacher's/Librarian's Resource.

ARBA, 88, n.1435; BL, 15 March 88, p.1232; Choice, March 88, p.1120; R&RBkN, February 88, p.25; SciTech, January 88, p.30; STARR, 89, n.253.

48. Science for Children: Resources for Teachers.
National Science Resources Center. Washington, DC: National Academy Press; 1988. 176p., illus., index. $7.95. 0-309-03934-7.

This excellent resource guide is divided into three sections. The first section covers curriculum materials, giving for each entry full bibliographical information, price, and annotation. The second section gives supplementary resources: "Science Activities Books," "Books on Teaching Sciences," "Science Book Lists and Other References," and "Magazines for Children and Teachers." The final section gives information on museums, professional associations, science curriculum projects, publishers, and suppliers of science materials. This is an excellent guide to the literature and a directory of information. *Grade Level:* Grades 3–5. Grades 6–8. Grades 9–12. Teacher's/Librarian's Resource.

Choice, May 89, p.1500; Instructor, March 89, p.53; LJ, 15 March 89, p.68; SB, May 89, p.274.

Histories

49. Asimov's New Guide to Science.
Isaac Asimov. New York, NY: Basic Books; 1984. 940p., illus., bibliog., index. $29.95. 0-465-00473-3.

This is a revised edition of *Asimov's Guide to Science*, a popular history of science that appeals to the layperson who has little or no formal background in the sciences. *Grade Level:* Grades 6–8. Grades 9–12.

50. Breakthroughs: A Chronology of Great Achievements in Science and Mathematics, 1200-1930.
Claire L. Parkinson. Boston, MA: G.K. Hall; 1985. 576p., illus., bibliog., index. $29.95. 0-8161-8706-1.

This is an excellent chronology with the entries under specific years or short historical periods. In addition to listing the event or publication, the author briefly discusses the significance of the discovery or publication and links it to older and future developments. This book is intended to arouse the reader to do further research. *Grade Level:* Grades 9–12.
ARBA, 86, n.1743; Choice, February 86, p.852; LJ, 1 March 86, p.50; SB, September 86, p.47; WLB, December 85, p.61.

51. Milestones in Science and Technology: The Ready Reference Guide to Discoveries, Inventions, and Facts.
Ellis Mount; Barbara A. List. Phoenix, AZ: Oryx Press; 1987. 152p., bibliog., index. $35.00. 0-89774-260-5.
This encyclopedic work covers basic discoveries and inventions in all areas of science and technology. It is arranged alphabetically by the name of the invention or the discovery followed by a brief description of the topic, including dates the event occurred, names of the people involved, and the nationalities of the persons named. *Grade Level:* Grades 9–12.
BL, 1 April 88, p.1324; Choice, April 88, p.1223; LJ, 1 March 88, p.32; SLJ, May 88, p.33; STARR, 89, n.251; VOYA, April 88, p.52; WLB, January 88, p.102.

How-to-do-it Books

52. Simple Science Experiments with Everyday Materials.
Muriel Mandell. New York, NY: Sterling Publishing Co; 1989. 128p., illus., index. $11.95. 0-8069-6794-3.
More than 100 ideas for science experiments are included in this compact guide. All experiments are explained in short passages and accompanied with at least one drawing. Each experiment contains step-by-step outlines of materials needed, equipment required, methods for setting up the experiment, results, and further explanations. *Grade Level:* Grades 6–8. Grades 9–12.

Indexes

53. Applied Science and Technology Index.
New York, NY: H.W. Wilson; 1913–. index. Monthly. Service basis. 0003-6986.
From 1913 to 1957 this title was known as the *Industrial Arts Index*. It is a subject index to English-language periodicals that cover both the theoretical sciences and their engineering applications. It includes pure physics, chemistry, geology, engineering, computer technology, mathematics, transportation, and other related fields. It is arranged by subject with each article providing title, name of periodical, volume,

paging, date, and author. There is a separate section of book reviews. *Grade Level:* Grades 9–12.
ARBA, 85, n.1340; RSR, Winter 86, p.77; SerR, October 77, p.26.

54. General Science Index.
New York, NY: H.W. Wilson; 1978–. index. Monthly. Service basis. 0162-1963.

This cumulative subject index to a core collection of English-language periodicals covers the subject areas of astronomy, atmospheric science, biology, botany, chemistry, earth sciences, environment and conservation, food and nutrition, genetics, mathematics, medicine and health, microbiology, oceanography, physics, physiology, psychology, and zoology. It is arranged by subject and has a book review section. *Grade Level:* Grades 9–12.
ARBA, 82, n.1415; Choice, April 79, p.202; RSR, October 79, p.14; WLB, January 79, p.409.

55. Science Experiments Index for Young People.
Mary Anne Pilger. Englewood, CO: Libraries Unlimited; 1988. 239p. $35.00. 0-87287-671-3.

This guide indexes science experiments and demonstrations that appear in 694 elementary and intermediate science books for the years 1941–1988. First arranged alphabetically by subject, each entry has a description, a book number, and the pages in the book where the experiment is explained. The second section is a list of the book references by book number. *Grade Level:* Grades 3–5. Grades 6–8. Teacher's/Librarian's Resource.
ARBA 89, n.1360; BL, 1 June 89, p.1709; SciTech, January 89, p.5; SLJ, May 89, p.25; STARR, 90, n.351; WLB, March 89, p.117.

56. Science Fair Project Index, 1960–72, 1973–80, 1981–84.
Metuchen, NJ: Scarecrow; 1975–1986. 3v., bibliog. $47.50 per volume. 0-8108-0783-1, 1960–72; 0-8108-1605-9, 1973–80; 0-8108-1892-2, 1981–84.

The sources in which specific mathematical, scientific, and technological projects are indexed on a regular basis are included in this index. Janet Y. Stoffer edited the 1960–72 volume; Cynthia Bishop and Deborah Crowe edited the 1981–84 volume; and the Science and Technology Division of the Akron-Summit County Public Library compiled the 1973–80 volume. The volumes are arranged alphabetically by subject and designed for students and teachers in schools or with such organizations as 4H Clubs and Scouts. *Grade Level:* Grades 3–5. Grades 6–8. Grades 9–12. Teacher's/Librarian's Resource.
ARBA, 87, n.1395; R&RBkN, Winter 87, p.22; SB, January 87, p. 282; SLJ, May 87, p.25; VOYA, February 87, p.306.

Yearbooks/Annuals/Almanacs

57. The Facts on File Scientific Yearbook.

Margaret DiCanio, ed. New York, NY: Facts on File; 1985–. illus. (part in color), index. Annual. $27.50. 0883-0800.

Published since 1985, this well-written and illustrated annual reviews recent scientific milestones in unsigned articles. It is well-indexed and includes lists of the winners of major scientific awards and prizes for the year under review. *Grade Level:* Grades 6–8. Grades 9–12.

ARBA, 89, n.1355; BRpt, January 89, p.49; R&RBkN, August 88, p.26; SB, January 89, p.154.

58. McGraw-Hill Yearbook of Science and Technology.

New York, NY: McGraw-Hill; 1962–. illus. (part in color), bibliog., index. Annual. $46.00.

This comprehensive yearbook updates the *McGraw-Hill Encyclopedia of Science and Technology*. The articles are all signed and cover the key advances, discoveries, and developments in science and technology during the year. It also contains major review articles on topics of broad interest and growing significance. *Grade Level:* Grades 9–12.

ARBA, 76, n.1317; SB, May 79, p.14.

59. Science Year: The World Book Science Annual.

Chicago, IL: World Book; 1965–. illus., bibliog., index. Annual. $19.95.

This annual update of science events is intended for school children. Each article is signed and there are excellent illustrations. *Grade Level:* Grades 6–8. Grades 9–12.

ARBA, 80, n.1320; BL, 1 July 81, p.1407; SB, September 87, p.26.

60. Science Year: The World Book Annual Science Supplement.

Chicago, IL: World Book, Inc; 1965–. color illus., bibliog., index. Price varies according to type of institution. 0080-7621.

This annual supplements the *World Book Encyclopedia* and contains special reports and short scientific articles of recent events in science. *Grade Level:* Grades 6–8. Grades 9–12.

ASTRONOMY

Astronomy, the fascinating physical science that has interested people for hundreds of years, is the study of all the forces and objects outside the earth and its atmosphere. Young people have always had an interest in astronomy, coming partly from the intrigue of looking through a telescope at distant planets and moons and partly from the prolific science fiction literature. Today, space probes, both with and without human crews, have greatly increased this interest in outer space. *Observational astronomy* is that branch of the science that covers any type of visual observation of planets, stars, galaxies, nebulae, moons, comets, or meteors, whether by the unaided eye, by the simplest telescope, or by the highly sophisticated Hubble telescope that was placed into orbit around the earth by the shuttle crew in 1990. *Theoretical astronomy* is tied closely to physics and mathematics and concerns itself with the theories of how the universe was created, the motions of the heavenly bodies, and the predictions of what has and what will happen derived from astronomical observations.

There are many highly specialized subfields of astronomy. *Astrophysics* is a growing field of research that applies modern physics to the problems of astronomy. *Photometry* is concerned with calculations and measurement of light or its time rate of flow, a primary consideration in calculating distances of stars and the age of the universe. Another important process for measurement uses gamma rays or electromagnetic radiation. As a result of this process, there is a subfield of astronomy called *gamma-ray astronomy.* *Infrared astronomy* studies the electromagnetic spectrum in the one micrometer to plus one millimeter wavelength. Another electromagnetic wave is the X-ray, and the subfield of *X-ray astronomy* exists because all astronomic objects in the universe emit X-rays. Finally, the field of *cosmology* theorizes about the origin of the universe.

The reference materials for astronomy are voluminous, and many older materials are still used today. Because astronomy is popular with young people, this chapter includes a large number of these reference works. Excellent star charts or star atlases, field guides, manuals, and handbooks abound. Atlases exist for every planet, for earth's moon, and for some of the moons of other planets. A representative number have been included, such as *Atlas of the Planets, Cambridge Photographic Atlas of the Planets*, and *New Atlas of the Universe.* Field guides include star charts with additional information on how to observe a particular heavenly body, the best time to observe it, and, in some cases, how to photograph it. Patrick Moore is a prolific writer on popular astronomy with numerous atlases, handbooks, and field guides, such as *Pocket Guide to Astronomy* and *Amateur Astronomer* (a handbook and a textbook) to his credit. Other good handbooks include the identically titled (and frequently confused) *Amateur Astronomer's Handbook* by James Muirden and *Amateur Astronomer's Handbook* by John Benson Sidgwick. The *Facts on File Dictionary of Astronomy* and *Longman Illustrated Dictionary of Astronomy and Astronautics: The Terminology of Space* are two good dictionaries. McGraw-Hill has a good spin-off encyclopedia, *McGraw-Hill Encyclopedia of Astronomy,* but Richard S. Lewis's *Illustrated Encyclopedia of the Universe: Exploring and Understanding the Cosmos* is also very good. Finally, the *Yearbook of Astronomy* is a small annual full of practical information for the amateur astronomer on motions of stars and planets, eclipses, and setting times of the moon and sun.

Atlases—Science

61. Atlas of the Planets.
Paul Doherty. New York, NY: McGraw-Hill; 1980. 143p., illus. (part in color), bibliog., index. $18.95. 0-07-017341-9.
This handbook/atlas for amateur observers provides observational history, observing hints, detailed descriptions of planetary features, nomenclature, and other useful information for each planet. The material is presented in clear, interesting, and highly readable text. The author has furnished drawings of each planet as seen through the telescope, and imagined scenes, such as planetary landscapes, based on current knowledge. *Grade Level:* Grades 9–12.
ARBA, 81, n.1380; BL, 1 September 84, p.40; Choice, November 80, p.418; LJ, 1 October 80, p.2093.

62. Cambridge Photographic Atlas of the Planets.
Geoffrey Briggs; Fredric Taylor. New York, NY: Cambridge University Press; 1988 (c1986). 246p., illus. (part in color), maps. $32.50, $11.96pbk. 0-521-23976-1, 0-521-31058-Xpbk.
This well-illustrated and documented atlas of the planets contains numerous high quality photographs. *Grade Level:* Grades 6–8. Grades 9–12.
BL, 1 November 82, p.343; BRpt, May 87, p.51; Choice, March 83, p.953; LJ, 1 March 83, p.444; SB, March 83, p.190; SchLib, March 83, p.77.

63. Color Star Atlas.
Patrick Moore. New York, NY: Crown; 1973. 112p., index. Out-of-print. 0-517-51403-6.

Now out-of-print, this beginner's star atlas has excellent star maps and constellation charts. It also includes an introductory text on theory, stellar types, and galaxies. *Grade Level:* Grades 6–8. Grades 9–12.

64. National Geographic Picture Atlas of Our Universe.
Revised. Roy A. Gallant; Margaret Sedeen. Washington, DC:
National Geographic Society; 1986. 276p., illus. (part in color), maps, index. $18.95. 0-87044-357-7.
This well-written and beautifully illustrated picture atlas of astronomy is meant for the amateur. It begins with an informative history of astronomy, including the development of astronomical instruments. The individual members of the solar system are then covered, followed by the stars and galaxies, including stellar evolution, radio astronomy, and black holes. *Grade Level:* Grades 9–12.
ARBA, 82, n.1421; ASBYP, Fall 82, p.24; BL, 15 January 81, p.684, 15 October 83, p.369; SB, November 81, p.92; S&T, May 81, p.440.

65. New Atlas of the Universe.
2nd. Patrick Moore. New York, NY: Crown; 1984. 271p., illus.
$40.00. 0-517-55500-X.
This good general atlas for the amateur covers the universe with clear charts and illustrations that are easy to follow. Its previous title was *Concise Atlas of the Universe. Grade Level:* Grades 9–12.
SB, September 85, p.17; ST, June 85, p.17.

66. Norton's Star Atlas and Reference Handbook.
17th. Arthur P. Norton. New York, NY: Wiley; 1986. 116p., illus.
$29.95. 0-470-20678-0.
One of the best known star atlases, *Norton's* is used by the amateur as well as the professional. The first edition was published in 1910. Almost all objects are listed, including stars of the seventh magnitude. It also contains over 300 named features on the moon and 128 on the planet Mars. *Grade Level:* Grades 9–12.
S&T, February 65, p.107.

67. Patrick Moore's Color Star Atlas.
Patrick Moore. New York, NY: Crown; 1973. 112p., illus. (part in color), index. Out-of-print. 0-517-31403-6.
A small, now out-of-print, atlas for the amateur with excellent star maps and constellation charts. The introductory chapters cover theory, stellar types, and the galaxies. *Grade Level:* Grades 9–12.
ARBA, 75, n.1448; Choice, July 74, p.784; LJ, August 74, p.1927; WLB, April 74, p.674.

68. Rand McNally New Concise Atlas of the Universe.
Patrick Moore. Chicago, IL: Rand McNally; 1978. 190p., illus. (part in color), maps, index. Out-of-print. 0-528-83031-7.
Rand McNally has long been known as a producer of excellent atlases. This one on the universe is now out-of-print. More an encyclopedia than an atlas, it is divided into four parts: "Atlas of the Earth from

Space," "Atlas of the Moon," "Atlas of the Solar System," and "Atlas of the Stars." *Grade Level:* Grades 9–12.
ARBA, 80, n.1331; BL, 15 Octobrer 79, p.370; Choice, March 79, p.58; LJ, 1 February 79, p.394; SB, December 79, p.144; S&T, March 79, p.289; WLB, January 79, p.407.

Biographical Sources

69. Astronomical Scrapbook: Skywatchers, Pioneers, and Seekers in Astronomy.
Joseph D. Ashbrook. Leif J. Robinson, ed. New York, NY: Cambridge University Press; 1984. 468p., illus., bibliog. $19.95. 0-521-30045-2.
This interesting book is a general biographical account of individuals who have figured prominently in the history of astronomy. *Grade Level:* Grades 9–12.
ST, May 85, p.417; SB, November 85, p.85; WCRB, September 85, p.34, November 85, p.43.

70. Wild Abyss: The Story of the Men Who Made Modern Astronomy.
Gale E. Christianson. New York, NY: Free Press; 1978. 461p., illus. Out-of-print. 0-02-905380-3.
This is a respected biographical encyclopedia with biographies and stories of the astronomers who have figured in modern astronomy. It is, unfortunately, now out-of-print. *Grade Level:* Grades 9–12.
Choice, July 78, p.712; KR, December 77, p.1299; LJ, 1 February 78, p.374; PW, 26 December 77, p.62; SB, March 79, p.214; SLJ, September 78, p.171; S&T, September 78, p.243.

Catalogs

71. Messier Catalogue.
Charles Messier. P.H. Niles, ed. Clifton Park, NJ: Auriga; 1981. 52p. $1.50. 0-9602738-2-4.
This is a translation of Charles Messier's 1787 catalog listing star clusters, galaxies, and nebulae with descriptions and tables of their right ascensions and declinations. This famous list is often used by amateur astronomers who want to observe each of Messier's clusters and nebulae. *Grade Level:* Grades 9–12.
ARBA, 83, n.1277.

72. Messier's Nebulae and Star Clusters.
Kenneth Glyn Jones. New York, NY: American Elsevier; 1969 (c1968). 480p., illus., bibliog., index. Out-of-print.

This catalog describes in detail all of the objects found in Messier's 1787 catalog. It gives both historical and biographical information about the objects plus information about the astronomers who identified the objects. Illustrations, star charts, and classifications are included. *Grade Level:* Grades 9–12.
Choice, October 69, p.1036; SB, December 69, p.224; S&T, September 69, p.183, November 69, p.335.

Dictionaries

73. Dictionary of Astronomy: Terms and Concepts of Space and the Universe.
Iain Nicolson. New York, NY: Barnes and Noble; 1980 (c1977). 249p., illus., bibliog. $4.95. 0-06-463524-4.
This dictionary of scientific terminology and concepts provides good coverage, accurate information, and useful diagrams. It discusses such topics as intelligent life in the universe. *Grade Level:* Grades 9–12.
ARBA, 81, n.1381; Kliatt, Winter 81, p.58.

74. Dictionary of Astronomy, Space, and Atmospheric Phenomena.
David F. Tver. New York, NY: Van Nostrand Reinhold; 1979. 281p., illus., tables. $19.95. 0-442-24045-7.
This general dictionary contains brief definitions of terms pertaining to astronomy, space, atmospheric phenomena, physics, and mathematicals. *Grade Level:* Grades 9–12.
ARBA, 80, n.1333; BL, 15 July 80, p.1695; Choice, April 80, p.206; SB, September 80, p.14; SLJ, December 80, p.21; WLB, February 80, p.399.

75. Facts on File Dictionary of Astronomy.
2nd. Valerie Illingworth, ed. New York, NY: Facts on File; 1987 (c1985). 437p., illus. $19.95, $12.95pbk. 0-8160-1357-8, 0-8160-1892-8pbk.
This dictionary contains over 2,300 entries, along with more than 85 diagrams and illustrations and 12 tables as appendices. It gathers into one book most of the astronomical data and terminology a nonspecialist is likely to require. The definitions are clear and usually succinct, ranging from a line or two up to a page or more. *Grade Level:* Grades 6–8. Grades 9–12.
Kliatt, September 88, p.55; STARR, 89, n.50; VOYA, October 88, p.211.

76. Glossary of Astronomy and Astrophysics.
2nd revised and enlarged. Jeanne Hopkins. Chicago, IL: University of Chicago Press; 1980. 196p. $17.50. 0-226-35171-8.
This is a comprehensive and accurate dictionary of over 2,000 astronomical, astrophysical, and related physical and chemical terms. Although intended for the professional, it is also of use to the student and layperson. *Grade Level:* Grades 9–12.

ARBA, 82, n.1422; BL, 1 September 84, p.40; Choice, September 76, p.798; SB, November 81, p.73.

77. Key Definitions in Astronomy.
Jacqueline Mitton. Totowa, NJ: Littlefield, Adams; 1982 (c1980).
168p., illus., tables. $4.95. 0-8226-0375-6.
Only 230 words and phrases are included in this dictionary, but they are the "key" words that are encountered in popular reading. The definitions are detailed and easy to comprehend. *Grade Level:* Grades 6–8. Grades 9–12.
ARBA, 83, n.1275; WLB, December 82, p.350.

78. Longman Illustrated Dictionary of Astronomy and Astronautics: The Terminology of Space.
Ian Ridpath. New York, NY: Longman; 1987. 224p., illus., index. $7.45. Longman Illustrated Science Dictionaries. 0-583-89381-X.
This well-written general dictionary defines the latest terms used in space exploration as well as the standard terms of astronomy. *Grade Level:* Grades 9–12.
ARBA, 88, n.1732.

79. Macmillan Dictionary of Astronomy.
2nd. Valerie Illingworth. New York, NY: Macmillan; 1985. 437p., illus. $30.00, $15.95pbk. 0-333-39062-8, 0-333-39243-4pbk.
This is a very good general dictionary of astronomical terms intended for students, laypersons, and professionals. The definitions of terms are concise and accurate. *Grade Level:* Grades 9–12.

80. Patrick Moore's A-Z of Astronomy.
Patrick Moore. New York, NY: Norton; 1987. 240p., illus. $13.20. 0-393-30505-8.
This glossary for the amateur astronomer covers astronomical terms, instruments, events, places, phenomena, observatories, and principles. The more important astronomers are given brief biographical discussions. Originally published as *Amateur Astronomer's Glossary* and then as *A-Z of Astronomy. Grade Level:* Grades 6–8. Grades 9–12.
BL, 1 March 88, p.1121; SciTech, March 88, p.8; S&T, February 88, p.161..

Encyclopedias

81. Cambridge Encyclopaedia of Astronomy.
Simon Mitton, ed. New York, NY: Crown; 1977. 481p., illus. (part in color), index. $35.00. 0-517-52806-1.
This is a standard encyclopedia covering the nature of cosmic matter, the sun, solar system, intergalactic space, galaxies, radio galaxies, cosmology, and life in the universe. *Grade Level:* Grades 9–12.

ARBA, 79, n.1313; BL, 1 September 84, p.40; Choice, July 78, p.666; LJ, 1 April 78, p.721, 762, 15 April 78, p.818; S&T, June 78, p. 528, October 78, p.337.

82. Catalogue of the Universe.
Paul Murdin; David Allen. New York, NY: Crown; 1979. 256p., illus. (part in color), index. $15.95. 0-517-53616-1.
This nontraditional encyclopedia presents theories and concepts in astronomy through descriptions of the individual objects in the universe. Objects such as galaxies, constellations, double stars, and planets are given a historical perspective followed with an indication of why astronomers think the object is important. The *Catalogue* contains excellent photographs and illustrations. *Grade Level:* Grades 9–12.
ARBA, 80, n.1338; BL, 1 April 81, p.1120; Choice, February 80, p.1604; LJ, 15 May 81, p.1043; SB, May 80, p.260; SchLib, March 80, p.82; S&T, November 79, p.458; WLB, March 80, p.463.

83. Extraterrestrial Encyclopedia: Our Search for Life in Outer Space.
Joseph A. Angelo. New York, NY: Facts on File; 1985. 254p., illus., bibliog. $24.95. 0-87196-764-2.
More than 400 entries cover basic astronomy, UFOs, life on other planets, and the origin of life on earth. This encyclopedia also includes ideas and speculations based on both scientific fact and science fiction. *Grade Level:* Grades 9–12.
ARBA, 86, n.1758; BL, 15 April 86, p.1194; Choice, March 86, p.1035; LJ, 1 February 86, p.73, 1 March 86, p.51; SB, September 86, p.39, 41; SciTech, December 85, p.6; VOYA, August 86, p.183; WLB, February 86, p.62.

84. Illustrated Encyclopedia of Astronomy and Space.
Revised. Ian Ridpath, ed. New York, NY: Crowell; 1979. 240p., illus. (part in color), index. $19.45. 0-690-01838-X.
This good general encyclopedia includes over 1,000 entries that cover the fields of astronomy and astrophysics. Biographies of researchers in these areas are also included. The text is more advanced than other general encyclopedias, but it also contains more illustrations. *Grade Level:* Grades 9–12.
ARBA, 81, n.1382; BL 1 September 84, p.40; SLJ, May 80, p.94, April 83, p.114.

85. Illustrated Encyclopedia of the Universe: Exploring and Understanding the Cosmos.
Richard S. Lewis. New York, NY: Harmony Books; 1983. 320p., illus. (part in color), maps, index. $24.95. 0-517-55109-8.
This is an excellent general encyclopedia with outstanding photographs. It is divided into three sections, with section one covering the origin and evolution of the universe, section two covering each planet in detail, and section three being a chronology of space flight for 1957–83. *Grade Level:* Grades 9–12.
ARBA, 85, n.1675; Choice, April 84, p.1158; SB, November 84, p.79; SLJ, May 84, p.24, 109; WLB, April 84, p.594.

86. McGraw-Hill Encyclopedia of Astronomy.
Sybil P. Parker, ed. New York, NY: McGraw-Hill; 1983. 450p., illus.,
index. $59.50. 0-07-045251-2.
All aspects of astronomy are covered in this well-documented ency-
clopedia. All of the articles are from the fifth edition of the *McGraw-
Hill Encyclopedia of Science and Technology.* Includes excellent il-
lustrations. *Grade Level:* Grades 9–12.
ARBA, 84, n.1279; BL, 15 January 84, p.735; SB, November 83, p.73;
WLB, June 83, p.883.

87. 1001 Questions Answered About Astronomy.
2nd revised. James S. Pickering. New York, NY: Dodd, Mead; 1975
(c1965). 420p., illus., index. Out-of-print.
Using a question and answer format, this book covers information
about the sun, earth, moon, planets, stars, comets, galaxies, and other
astronomical phenomena. It is easy to use and intended for the amateur. *Grade Level:* Grades 9–12.
SB, March 67, p.263, March 74, p.292.

88. What's in the Names of Stars and Constellations.
Peter Limburg. New York, NY: Coward, McCann and Geoghegan;
1976. 193p., illus. Out-of-print. 0-698-20359-3.
This good encyclopedic description of astronomical topics is now out-
of-print. Facts, name origin, and associated mythological stories are
given for the nine planets, the sun and moon, and 13 stars and 18
constellations. *Grade Level:* Grades 9–12.
KR, 15 November 76, p.1220; SB, December 77, p.163; SLJ, February
77, p.72.

Field Books

**89. Field Guide to the Stars and Planets, Including the Moon,
Satellites, Comets, and Other Features of the Universe.**
2nd completely revised and enlarged. Donald Howard Menzel; Jay M.
Pasachoff. Boston, MA: Houghton Mifflin; 1983. 473p., illus., index.
$17.95, $12.95pbk. Peterson Field Guide Series, 15. 0-395-34641-X,
0-395-34835-8pbk.
This popular field guide for the amateur is part of the well-known
Peterson Field Guide Series. It includes numerous star charts and a
photographic   atlas,   plus   information   about   telescopes   and
photographing stars. *Grade Level:* Grades 9–12.
Choice, July 65, p.312; LJ, 1 March 84, p.429; SB, November 84,
p.80; S&T, December 83, p.530, September 84, p.227.

90. Skyguide: A Field Guide for Amateur Astronomers.
Mark R. Chartrand, III. Racine, WI: Western Publishing; 1982.
280p., illus. (part in color), bibliog., index. $9.95, $6.95pbk.
0-307-47020-5, 0-307-13667-1pbk.

As with all *Golden Field Guides*, this one is for the novice and educated layperson. Topics cover the sun, moon, planets, stars, galaxies, nebulae, astronomical coordinates, time, and other subjects of interest to the amateur astronomer. There are eight seasonal sky maps and 88 individual constellation charts. The charts are arranged alphabetically and include pronunciation, origin, special objects for viewing, and notes. *Grade Level:* Grades 6-8. Grades 9-12.
ARBA, 84, n.1278; BL, 1 March 83, p.848; SB, May 83, p.252; SLJ, August 83, p.83; S&T, March 83, p. 242, September 83, p.218.

91. Universe Guide to Stars and Planets.
Ian Ridpath. New York, NY: Universe Books; 1984. 384p., illus.
(part in color), maps, index. $19.95, $10.95pbk. 0-87663-366-1, 0-87663-859-0pbk.
This is a very good general guide to the night sky for the amateur. The maps are specially designed to be read by flashlight. Monthly sky maps for both the northern and southern hemispheres, and individual star maps for each of the 88 constellations are included. *Grade Level:* Grades 9-12.
ARBA, 86, n.1750; Kliatt, Winter 86, p.59; LJ, 15 October 85, p.96; SB, January 86, p.142; SciTech, September 85, p.7; S&T, January 86, p.35.

92. Whitney's Star Finder: A Field Guide to the Heavens.
4th. Charles A. Whitney. New York, NY: Knopf; 1985. 111p., illus.
$12.95. 0-394-72717-7.
This compact and clearly written field guide to the heavens covers star finding, planet watching, time telling, eclipses, and other topics. This edition is updated and expanded for 1986 through 1989. A separate star finder is included. *Grade Level:* Grades 9-12.
ARBA, 82, n.1425; BL, 1 September 84, p.42; CSM, 16 December 81, p.17; VOYA, June 82, p.48.

Glossaries

93. Amateur Astronomer's Glossary.
Patrick Moore. New York, NY: Norton; 1967. 162p., illus., charts.
$20.00. Amateur Astronomer's Library, v. 6.
For the amateur astronomer, this is a very good small glossary of terms that might be encountered in the astronomy literature. Although published in 1967, it is still useful. *Grade Level:* Grades 9-12.
BL, 15 December 67, p.478; Choice, July 68, p.610; KR, 1 August 67, p.949; SB, March 68, p.295.

Guides

94. Exploring the Sky: 100 Projects for Beginning Astronomers.
Richard Moeschl. Chicago, IL: Chicago Review Press; 1989. 339p., illus., bibliog., glossary, index. $14.95pbk. 1-556-52039-5pbk.

This is a collection of projects for school-age children, covering the earth, sky-gazing, tools, the sun, the stars, sky measurements, time, and historical views of the sky. It includes numerous illustrations, a glossary, and further reading lists. *Grade Level:* Grades 6–8. Grades 9–12. STARR, 90, n.77.

95. Exploring with a Telescope.
Glenn F. Chaple, Jr. New York, NY: Franklin Watts; 1988. 142p., illus., bibliog., index. $11.90. 0-531-10581-4.

This well-written introduction to the use of telescopes describes types of telescopes, mounts, eyepieces, and available accessories in the first third of the book. The remainder of the book discusses the celestial bodies, including the moon, sun, planets, and other astronomical objects, giving pointers on how to observe these bodies. *Grade Level:* Grades 6–8. Grades 9–12. STARR 90, n.70.

96. Grand Tour: A Traveler's Guide to the Solar System.
Ron Miller; William K. Hartmann. New York, NY: Workman Publishing; 1981. 187p., illus. (part in color), index. $19.95, $9.95pbk. 0-89480-147-3, 0-89480-146-5pbk.

This is a beautifully illustrated text on the universe with art by Ron Miller. It covers the planets, asteroids, and comets. The well-written narrative makes this an excellent book for school and college students as well as for laypersons. *Grade Level:* Grades 9–12. ARBA, 83, n.1278; BL, 15 December 81, p.527; Kliatt, Winter 82, p.74; LJ, 1 December 81, p.2323; SB, May 82, p.254; S&T, June 82, p.579; WLB, February 82, p.468.

97. How to Use an Astronomical Telescope: A Beginner's Guide to Observing the Cosmos.
James Muirden. New York, NY: Simon and Schuster; 1988. 400p., illus. $9.95. 0-671-66404-2.

This is an excellent guide for the amateur that discusses the various types of telescopes and their relative costs. It includes a general introduction to the night sky and how to observe the heavenly bodies. Separate chapters cover the sun, moon, planets, comets, stars, and galaxies. *Grade Level:* Grades 9–12. BL, 1 May 85, p.1223; Choice, October 85, p.319; SB, November 85, p.87; SciTech, June 85, p.6.

98. Larousse Guide to Astronomy.
David Baker. New York, NY: Larousse; 1980 (c1978). 288p., color illus., index. Out-of-print. 0-88332-094-0.

This very well-written guide to astronomy for the amateur is now out-of-print. It covers telescopes, stellar dynamics, the solar system, and galactic theory, and provides a brief history of astronomy, all with a British slant. The illustrations are very good. *Grade Level:* Grades 9–12.
ARBA, 80, n.1334; BL 1 December 79, p.574; LJ, 15 September 78, p.1757; SB, March 80, p.202.

99. Leslie Peltier's Guide to the Stars.
Leslie C. Peltier. New York, NY: Cambridge University Press; 1986. 185p., illus. $11.95pbk. 0-521-33595-7pbk.
This guide is an inviting introduction to astronomical observation using only binoculars and the unaided eye. Written as a trail guide and organized around seasonal observations, the guide provides special insights on observing the lunar surface and on variable stars. *Grade Level:* Grades 9–12.
BL, 1 February 87, p.813; BRpt, September 87, p.55; R&RBkN, Summer 87, p.33; SB, March 87, p.216; STARR, 89, n.51.

100. New Guide to the Planets.
Patrick Moore. New York, NY: Norton; 1972 (c1971). 224p., illus. Out-of-print. 0-393-06319-4.
This quick reference guide, now out-of-print, covers the planets, including information on wandering stars, birth of the planets, and movement of the planets. It is well-written and illustrated by Patrick Moore, a prolific writer of books on astronomy. Its previous title was *Guide to the Planets. Grade Level:* Grades 9–12.

101. New Guide to the Stars.
Patrick Moore. New York, NY: Norton; 1975 (c1974). 250p., illus. Out-of-print. 0-393-06406-9.
Now out-of-print, this excellent guide to the stars by a prolific author in astronomy is still one of the better quick reference books on the stars for the amateur. It was previously published as *Guide to the Stars. Grade Level:* Grades 9–12.

102. Pictorial Guide to the Moon.
3rd revised. Dinsmore Alter. Joseph H. Jackson, ed. New York, NY: Crowell; 1973. 216p., illus., index. Out-of-print. 0-690-01824-X.
Even though this guide to the moon is now out-of-print, it still continues to be a good pictorial guide with excellent photographs and illustrations. *Grade Level:* Grades 9–12.
ARBA, 74, n.1453; BL, 1 February 74, p.561; Choice, June 74, p.620, February 75, p.1744; S&T, March 74, p.188, August 74, p.63.

103. Pictorial Guide to the Planets.
3rd. Joseph H. Jackson; John H. Baumert. New York, NY: Harper and Row; 1981. 246p., illus. (part in color), index. $22.50. 0-06-014869-1.

This guide provides a good treatment of the solar system. The planets, including earth, are analyzed in detail. The pictures are current with the publication date. Useful tables that follow the chapters cover data on celestial bodies in the solar planetary system and space exploration therein, with special emphasis on the earth and moon. *Grade Level:* Grades 6–8. Grades 9–12.
ARBA, 82, n.1424; BL, 1 September 84, p.40; LJ, July 81, p.1406; SLJ, May 83, p.26.

104. Pocket Guide to Astronomy.
Patrick Moore. New York, NY: Simon and Schuster; 1985 (c1980). 144p., illus. (part in color), maps, index. $7.95. 0-671-25309-3.
The beginning observer will find this a very useful pocket guide to astronomy. It contains the usual star charts, data about celestial bodies, color plates, indexes to moon features, and a general index. *Grade Level:* Grades 9–12.
ARBA, 81, n.1386; S&T, November 80, p.413.

105. Stars and Planets.
Robin Kerrod; Ron Jobson. New York, NY: Arco; 1984 (c1979). 125p., color illus. $6.95. Arco Fact Guide in Color Series. 0-668-06263-0.
This is a good general book containing information on the sun, moon, earth, other planets, stars, asteroids, comets, meteors, telescopes, and such topics as black holes and quasars. It includes a list of key dates pertaining to stars and planets and a glossary of terms. *Grade Level:* Grades 3–5. Grades 6–8.
ASBYP, Winter 81, p.40; BL, 15 May 81, p.1273; SB, November 80, p.71.

106. Universe.
Con Dixon. Boston, MA: Houghton Mifflin; 1981. 240p., illus. (part in color), index. $35.00. 0-395-31290-6.
This is a good introductory guide to the solar system that includes some excellent space art. It is well-written and applicable for student use as well as a good book for the layperson. *Grade Level:* Grades 9–12.
ARBA, 83, n.1276; Choice, March 82, p.948; LJ, 1 March 82, p.554; SB, May 82, p.253; S&T, June 82, p.579; WLB, February 82, p.468.

Guides to the Literature

107. Astronomy and Astronautics: An Enthusiast's Guide to Books and Periodicals.
Andy Lusis. New York, NY: Facts on File; 1986. 292p., index. $24.95. 0-8160-1469-8.
A fully annotated bibliographic guide to books and periodicals in all areas of astronomy and astronautics is included in this guide to the literature. Over 900 entries are arranged by subject with brief but

informative annotations. There are many references to similar titles, published reviews, and level of readership. Only books published after 1976 are included. *Grade Level:* Grades 6–8. Grades 9–12.
ARBA, 87, n.1691; Choice, December 86, p.608; SB, January 87, p.168.

Handbooks

108. Amateur Astronomer's Catalog of 500 Deep-Sky Objects: Volume 1.
Ronald J. Morales. Tucson, AZ: Aztex Corp; 1986. 128p. $12.50. 0-89404-076-6.
For the amateur astronomer, this is a good general information handbook with accurate descriptions of deep-sky objects. Considered one of the better supplements to other observers' handbooks. *Grade Level:* Grades 9–12.
ST, March 87, p.281.

109. Amateur Astronomer's Handbook.
3rd. James Muirden. New York, NY: Harper and Row; 1987. 472p., illus., bibliog., index. $19.45. 0-06-181622-1.
This practical guide for the amateur astronomer includes instructions on techniques for viewing various celestial bodies and information on astronomical photography. A glossary, reading lists, and tables of recurring astronomical phenomena are included. *Grade Level:* Grades 9–12.
BL, 1 September 84, p.40.

110. Amateur Astronomer's Handbook.
4th. John Benson Sidgwick. James Muirden, ed. Hillside, NJ: Enslow; 1980 (c1955). 568p., illus., bibliog. $25.95. 0-89490-049-8.
Although similar to James Muirden's other handbook of the same title, this handbook is more technical, with information on the instrumental and theoretical concepts of practical astronomy. A bibliography is included. This is a companion to Sidgwick's *Observational Astronomy for Amateurs. Grade Level:* Grades 9–12.
ST, January 81, p.61, April 81, p.339, January 82, p.49; SB, September 81, p.14.

111. Amateur Radio Astronomer's Handbook.
John Potter Shields. New York, NY: Crown; 1986. 104p., illus. $17.95. 0-517-55810-6.
This well-written and straightforward general handbook contains information of interest to the specialized group of amateur radio astronomers. *Grade Level:* Grades 9–12.
ST, June 87, p.624.

112. Astronomy Handbook.
James Muirden. New York, NY: Prentice-Hall; 1987 (c1982). 189p., color illus., index. $8.95. 0-668-0623-5.

James Muirden has written an excellent handbook for the amateur astronomer. It covers the moving sky, the sun, the stars, nebulae and star clusters, the constellations, the moon, the planets, meteors and comets, atmospheric astronomy, the Milky Way, astrophotography, and astronomy projects. Eight star maps and many color illustrations are included. *Grade Level:* Grades 9–12.
ARBA, 83, n.1279; BL, 1 October 83, p.247, 1 September 84, p.40; Choice, December 82, p.601; LJ, 15 January 83, p.139; SB, March 83, p.191.

113. Astronomy Today.
Dinah L. Moché. New York, NY: Random House; 1986 (c1982). 96p., color illus. $8.00, $6.95pbk. Random House Library of Knowledge. 0-394-94423-2, 0-394-84423-8pbk.
This well-indexed book covers planets, stars, and space exploration with articles that are encyclopedic in content. *Grade Level:* Grades 9–12.
ASBYP, Fall 83, p.41; BL, 1 April 83, p.1036, 15 January 84, p.730; CBRS, February 83, p.71; SB, September 83, p.30; SLJ, January 83, p.72.

114. Beginner's Guide to the Skies: A Month-By-Month Handbook for Stargazers and Planet Watchers.
Clarence H. Cleminshaw. New York, NY: Crowell; 1977. 152p., illus., index. $14.45. 0-690-01214-4.
This general guide to astronomy covers the names of stars and constellations, descriptions and locations of the planets, and information about the sun and moon. *Grade Level:* Grades 9–12.
ARBA, 79, n.1314; LJ, 15 April 77, p.937; ST, December 83, p.529.

115. Beginning Knowledge Book of Stars and Constellations.
Ann Ivins. New York, NY: Macmillan; 1969. 35p. Out-of-print.
Although this is an older out-of-print book, it is still a good introduction to the constellations for preteen and teen readers. Nineteen constellations are described in clear terms. *Grade Level:* Grades 9–12.
PW, 17 November 69, p.81; SB, March 70, p.308.

116. Complete Manual of Amateur Astronomy: Tools and Techniques for Astronomical Observations.
P. Clay Sherrod; Thomas L. Koed. Englewood Cliffs, NJ: Prentice-Hall; 1981. 319p., illus. Out-of-print. 0-13-162115-7.
Another standard amateur astronomer's handbook covering all of the information that is needed to do astronomical observations. It includes tools and techniques. Unfortunately, it is now out-of-print. *Grade Level:* Grades 9–12.
BL, 15 November 81, p.416; Choice, December 81, p.522; CSM, 16 December 81, p.17; LJ, 1 January 82, p.101; SB, September 82, p.13; S&T, December 81, p.595.

117. Guinness Book of Astronomy: Facts and Feats.
3rd. Patrick Moore. Enfield, Great Britain: Guinness Superlatives;
Dist. by Sterling; New York; NY; 1988. 288p., illus. (part in color),
index. $19.95. 0-85112-375-9.
This is a book of astronomical first facts and various astronomical
tables for the amateur astronomer. It is arranged by subject. The tables
of data include stellar positions, planetary characteristics, and information on periodic comets. *Grade Level:* Grades 9–12.
ARBA, 84, n.1280; BL, 1 January 81, p.642; Choice, September 81,
p.41; LJ, 15 May 80, p.1175; SB, November 84, p.80.

118. The Moon Observer's Handbook.
Fred W. Price. New York, NY: Cambridge University Press; 1988.
309p., illus., bibliog., index. $27.50. 0-521-33500-0.
This well-written and excellently illustrated handbook covers everything one would want to know about the moon, including the mythological events. There is an excellent chapter that describes the telescope. *Grade Level:* Grades 9–12.
STARR, 90, n.73.

119. Observational Astronomy for Amateurs.
4th. John Benson Sidgwick, ed. Hillside, NJ: Enslow; 1982. 348p.,
illus., bibliog., index. $20.95, $8.95pbk. 0-89490-067-6,
0-89490-068-4pbk.
This advanced handbook for amateur astronomers describes the various heavenly bodies and indicates how one is to observe and identify
them. *Grade Level:* Grades 9–12.
BL, 1 September 84, p.40; SchLib, June 82, p.180; S&T, January 83,
p.40.

120. Sky Observers Guide: Handbook for Amateur Astronomers.
R. Newton Mayall; Margaret Mayall; Jerome Wyckoff. New York,
NY: Golden Press; 1985. 160p., illus. $2.95. Golden Guide.
0-307-24009-6.
This is a small handbook for junior high amateur astronomers. It
covers all aspects of observing the stars and planets and has brief
information about various telescopes. *Grade Level:* Grades 9–12.

121. Standard Handbook for Telescope Making.
Revised. Neale E. Howard. New York, NY: Harper and Row; 1984.
356p., illus., index. $25.45. 0-06-181394-X.
All aspects of building your own telescope are clearly presented in this
handbook. In particular, this work describes how to build an 8-inch, 5/
7 Newtonian reflector. Previously titled *Handbook for Telescope Making. Grade Level:* Grades 9–12.
ST, March 84, p.238.

**122. Star Guide: A Unique System for Identifying the Brightest Stars
in the Night Sky.**
Steven L. Beyer. New York, NY: Little, Brown; 1986. 404p., illus.,

maps, bibliog., index. $22.95, $11.95pbk. 0-316-09267-3, 0-316-09268-1pbk.
A general handbook for the amateur, this book helps to identify stars and their names. Some historical introductory information is also given. *Grade Level:* Grades 9–12.
BL, 15 May 86, p.1345; Choice, July 86, p.1695; Kliatt, Fall 86, p.67; SB, November 86, p.87.

123. Stargazer's Bible.
W.S. Kals. Garden City, NY: Doubleday; 1980. 168p., illus. $4.50. 0-385-13057-0.
This is an introduction to observational astronomy for the amateur. It includes material on identifying constellations, finding bright stars and planets, stargazing at other latitudes, using binoculars and telescopes, astrophotography, and an appendix of observational data. *Grade Level:* Grades 9–12.
LJ, 15 March 80, p.733; SB, November 80, p.71.

124. Stars: A Guide to the Constellations, Sun, Moon, Planets, and Other Features of the Heavens.
Revised. Herbert S. Zim; Robert H. Baker. Mark R. Chartrand, III, ed. New York, NY: Golden Press; 1985. 160p., illus. $2.95. 0-307-24493-8.
This authoritative handbook for the young adult covers stars, constellations, and the solar system. This book tells why, how, and when to observe the skies and what kinds of equipment are needed. *Grade Level:* Grades 9–12.
BW, 11 November 73, p.6.

125. Telescope Handbook and Star Atlas.
2nd. Neale E. Howard. New York, NY: Crowell; 1975. 226p., illus., bibliog., index. $21.10. 0-690-00686-1.
This is a very good amateur's book to telescopes and practical astronomy. It discusses telescopes and the types of celestial objects that may be viewed by using telescopes, followed by star maps, a gazetteer, and a Messier catalog. *Grade Level:* Grades 9–12.
ARBA, 76, n.1337; Choice, February 76, p.1593; SB, May 76, p.17; S&T, January 76, p.51.

126. The Universe from Your Backyard: A Guide to Deep-Sky Objects from *Astronomy Magazine*.
David J. Eicher. New York, NY: Cambridge University Press; 1988. 188p., illus. (part in color), bibliog., index. $24.95. "AstroMedia Milwaukee." 0-521-36299-7.
This is a sky-watcher's handbook containing four-page, alphabetically arranged entries that cover from one to three constellations. Each entry includes a star chart, list of the most prominent features, color photographs, mythological basis of the constellation, and an indication of the best season for viewing. This handbook is intended for use with the telescope. *Grade Level:* Grades 9–12.
STARR, 90, n.72.

127. Webb Society Deep-Sky Observer's Handbook.
2nd. Webb Society, comp. Short Hills, NJ: Enslow; 1979–1987. 7v., illus. See text for prices. See text for ISBN.
This is an advanced level observational guide to the stars for the amateur astronomer. Each volume covers a different area of the deep sky. These volumes provide background information and instructions for observing astronomical bodies. The seven volumes are: Volume 1, "Double Stars," 2nd ed., 0-89490-122-2, $14.95; Volume 2, "Planetary and Gaseous Nebulae," 0-89490-028-5, $11.95; Volume 3, "Open and Globular Clusters," 0-89490-034-X, $15.95; Volume 4, "Galaxies," 0-89490-050-1, $17.95; Volume 5, "Clusters of Galaxies," 0-89490-066-8, $17.95; Volume 6, "Anonymous Galaxies," 0-89490-133-8, $12.95; and Volume 7, "The Southern Sky," 0-89490-134-6, $16.95. *Grade Level:* Grades 9–12.
ARBA, 80, n.1336, 81, n.1383.

Histories

128. Daytime Star: The Story of Our Sun.
Simon Mitton. New York, NY: Scribner's; 1983 (c1981). 191p., illus. $6.95. 0-684-17829-X.
This interesting historical account of our sun covers what has been recorded about the sun from prehistoric times to the present, including the findings of early astronomers. *Grade Level:* Grades 6–8. Grades 9–12.
BL, 1 July 81, p.1376; Choice, October 81, p.260; Kliatt, Fall 83, p.71; KR, 1 April 81, p.486, 15 May 81, p.641; LJ, August 81, p.1556; PW, 17 April 81, p.56.

129. Echoes of the Ancient Skies: The Astronomy of Lost Civilizations.
E.C. Krupp. New York, NY: Harper and Row; 1983. 386p., illus. $19.45. 0-06-01510-3.
This book is a general history of astronomy and its close relationship to archaeology. It discusses the seasonal night skies and then relates this to the primitive and vanished cultures that have used astronomy in their daily and spiritual lives. *Grade Level:* Grades 9–12.
BL, 1 April 83, p.1001; Choice, September 83, p.125; KR, 1 April 83, p.435; LJ, 15 May 83, p.1009; PW, 22 April 83, p.91, 11 May 84, p.271; S&T, March 84, p.234.

130. Patrick Moore's History of Astronomy.
6th revised. Patrick Moore. London, Great Britain: Macdonald; 1983. 327p., illus. (part in color). $19.95. 0-356-08607-0.
This is a very good general history of astronomy for the amateur and layperson. The illustrations are good. It was previously published as *The Story of Astronomy. Grade Level:* Grades 9–12.

Manuals

131. All About Telescopes.
6th. Sam Brown. Barrington, NJ: Edmund Scientific; 1985. 192p.,
illus., index. $20.00. 0-93334-620-4.
This how-to book on building your own telescope contains chapters on
the use of the telescope, observing the sky, photography, mirror grind-
ing and testing, mounts, collimation and adjustments, and optics.
Grade Level: Grades 9–12.

Textbooks

132. Amateur Astronomer.
11th. Patrick Moore. New York, NY: Cambridge University Press;
1989. 356p. $25.00. 0-521-34511-1.
This general textbook covers telescopes, the solar system, the sun,
moon, aurorae, planets, comets, meteors, stars, nebulae, and galaxies.
Astronomical charts and tables are included. *Grade Level:* Grades
9–12.
SB, September 66, p.102.

Yearbooks/Annuals/Almanacs

133. Astronomical Almanac.
Washington, DC: U.S. Naval Observatory; 1852–. index. Annual.
$16.00.
Until 1981, this annual was two publications: *American Ephemeris and
Nautical Almanac* and *Nautical Almanac and Astronomical Ephemeris.*
In addition to the heliocentric ephemerides of major planets and the
geocentric ephemerides of major and minor planets, it covers eclipses;
universal and sidereal time; information about the sun, moon, and
major planets; day numbers; and tables of risings and settings. *Grade
Level:* Grades 9–12.

**134. Space Almanac: Facts, Figures, Names, Dates, Places, Lists,
Charts, Tables, Maps Covering Space from Earth to the Edge of the
Universe.**
Anthony R. Curtis. Woodsboro, MD: Arcsoft Publishers; 1990. 955p.,
illus., maps, tables, charts, index. $19.95pbk. 0-86668-065-9pbk.
This almanac contains a wealth of information about space subjects,
including astronauts, stations, shuttles, rockets, satellites, solar system,
and deep space. Contains a calendar of events from 1903 to 1989.
Grade Level: Grades 6–8. Grades 9–12.

135. Yearbook of Astronomy.
New York, NY: Norton; 1962–. illus. Annual. $16.95. 0084-3660.
This yearbook for the amateur astronomer reports astronomical events for the year with appropriate tables, articles, and directory information. *Grade Level:* Grades 9–12.
ARBA, 87, n.1692; BL, 15 July 74, p.1220; Choice, July 78, p.713; SB, September 85, p.36.

MATHEMATICS/
COMPUTER SCIENCE

Although mathematics is usually treated separately, in this book, it is included with computer science because computer science is related to mathematics and also because there are a limited number of reference works covering just mathematics that are of interest to young people. Mathematics is not a branch of natural science but the language by which all other sciences can interrelate. Without mathematics, the scientific fields of physics, astronomy, and chemistry would flounder in trying to explain theories, concepts, and laws. When one has a firm grasp of mathematics, all other sciences become much easier to understand. There are many subfields in mathematics, including *algebra*—the use of symbols in equations to solve problems; *analytical geometry*—the study of geometry by the use of algebra, also called *cartesian geometry*; *calculus of vectors*—the use of directed line segments to solve problems, especially in physics; *geometry*—that part of mathematics concerned with the properties of space, which includes points, lines, curves, planes, and surfaces; *probability*—the construction of abstract models to predict what may happen; *statistics*—the collection, analysis, and presentation of data; and *topology*—a complex area of mathematics dealing with spaces and continuous maps.

Computer science is one of the fastest growing fields in the production of literature because of the creation of highly sophisticated programming languages, the growth of networking, and the increasing number of personal computers. Computers are becoming as common as typewriters. Today, computer science is considered a basic course in most schools, and computer programs are becoming standard tools. It is surprising, then, that some in the computer science field continue to advocate and predict a paperless society when the number of computer science manuals that are published far exceed the printed reference materials in other disciplines.

Computer science is not a pure science because it uses the knowledge and processes of many other scientific areas and because all scientific or technological disciplines utilize computers. This science, however, does have some subfields. There are *analog* or *mechanical computers* and *digital* or *symbolic computers. Data processing* has a prominent place in computer science as does *word processing*, which has greatly increased the production speed of documents. Anything having to do with *robotics* also has a direct connection to computers. Finally, *artificial intelligence*, a growing research area in computer science, is concerned with the understanding of intelligent action, including problem solving, perception, learning, symbolic activity, creativity, and language.

Reference books for computer science and mathematics are mostly dictionaries, encyclopedias, and handbooks, with the majority being for computer science. There are numerous dictionaries for computer science, with new titles and new editions published each year. The terminology is ever changing, so it is important for any library to have at least one of the newest titles. Douglas Downing's *Dictionary of Computer Terms* is a very good up-to-date dictionary for computer science. Downing also has a good mathematics dictionary, *Dictionary of Mathematics Terms*. The *Facts on File Dictionary of Mathematics* is also well written and very useful for young people. For encyclopedic coverage, *McGraw-Hill Encyclopedia of Electronics and Computers* and *VNR Concise Encyclopedia of Mathematics* are recommended. The *History of Computing Technology* and *History of Mathematics* cover the histories of these two fields very well.

Biographical Sources

136. Makers of Mathematics.
Alfred Hooper. New York, NY: Random House; 1948. 402p., illus., bibliog. Out-of-print.
    Although out-of-print, this is a very good biography and history of mathematics work. It covers those personalities who have shaped modern mathematics. It does not require any prior mathematical knowledge. *Grade Level:* Grades 9–12.

137. Men of Mathematics.
Eric Temple Bell. New York, NY: Simon and Schuster; 1986 (c1937). 591p., illus. $11.95. 0-671-62818-6.
    Published in the 1930s, this well-known biographical work covers 34 men who were prominent in the development of mathematics from its beginning. Two criteria were used to determine inclusion: first, the known appeal of the man's life and character; and second, the importance of the man's works to modern mathematics. It is arranged in chronological order. *Grade Level:* Grades 9–12.

Dictionaries

138. Barnes and Noble Thesaurus of Computer Science.
Arthur Godman. New York, NY: Barnes and Noble/Harper and Row; 1984. 262p., color illus., index. $13.95, $6.95pbk. 0-06-015270-2, 0-06-463594-5pbk.

The entries in this small dictionary are grouped by topic with cross-references. The emphasis in the concise definitions is on how words are interconnected. Since this is written by a Briton, it has a British slant. *Grade Level:* Grades 9–12.
ARBA, 86, n.1694.

139. The Beginner's Computer Dictionary.
Elizabeth S. Wall; Alexander C. Wall. New York, NY: Avon; 1984.
80p., illus. $2.25pbk. 0-380-87114-9pbk.
This is a school-level dictionary of the more common computer terms encountered in everyday reading. It is well-illustrated with numerous cross-references. *Grade Level:* Grades 6–8. Grades 9–12.
ARBA, 85, n.1615.

140. Computer Dictionary.
4th. Charles J. Sippl. Indianapolis, IN: Sams; 1985. 562p., illus.
$24.95pbk. 0-672-22205-1pbk.
This comprehensive dictionary by a well- known author of computer books has more than 12,000 terms related to every aspect of computers. The definitions are concise and some related fields are included, such as robotics and artificial intelligence. *Grade Level:* Grades 9–12.
ARBA, 87, n.1652; Choice, April 75, p.202.

141. Computer Dictionary.
Patricia Conniffe. New York, NY: Scholastic Book Services; 1984.
96p., illus. $4.95pbk. 0-590-34315-7pbk.
This small dictionary of over 500 terms with definitions for the student and layperson stresses hardware and software terms and includes some biographical entries. *Grade Level:* Grades 9–12.
ARBA, 85, n.1603; CurR, March 85, p.38.

142. Computer Glossary: Complete Desk Reference.
4th. Alan Freedman, ed. Point Pleasant, PA: AMACOM; 1989. 776p.
$24.95pbk. 0-8144-7709-7pbk.
This book, a revision of *Computer Glossary for Everyone*, is a well-written glossary of general computer terminology. It is nontechnical and includes good illustrations. *Grade Level:* Grades 9–12.
STARR, 90, n.200.

143. Concise Encyclopedia of Information Technology.
3rd. Adrian V. Stokes. Brookfield, VT: Gower; 1986. 305p.
$16.50pbk. 0-7045-0520-7pbk.
This is an encyclopedic glossary of over 3,500 terms related to computers and other information technology areas. The definitions are concise and suitable for the layperson. Selectively includes the names of some computer equipment manufacturers and specific product names. *Grade Level:* Grades 9–12.
ARBA, 85, n.1613; BL, 1 February 84, p.797.

144. Dictionary of Computer Terms.
2nd. Douglas Downing; Michael Covington. New York, NY: Barron's; 1989. 288p. $8.95pbk. 0-8120-4152-6pbk.
This is a good, inexpensive dictionary of over 600 computer terms related to concepts and functions in computer programming. It includes electronics and computer hardware and peripheral terms. Some programming knowledge is assumed. *Grade Level:* Grades 9–12.
ARBA, 87, n.1647; Choice, July 86, p.1652.

145. Dictionary of Computers, Information Processing, and Telecommunications.
2nd. Jerry Martin Rosenberg. New York, NY: Wiley; 1987. 734p. $39.95. 0-471-85558-8.
This very good dictionary was formerly titled *Dictionary of Computers, Data Processing, and Telecommunications.* It has over 10,000 terms from all areas of computers, information processing, data processing, and telecommunications. The most recent or popular term is used with cross-references from other terms. It attempts to standardize the terminology and definitions and indicates multiple uses of terms where necessary. *Grade Level:* Grades 9–12.
ARBA, 88, n.1707; SciTech, February 88, p.7.

146. Dictionary of Computing.
2nd. Valerie Illingworth, ed. New York, NY: Oxford University Press; 1986. 430p., illus. $29.95. 0-19-853913-4.
More than 4,000 alphabetically arranged terms in all areas of computer technology are included in this excellent dictionary. It is intended for all levels of users with some terms defined at the basic level and others at the graduate level. *Grade Level:* Grades 9–12.
ARBA, 84, n.1249; SB, September 84, p.6.

147. Dictionary of Mathematics.
J.A. Glenn; G.H. Littler. Totowa, NJ: Barnes and Noble; 1984. 230p., illus. $18.95. 0-389-20451-X.
Although this dictionary has a British slant, it is a good general dictionary for the school-aged student. The definitions are concise and include diagrams and illustrations. *Grade Level:* Grades 9–12.
ARBA, 86, n.1767; Choice, July 85, p.1614.

148. Dictionary of Mathematics.
T. Alaric Millington; William Millington. New York, NY: Barnes and Noble; 1971 (c1966). 249p. $5.95. 0-06-463311-X.
This small dictionary is for the beginning student and contains brief definitions of terms that appear in all areas of mathematics. *Grade Level:* Grades 6–8. Grades 9–12.
ARBA, 72, n.1473; SB, September 72, p.114.

149. Dictionary of Mathematics Terms.
Douglas Downing. Hauppauge, NY: Barron's; 1987. 241p. $8.95pbk. 0-8120-2641-1.

Over 600 definitions are included in this small dictionary covering terminology used in algebra, geometry, analytic geometry, trigonometry, probability, statistics, logic, computer math, and calculus. *Grade Level:* Grades 9–12.
ARBA, 88, n.1773; BRpt, May 88, p.45; SciTech, May 88, p.5.

150. The Facts on File Dictionary of Mathematics.
Revised and expanded. Carol Gibson. New York, NY: Facts on File; 1988. 235p., illus. $19.95. 0-8160-1867-7.
This is one of the well-written Facts on File dictionaries that are intended for the layperson and undergraduate. It covers all areas of mathematics with clear and concise definitions. *Grade Level:* Grades 6–8. Grades 9–12.
ARBA, 89, n.1674; STARR, 90, n.355.

151. Illustrated Dictionary of Microcomputers.
2nd. Michael Hordeski. Blue Ridge Summit, PA: TAB; 1986. 352p., illus. $24.95, $14.95pbk. 0-8306-0488-X, 0-8306-2688-3pbk.
Brief but complete definitions of over 8,000 microcomputer and related terms are included in this good dictionary. It includes definitions of both hardware and software terms, including examples. *Grade Level:* Grades 9–12.
ARBA, 87, n.1667; Choice, November 86, p.454.

152. Mathematics Dictionary.
4th. Glenn James; Robert C. James. Princeton, NJ: Van Nostrand; 1976. 509p., illus., index. $32.95. 0-442-24091-0.
This is the standard mathematical dictionary for general coverage. It includes biographical sketches of those mathematicians who have contributed to the development of mathematics. *Grade Level:* Grades 9–12.
ARBA, 77, n.1302; BL, 15 May 77, p.1452; Choice, Februrary 77, p.1572; SB, September 77, p.74; WLB, December 76, p.366.

153. Mathematics Illustrated Dictionary: Facts, Figures, and People.
Revised. Jeanne Bendick. New York, NY: Franklin Watts; 1989. 247p. illus. $14.90. 0-531-10664-0.
This dictionary contains brief definitions of mathematical terms, biographies of famous and not-so-famous mathematicians and scientists, and an assortment of tables. *Grade Level:* Grades 3–5. Grades 6–8.

154. McGraw-Hill Dictionary of Computers.
Sybil P. Parker, ed. New York, NY: McGraw-Hill; 1984. 452p. $15.95pbk. 0-07-045415-9pbk.
This spin-off from the *Dictionary of Scientific and Technical Terms* includes all of the terms that relate to computers and associated terminology from electronic engineering. The definitions are intended for the layperson. *Grade Level:* Grades 9–12.
ARBA, 86, n.1684.

155. Penguin Dictionary of Computers.
3rd. Anthony Chandor; John Graham; Robin Williamson, eds. New York, NY: Penguin Books; 1985. 488p. $6.95. 0-14-051127-X.
Also known as the *Dictionary of Computers*, this dictionary contains over 3,000 words, phrases, and acronyms used in connection with computers. The definitions are concise and easy to understand. When necessary, basic concepts are also explained at length. *Grade Level:* Grades 9–12.
ARBA, 79, n.1560; Choice, December 70, p.1353.

156. Personal Computers A-Z.
Joel Makower. Garden City, NY: Quantum Press/Doubleday; 1984. 185p., illus., index. $14.95pbk. 0-385-19054-9pbk.
This is an entertaining dictionary of 350 computer terms relating to microcomputer hardware, software, and services. The definitions are well-written, and the small caveats of humor throughout the book make this one of the more enjoyable dictionaries to use. *Grade Level:* Grades 9–12.
ARBA, 85, n.1632.

157. The Prentice-Hall Standard Glossary of Computer Terminology.
Robert A. Edmunds. Englewood Cliffs, NJ: Prentice-Hall; 1985. 489p., illus. $34.95, $24.95pbk. 0-13-698234-4, 0-13-698226-3pbk.
This is a comprehensive dictionary of computer terms with definitions that are not too technical but still sophisticated enough for the computer professional. Includes acronyms, abbreviations, and commercial suppliers of software and hardware. The definitions of terms make reference to more general terms that have to be consulted to obtain a full definition. *Grade Level:* Grades 9–12.
ARBA, 86, n.1683; Choice, April 85, p.1140.

158. Spencer's Computer Dictionary for Everyone.
3rd. Donald D. Spencer. New York, NY: Scribner's; 1985. 290p., illus. $15.95, $8.95pbk. 0-684-18250-5, 0-684-18251-3pbk.
This dictionary for those who know little about computers contains more than 3,000 entries with concise and readable definitions. It was previously published as the *Computer Dictionary for Everyone. Grade Level:* Grades 9–12.
ARBA, 86, n.1686.

Encyclopedias

159. Encyclopedia Macintosh.
Craig Danuloff; Deke McClelland. San Francisco, CA: SYBEX; 1990. 1v. various paging, tables, charts, glossary, index. $24.95pbk. 0-89588-628-6pbk.
This is a comprehensive encyclopedia of information about the hardware, software, and peripherals pertaining to the Macintosh computer. The encyclopedia is more for the teacher, since it is technical, but high

school students will find it an interesting reference source for the computer that is used a great deal in schools. *Grade Level:* Grades 9–12.

160. Encyclopedia of Computers and Electronics.
Chicago, IL: Rand McNally; 1983. 140p., illus. (part in color), index. $9.95. 0-528-82389-2.
This is a book for school-aged children who need a brief introduction to computer terminology and concepts. The encyclopedia includes numerous illustrations. Although the discussion of concepts is very brief, the book covers many areas, such as microwaves, binary numbers, computer graphics, and other computer and electronic topics. *Grade Level:* Grades 9–12.
ARBA, 84, n.1248.

161. McGraw-Hill Encyclopedia of Electronics and Computers.
2nd. Sybil P. Parker, ed. New York, NY: McGraw-Hill; 1988. 1,047p., illus., bibliog., index. $75.00. 0-07-045499-X.
This spin-off from that venerable reference book, the *McGraw-Hill Encyclopedia of Science and Technology*, contains some 520 articles relating to electricity, semiconductors, integrated circuitry, computer hardware and software, robotics, data management, communications, and consumer products employing microprocessors. Also included is information on artificial intelligence, radar, computer-aided engineering, and a variety of electronic circuits, chips, and components. Although somewhat expensive, but it should still be considered. *Grade Level:* Grades 9–12.
ARBA, 89, n.1608; BL, 1 October 88, p.242; STARR, 89, n.462.

162. Universal Encyclopedia of Mathematics.
James R. Newman. New York, NY: Simon and Schuster; 1969. 598p., illus. $8.95pbk. 0-671-20348-7pbk.
This translation of *Meyers Rechenduden* is designed for secondary school and college students. The encyclopedia covers arithmetic through calculus, and even though published in 1969, it is still a useful encyclopedia. *Grade Level:* Grades 9–12.
ARBA, 70(2), p.104.

163. VNR Concise Encyclopedia of Mathematics.
2nd. W. Gottwald, ed. New York, NY: Van Nostrand Reinhold; 1989. 816p., illus. $28.95. 0-442-20590-2.
This English version of *Kleine Enzyklopadie der Mathematik* was also originally published as *Mathematics at a Glance* and is sometimes known as just the *Concise Encyclopedia of Mathematics*. It is divided into three parts, with part one covering the traditional areas of elementary mathematics, part two covering higher mathematics, and part three covering contemporary mathematics. *Grade Level:* Grades 9–12.
ARBA, 78, n.1228; LJ, 1 April 78, p.723; WLB, September 77, p.84.

Guides

164. **Understanding Artificial Intelligence.**
2nd. Henry C. Mishkoff; Dan Shafer; Daniel W. Rasmus.
Indianapolis, IN: Sams; 1988. 284p., illus., bibliog., glossary, index.
$17.95. 0-672-27271-7.
A well-written guide on an important topic, artificial intelligence (AI),
written for the layperson and the scholar. The first three chapters
cover definitions, history, and trends. The remaining chapters each
cover a specific area of AI. The chapters are arranged in the format of
introduction, discussion, summary, and quiz. A good glossary is included. *Grade Level:* Grades 9–12.
STARR, 90, n.211.

Guides to the Literature

165. **The High School Mathematics Library.**
8th. William L. Schaaf, comp. Reston, VA: National Council of
Teachers of Mathematics; 1987. 83p. $7.80pbk. 0-87353-238-4pbk.
This is an essential selection aid for high school librarians, teachers,
and students, listing some 800 titles. It includes books on modern
algebra, topology, and recreational topics. *Grade Level:* Grades 9–12.
Teacher's/Librarian's Resource.

166. **Mathematics Library: Elementary and Junior High School.**
5th. Margariete Wheeler. Reston, VA: National Council of Teachers
of Mathematics; 1986. 35p. $6.75pbk. 0-87353-228-7pbk.
This is a bibliography of selected books in mathematics that may be
sources for recreational and informational reading. It is revised on a
regular basis. *Grade Level:* Grades 3–5. Grades 6–8. Grades 9–12.
Teacher's/Librarian's Resource.
ARBA, 79, n.1311.

Handbooks

167. **Handbook of Mathematical Tables and Formulas.**
5th. Richard S. Burington. New York, NY: McGraw-Hill; 1973.
500p., illus., bibliog., index. $31.95. 0-07-009015-7.
This is a standard book for mathematical tables and formulas. The
first part includes the main formulas and theorems of algebra, geometry, trigonometry, calculus, vector analysis, sets, logic, matrices, linear
algebra, numerical analysis, differential equations, some special functions, Fourier and Laplace transforms, complex variables, and statistics. The second part includes tables of logarithms, trigonometry, exponential and hyperbolic functions, powers and roots, probability dis-
tributions, annuity, and others. *Grade Level:* Grades 9–12.

ARBA, 74, n.1450; BL, 1 September 84, p.40; WLB, March 73, p.613.

168. SI Metric Handbook.
John L. Feirer. New York, NY: Scribner's; 1977. 1v. various paging, illus., index. $27.50. 0-87002-908-8.
This handbook is designed "to serve as a reference for all individuals interested in metric conversion in basic occupational areas." It contains a history and definition of the SI measuring system, discussion of precision measuring tools, and information on ISO and SI metric standards. It applies the metric system to the occupations of woodworking, graphic arts, auto mechanics, office and business practice, food, clothing, agriculture, and health. *Grade Level:* Grades 9–12.
ARBA, 78, n.1231; LJ, 15 April 77, p.936.

169. Workshop Formulas, Tips and Data.
Revised. Kenneth M Swezey; Robert Scharff. New York, NY: Sterling Publishing Co., Inc; 1989. 340p., illus., tables, charts, index. $14.95pbk. 0-8069-6791-9pbk.
This useful handbook of information that would be of interest to the handy person covers such topics as selecting woods, weathering of woods, paints and painting, masonry, formulas used in woodworking, and the selection of various mechanical and electrical materials. *Grade Level:* Grades 6–8. Grades 9–12.

Histories

170. Bit by Bit: An Illustrated History of Computers and Their Inventors.
Stan Augarten. New York, NY: Ticknor and Fields; 1984. 324p., illus. (part in color), index. $29.95, $17.95pbk. 0-89919-268-8, 0-89919-302-1pbk.
This is a very readable history of computing from the introduction of logarithms in the seventeenth century to the microcomputer and the founding of the Apple Computer Company in this century. The excellent illustrations add to the usefulness of this history for all age groups. *Grade Level:* Grades 6–8. Grades 9–12.
BL, 1 December 84, p.467; Choice, March 85, p.1017; KR, 1 November 84, p.1020; LJ, December 84, p.2289, 1 March 85, p.37; SLJ, February 85, p.91.

171. The Computer Story.
Irving E. Fang. Saint Paul, MN: Rada Press; 1988. 104p., illus., bibliog., glossary. $12.50. Tools of Communication. 0-9604212-4-6.
This interesting history covers information processing from earliest writing to artificial intelligence. Written for students, it uses nontechnical language, and covers such topics as the development of the numbering systems, slide rule, Babbage's difference engine, and microcomputers. *Grade Level:* Grades 9–12.
BRpt, January 89, p.43; STARR, 90, n.205.

172. Concise History of Mathematics.
4th new. Dirk J.A. Struik, ed. New York, NY: Dover; 1987 (c1986).
195p., illus., index. $5.00pbk. 0-486-60255-9pbk.
This is one of the better general histories of mathematics that is
written for the student and nonprofessional. It is concise but accurate.
Grade Level: Grades 9–12.
Choice, February 68, p.1413.

173. From One to Zero: A Universal History of Numbers.
Georges Ifrah. New York, NY: Penguin Books; 1987 (c1985). 503p.,
illus., bibliog. $14.95. 0-14-009919-0.
This is a very entertaining and readable account of "How did numbers
start?" The evolution of worldwide numerical notation is traced, showing how the zero concept and the place-value principle were adopted.
There is no index, but that does not detract from the usefulness of this
well-written work. *Grade Level:* Grades 6–8. Grades 9–12.
BL, July 85, p.1487; Choice, February 86, p.885; KR, 15 July 85,
p.696; LJ, 1 March 86, p.48; Sci Tech, December 85, p.4.

174. History of Computing Technology.
Michael R. Williams. Englewood Cliffs, NJ: Pentice-Hall; 1985.
432p., illus., index. $36.95. 0-13-389917-9.
This very readable history of computing technology traces development
through the mid-1980s. *Grade Level:* Grades 9–12.
Choice, April 86, p.1233.

175. History of Mathematics.
2nd. Carl B. Boyer; Uta C. Merzbach. New York, NY: Wiley; 1989
(c1988). 717p., illus., bibliog. $12.50. 0-691-0239-3.
This good general history of mathematics is understandable to the
student as well as authoritative for the mathematician. *Grade Level:*
Grades 9–12.

176. History of Mathematics.
David Eugene Smith. New York, NY: Dover; 1958 (c1923–1925).
2v., illus., bibliog., index. $10.00 per volume. 0-486-20429-4, v.1;
0-486-20430-8, v.2.
Although this book is almost 60 years old, it is still the best book
covering the history of elementary mathematics through calculus. Volume one is a general survey of the history of elementary mathematics,
and volume two covers special mathematical topics. *Grade Level:*
Grades 9–12.

**177. History of Mathematics, From Antiquity to the Beginning of the
19th Century.**
2nd. Joseph Frederick Scott. New York, NY: Barnes and Noble; 1975
(c1960). 266p., illus., bibliog. $28.50. 0-06-496130-3.
This is a 2,000-year chronology of mathematical ideas. Some prior
knowledge of mathematics is presumed. The biographical notes in the
appendix are excellent. *Grade Level:* Grades 9–12.

178. World of Mathematics: A Small Library of the Literature of Mathematics from a'h'Mose the Scribe to Albert Einstein.
James R. Newman. Redmond, WA: Microsoft Press; 1988 (c1956–70). 4v., illus., bibliog. $99.95, $50.00pbk. 1-55615-149-7, 1-55615-148-9pbk.

Now reprinted by Microsoft Press, this interesting historical account of mathematics for those with little or no mathematics background is well-written and would be appropriate for school libraries. *Grade Level:* Grades 9–12.

How-to-do-it Books

179. Math Projects for Young Scientists.
David A. Thomas. New York, NY: Franklin Watts; 1988. 126p., illus., index. $11.90. Projects for Young Scientists. 0-531-10523-7.

This is a good "idea book" for science fair competitions. The problems are briefly explained without answers and cover combinatorics and probability, Fibonacci numbers, number theory, sequences and theories, geometry and topology, computer modelling, dynamical systems, Julia sets, and fractals. *Grade Level:* Grades 3–5. Grades 6–8. Teacher's/Librarian's Resource.
BRpt, November 88, p.50; STARR, 90, n.360.

Tables

180. CRC Standard Mathematical Tables.
28th. William H. Beyer, ed. Boca Raton, FL: CRC; 1987. 688p., illus., index. $29.95. 0-8493-0628-0.

This standard mathematical handbook contains both textual and tabular material. The contents include constants and conversion factors; algebra; combinatorial analysis; geometry; trigonometry; logarithmic, exponential, and hyberbolic functions; analytical geometry; calculus; differential equations; special functions; numerical methods; probability and statistics; and financial tables. *Grade Level:* Grades 9–12.
STARR, 90, n.361.

PHYSICS

Physics concerns itself with those fundamental laws and principles that govern all of nature. Early scientific journals referred to physics by the phrase "natural philosophy." Most of the laws and principles of physics are related to mechanics and field theory. *Mechanics* is concerned with anything that relates to the motion of objects or particles by the action of given forces; in other words, what happens when something is pushed, shoved, thrown, dropped, thrust, hurtled, or hit. *Field theory* looks at all of the various fields of energy that produce these forces, such as gravity, electricity, and nuclear power.

From the early designation of natural philosophy, physics has evolved into a complex area with many specialized subfields. These include *acoustics*—the science of sound; *astrophysics*—the application of physics to astronomy and the history of our universe; *atomic physics*—the study of the energy properties of atoms; *biophysics*—the study of the physical properties of living plants and animals; *classical mechanics*—the study of early physics which was concerned with the position of objects in space under the action of forces as a function of time; *electricity*—the study of electric charges at rest and in motion; *electromagnetism*—the study of physical laws and principles that connect electricity and magnetism; *geophysics*—the study of physical laws that affect the earth and its development; *heat*—the study of energy that is the result of a temperature change; *low-temperature physics*—the study of the properties of materials below minus 452 degrees Fahrenheit; *molecular physics*—the study of the interaction of atomic nuclei and their structure; *optics*—the study of light and vision; *solid-state physics*—the study of the physical properties of solids; and *theoretical physics*—the study of physics in the form of mathematics.

Reference books in this area tend to be highly specialized and intended for researchers, with compilations of physical tables being a typical type of physics reference book. With the use of computers, these tables have become more accurate and are available online or have special programs developed which permit the researcher to create tailored tables for a specific experiment or research need. For young people, the number of reference books is limited. Dictionaries are the most prominent type, with the *Barnes and Noble Thesaurus of Physics*, *The Facts on File Dictionary of Physics*, and *McGraw-Hill Dictionary of Physics* being recommended. The *McGraw-Hill Encyclopedia of Physics* is a good encyclopedia but would be unnecessary if the parent encyclopedia, the *McGraw-Hill Encyclopedia of Science and Technology* were already owned. For a good, readable history,

Discoveries in Physics for Scientists and Engineers is recommended. Finally, in the areas of physical tables that young people could use, one should consult *Fundamental Formulas of Physics, Handbook of Physical Calculations*, and *Tables of Physical and Chemical Constants, and Some Mathematical Functions.*

Dictionaries

181. A-Z of Nuclear Jargon.
Jonathon Green. London, Great Britain: Routledge and Kegan Paul; Dist. by Methuen; New York; NY; 1986. 199p., bibliog. $34.95. 0-7102-0641-0.
This is a dictionary of terms that one would encounter in day-to-day reading about nuclear research and politics. There are some 500 terms with definitions from an anti-nuclear viewpoint. Definitions range from a single sentence to two pages. *Grade Level:* Grades 9–12.
BL, July 87, p.1656; Choice, June 87, p.1532; SB, September 87, p.9; SciTech, April 87, p.38; WLB, April 87, p.63.

182. Barnes and Noble Thesaurus of Physics.
Teresa Rickars. R. C. Denney; Stephen Foster, eds. New York, NY: Barnes & Noble/Harper & Row; 1984. 256p., color illus. $13.95, $6.95pbk. 0-06-015214-1, 0-06-463582-1pbk.
Over 1,300 terms from all areas of physics are defined in this general dictionary. Excellent illustrations are used throughout the book. Four appendices cover units of measurement, the international system of units, physical constants, and physical quantities. It is also called the *Cambridge Illustrated Thesaurus of Physics. Grade Level:* Grades 9–12.
ARBA, 86, n.1774; SchLib, September 85, p.290.

183. Dictionary of Effects and Phenomena in Physics: Descriptions, Applictions, Tables.
Joachim Schubert. New York, NY: VCH; 1987. 140p., bibliog. $24.95. 0-89573-487-7.
This dictionary covers the various effects and phenomena in physics. The definitions are concise and for the layperson or undergraduate. *Grade Level:* Grades 9–12.
ARBA, 89, n.1681; Choice, October 88, p.296; SciTech, June 88, p.9.

184. Dictionary of Physical Sciences.
John Daintith. Totowa, NJ: Rowman and Allanheld; 1983 (c1976). 333p., illus. $9.95pbk. 0-8226-379-9pbk.
This is a good dictionary of the more commonly used scientific terms in the main branches of physics, including chemistry and astronomy, as well as relevant terms from the related fields of electronics, computer science, and mathematics. It is a companion to *Dictionary of Life Sciences. Grade Level:* Grades 9–12.

ARBA, 78, n.1207; BL, 1 November 77, p.490; Choice, December 77, p.1338; LJ, August 77, p.1625; SB, December 77, p.137.

185. The Facts on File Dictionary of Physics.
Rev. John Daintith, ed. New York, NY: Facts on File; 1988. 235p., illus. $19.95. 0-8160-1868-5.
This readable dictionary contains brief definitions of terms in physics intended for the layperson and student. It is not comprehensive but covers most of the basic terms in physics that a secondary school student would encounter. *Grade Level:* Grades 6–8. Grades 9–12.
ARBA, 89, n.1677; SB, May 89, p.288; STARR, 90, n.544.

186. McGraw-Hill Dictionary of Physics.
Sybil P. Parker, ed. New York, NY: McGraw-Hill; 1985. 646p. $15.95. 0-07-045418-3.
Some 11,200 terms in this dictionary are taken from the 1984 edition of the *McGraw-Hill Dictionary of Scientific and Technical Terms.* It includes all areas of physics such as acoustics, electricity, mechanics, optics, particle physics, quantum mechanics, and solid state physics. Included in the definitions are abbreviations, acronyms, variant spellings, symbols, and synonyms to the entry term. *Grade Level:* Grades 9–12.
ARBA, 87, n.1723; NewTechBks, November 86, p.63.

187. Minidictionary of Physics.
Revised. New York, NY: Oxford University Press; 1988. 384p., illus. $16.95. 0-19-866154-1.
This is a subject spin-off from the 1984 edition of the *Concise Dictionary of Science* and formerly called the *Concise Dictionary of Physics.* It includes "all the entries relating to physics. . .together with some of those entries relating to astronomy that are required for an understanding of astrophysics and many entries relating to physical chemistry." The definitions are clear and concise and identical to the parent dictionary. This dictionary would not be needed if the parent dictionary was available. *Grade Level:* Grades 9–12.
ARBA, 87, n.1720; NewTechBks, December 86, p.672; R&RBkN, Spring 86, p.9; S&T, March 87, p.282; SchLib, June 86, p.200.

188. New Dictionary of Physics.
2nd. Harold James Gray; Alan Isaacs. London, Great Britain: Longman; 1975. 619p., illus., bibliog. $40.00. 0-582-32242-1.
The first edition of this dictionary was published as the *Dictionary of Physics.* The definitions are brief and nontechnical with good explanations of terms and concepts. Some biographical information is included. *Grade Level:* Grades 9–12.
ARBA, 76, n.1350; Choice, November 75, p.1142; LJ, 1 April 75, p.654; WLB, September 75, p.72.

Encyclopedias

189. McGraw-Hill Encyclopedia of Physics.
Sybil P. Parker, ed. New York, NY: McGraw-Hill; 1983. 1343p.,
illus. $54.50. 0-07-045253-9.
All of the articles in this encyclopedia of physics are from the fifth
edition of the *McGraw-Hill Encyclopedia of Science and Technology*.
They cover all aspects of both classical physics and modern physics,
including acoustics, atomic physics, particle physics, molecular physics,
nuclear physics, classical mechanics, electricity, electromagnetism, fluid
mechanics, heat and thermodynamics, low-temperature physics, optics,
relativity, and solid-state physics. The appendices cover the International System of Units (SI); tables of conversion factors for SI, the
metric system, and the U.S. customary system; chemical symbols;
symbols and abbreviations used in scientific writing; mathematical
signs and symbols; mathematical notations; and the periodic table of
elements. *Grade Level:* Grades 9-12.
ARBA, 84, n.1293; BL, 15 February 84, p.866; SB, March 84, p.197;
WLB, June 83, p.883.

Handbooks

190. Fundamental Formulas of Physics.
Donald Howard Menzel. New York, NY: Dover; 1960. 2v., illus.
$17.00set. 0-486-60595-7, v.1; 0-486-60596-5, v.2.
This handbook of all of the formulas that would be used at all levels of
physics is an unabridged and revised version of a work first published
in 1955. *Grade Level:* Grades 9-12.

**191. Handbook of Physical Calculations: Definitions, Formulas,
Technical Applications, Physical Tables, Conversion Tables, Graphs,
Dictionary of Physical Terms.**
2nd enlarged and revised. Jan J. Tuma. New York, NY: McGraw-
Hill; 1983. 478p., illus., bibliog., index. $41.95. 0-07-065439-5.
This comprehensive handbook of every type of physical calculation
also includes definitions of terms, lists of formulas used in the field of
physics, conversion tables, and numerous supporting tables and graphs.
Grade Level: Grades 9-12.
RSR, October 77, p.24; SB, November 83, p.75.

Histories

192. Discoveries in Physics for Scientists and Engineers.
2nd. Leonard H. Greenberg. Philadelphia, PA: Saunders; 1975. 316p.,
illus. $20.95. 0-7216-4246-2.

An interesting history of discoveries in physics understandable to both the student and the layperson. *Grade Level:* Grades 9–12.

How-to-do-it Books

193. **Physics for Kids: 49 Easy Experiments with Mechanics.**
Robert W. Wood. Blue Ridge Summit, PA: TAB Books, Inc; 1989. 150p., illus., index. $16.95, $9.95pbk. 0-8306-9282-7, 0-8306-3282-4pbk.
This well-written guide covers 49 basic experiments in fluid and solid mechanics. The explanations and directions are clearly detailed and illustrated with line drawings. A list of materials and warning symbols is included. *Grade Level:* Grades 3–5. Grades 6–8. Teacher's/Librarian's Resource.

Tables

194. **Tables of Physical and Chemical Constants, and Some Mathematical Functions.**
15th. London, Great Britain: Longman; 1986. 477p., illus., bibliog. $39.95. 0-582-46354-8.
The earlier editions of this well-known handbook of tables were edited by G.W.C. Kaye and T.H. Laby. It is one of the standard sources to consult for tables in the fields of physics, chemistry, and mathematics. *Grade Level:* Grades 9–12.
Choice, October 75, p.1110.

CHEMISTRY

Chemistry, one of the basic physical sciences, is the study of the properties, composition, and structure of matter, its changes, and its generated energy. As with any scientific discipline, one is not just a chemist but rather a chemist with a speciality. *Physical chemists* are concerned with the physical state of chemical phenomena, whether solid, liquid, or gas. *Analytical chemists* may do qualitative analysis of chemicals in terms of descriptions of elements, compounds, and structural units, or they may do quantitative analysis in terms of measurements of amounts of elements, compounds, or structural units. *Biochemists* study the chemical processes of living organisms. *Inorganic chemists* study the chemical reactions and properties of all of the elements in the periodic table except carbon; *organic chemists* study just the chemical reactions and properties of carbon compounds.

The research literature of chemistry is sophisticated and, in many cases, quite complicated to use and interpret. Chemists depend on massive amounts of data on all compounds, with those data appearing in numerous formats. However, the reference literature for young people is quite simple. Dictionaries are the mainstay and include such well-known ones as D.W.G. Ballentyne's *Dictionary of Named Effects and Laws in Chemistry, Physics, and Mathematics*, Hawley's *Condensed Chemical Dictionary*, Grant and Hackh's *Chemical Dictionary*, and *Lange's Handbook of Chemistry*. Other good dictionaries and handbooks are published by McGraw-Hill and Facts on File. When needed, the following encyclopedias would be good to consult: *McGraw-Hill Encyclopedia of Chemistry* and *Van Nostrand Reinhold Encyclopedia of Chemistry*. Finally, no chemistry collection would be complete without the *CRC Handbook of Chemistry and Physics*, of which there is now a less expensive student edition.

Dictionaries

195. ABC's of Chemistry: An Illustrated Dictionary.
Roy A. Gallant. Garden City, NY: Doubleday; 1963. 88p., illus. Out-of-print.
Although now out-of-print, this is a good elementary picture book dictionary of chemistry. Concise definitions are given for over 500 basic chemical terms and concepts. There are useful tables covering

acids, food elements, plastics, and synthetic fibers. *Grade Level:* Grades 6–8. Grades 9–12.

196. Dictionary of Named Effects and Laws in Chemistry, Physics, and Mathematics.
4th. Denis William George Ballentyne; D.R. Lovett. New York, NY: Chapman and Hall; 1980. 346p. $19.95. 0-412-22390-2.
This useful dictionary identifies over 1,200 chemical reactions, procedures, theories, laws, and other scientific terminology that have been named after a person. Easy to use and concise in the information presented, this dictionary is especially useful for secondary school students, since this is their first encounter with the names that one takes for granted later in the educational process. *Grade Level:* Grades 9–12.
ARBA, 82, n.1407; Choice, June 71, p.529; SB, May 71, p.17.

197. The Facts on File Dictionary of Chemistry.
Revised. John Daintith, ed. New York, NY: Facts on File; 1988. 249p., illus. $19.95. 0-8160-1866-9.
This dictionary is for high school and college students as well as laypersons. Although limited in coverage, the more common chemical terms are included. Definitions are concise and nontechnical. A 1982 edition was published in paperback by Barnes and Noble under the title *Dictionary of Chemistry. Grade Level:* Grades 6–8. Grades 9–12.
ARBA, 89, n.1640; SB, January 89, p.156; STARR, 90, n.171.

198. Glossary of Chemical Terms.
2nd. Clifford A. Hampel; Gessner G. Hawley, eds. New York, NY: Van Nostrand Reinhold; 1982. 306p. $21.95. 0-442-23871-1.
This very good general chemical dictionary for the student contains more than 2,000 terms that emphasize major chemical classifications, important functional terms, basic phenomena and processes, the chemical elements, major compounds, general and miscellaneous terminology, and biographies of outstanding contributors in the chemical field. *Grade Level:* Grades 9–12.
ARBA, 83, n.1283; SB, November 82, p.73.

199. Grant and Hackh's Chemical Dictionary (American, International, European and British Usage): Containing the Words Generally Used in Chemistry, and Many of the Terms Used in the Related Sciences of Physics, Astrophysics, Mineralogy, Pharmacy, Agriculture, Biology, Medicine, Engineering, Based on Recent Chemical Literature.
5th revised. Ingo W.D. Hackh. Roger Grant, ed. New York, NY: McGraw-Hill; 1987. 641p., illus. $74.00. 0-07-024067-1.
One of the most authoritative dictionaries in print, it covers more than 56,000 terms and phrases in chemistry and related fields. It includes trademarks and presents both American and British usage. Although somewhat expensive for secondary school libraries, it should still be considered because of its reputation. *Grade Level:* Grades 9–12.
ARBA, 70(2), p.109; LJ, 15 April 70, p.1442; SB, May 70, p.19.

200. Hawley's Condensed Chemical Dictionary.
11th. N. Irving Sax; Richard J. Lewis; Gessner G. Hawley, eds. New
York, NY: Van Nostrand Reinhold; 1987. 1,135p., illus. $52.95.
0-442-28097-1.

This excellent dictionary and handbook of chemical data includes three
types of information: technical descriptions of chemicals and of raw
and processed materials; definitions of chemical entities, phenomena,
and terminology; and identification of trademarked products used in
the chemical industries. Information for each chemical entry includes
name, synonym, formula, properties, source or occurrence, derivation,
grades, containers, hazards, uses, and shipping regulations. Other types
of information include abbreviations commonly used in the chemical
literature, short biographies, and brief descriptions of U.S. chemical
and related societies and trade associations. Although somewhat advanced for secondary schools, it is still an excellent dictionary for their
use. *Grade Level:* Grades 9-12.
ARBA, 88, n.1739.

201. Hazardous Substances: A Reference.
Melvin Berger. Hillside, NJ: Enslow; 1986. 128p., bibliog. $12.95.
0-89490-116-8.

More than 230 substances that threaten life by contaminating food and
the environment are listed in this dictionary. The text is easy to read
with few highly technical terms. Each entry includes the acronym,
formula, substance's purpose and application, history of its usage, and
its health effects. Drugs are not included but chewing tobacco and
snuff are. *Grade Level:* Grades 9-12.
ARBA, 87, n.1451; BL, 15 November 86, p.494; SLJ, May 87, p.24;
VOYA, April 87, p.51.

202. McGraw-Hill Dictionary of Chemical Terms.
Sybil P. Parker, ed. New York, NY: McGraw-Hill; 1985. 470p.
$15.95. 0-07-045417-5.

All of the terms in this general dictionary of chemistry were taken
from the *McGraw-Hill Dictionary of Scientific and Technical Terms.*
The focus of this dictionary is pure chemistry, with some material
from related fields such as biochemistry. The definitions are brief;
there are no illustrations. *Grade Level:* Grades 9-12.
ARBA, 87, n.1699.

203. McGraw-Hill Dictionary of Chemistry.
Sybil P. Parker, ed. New York, NY: McGraw-Hill; 1984. 665p.
$32.50. 0-07-045420-5.

The 9,000 terms in this chemical dictionary were taken from the
McGraw-Hill Dictionary of Scientific and Technical Terms. It is more
comprehensive than the *McGraw-Hill Dictionary of Chemical Terms.*
The definitions are brief and the coverage includes analytical chemistry, biochemistry, chemical engineering, crystallography, geochemistry, inorganic chemistry, organic chemistry, physical chemistry, and
spectroscopy. *Grade Level:* Grades 9-12.

ARBA, 85, n.1681; BL, 15 April 85, p.1188, August 85, p.1648; Choice, January 85, p.662; LJ, January 85, p.76; SB, May 85, p.297; WLB, January 85, p.357.

204. Minidictionary of Chemistry.
John Daintith, ed. New York, NY: Oxford University Press; 1988. 400p., illus. $16.95. 0-19-866153-3.
These 3,000 terms in the fields of chemistry, physical chemistry, and biochemistry have been taken from the *Concise Science Dictionary*. The definitions are short, concise, and written for students and laypersons. This dictionary was formerly titled *Concise Dictionary of Chemistry*. *Grade Level:* Grades 9–12.
ARBA, 87, n.1695.

205. The Vocabulary of Organic Chemistry.
Milton Orchin. New York, NY: Wiley; 1980. 609p., illus., index. $35.00. 0-471-04491-1.
This dictionary of about 1,300 terms in organic chemistry is for the student and layperson. The terms are grouped according to general content, including symmetry, wave and quantum mechanics, hydrocarbons, classes other than hydrocarbons, stereochemistry, types of organic reaction mechanisms, name reactions, organometallic compounds, natural products, polymers, and fossil fuels. Definitions usually include the pertinent chemical reactions. *Grade Level:* Grades 9–12.
ARBA, 82, n.1439; Choice, May 81, p.1293.

Encyclopedias

206. McGraw-Hill Encyclopedia of Chemistry.
Sybil P. Parker, ed. New York, NY: McGraw-Hill; 1983. 1,195p., illus., index. $49.50. 0-07-045484-1.
This excellent encyclopedia contains articles that appeared in the *McGraw-Hill Encyclopedia of Science and Technology*. Seven hundred ninety signed articles cover all aspects of chemistry but do not cover all areas of biochemistry. Specific compounds, chemical processes, equipment used in the laboratory, and equipment used in the manufacture of chemicals are described. *Grade Level:* Grades 9–12.
ARBA, 84, n.1286; Choice, May 83, p.1267; LJ, 1 June 84, p.1127; SB, November 83, p.76; WLB, June 83, p.883.

207. Van Nostrand Reinhold Encyclopedia of Chemistry.
4th. Douglas M. Considine, ed. New York, NY: Van Nostrand Reinhold; 1984. 1,082p., illus., bibliog., index. $89.50. 0-442-22572-5.
This is a very good one-volume encyclopedia of chemistry with close to 1,300 alphabetically arranged entries. It covers general chemistry and related areas that include raw materials, chemistry of metals, pollution, and food chemistry. *Grade Level:* Grades 9–12.

ARBA, 85, n.1679; BL, 1 September 84, p.36, 15 December 84, p.577; SB, September 85, p.21.

Handbooks

208. CRC Handbook of Chemistry and Physics: A Ready-Reference Book of Chemical and Physical Data.
Boca Raton, FL: CRC; 1913–. 1st– , illus., bibliog., index. Annual. $74.95. 0-8493-0467-9, 67th ed.
Also known as the *Handbook of Chemistry and Physics*, this is the most reliable and most used of the chemistry and physics handbooks. It includes information on all areas of chemistry and physics, such as elements, atomic weights, organic compounds, and physical constants. Although revised on an annual basis, the basic information does not change, and a new edition is usually not needed each year for the general library. Research laboratories will need the latest edition. There is also a student edition. *Grade Level:* Grades 9–12.
ARBA, 76, n.1344; Choice, March 71, p.46; SB, September 72, p.126; STARR, 90, n.188.

209. CRC Handbook of Chemistry and Physics: 1st Student Edition.
Robert C. Weast, ed. Boca Raton, FL: CRC; 1988. 1,760p., index. $29.95. 0-8493-0740-6.
This is an excellent condensed version of the well-known handbook at a very reasonable price. The section on organic compounds is identical to the parent volume as are some of the general tables. The more specific tables used in advanced research have been left out. *Grade Level:* Grades 9–12.
Choice, June 88, p.1532; STARR, 90, n.189.

210. Handbook of the Atomic Elements.
R.A. Williams. New York, NY: Philosophical Library; 1970. 125p. Out-of-print.
Although out-of-print, this handbook of 103 atomic elements is a good source of information on their physical values based on Carbon-12 and values released by the International Union of Pure and Applied Chemistry. *Grade Level:* Grades 9–12.
ARBA, 71, n.1566; Choice, October 70, p.1018; SB, December 70, p.213.

211. Hazardous Chemical Desk Reference.
N. Irving Sax. New York, NY: Van Nostrand Reinhold; 1987. 1,084p., illus., bibliog., index. $69.95. 0-442-28208-7.
Sax has compiled a handbook of information taken from his more comprehensive and expensive work, *Dangerous Properties of Industrial Materials. The Hazardous Chemical Desk Reference* covers those hazardous chemicals that are encountered in industry on a daily basis, and includes warnings as to what hazards result from the chemical reactions. *Grade Level:* Grades 9–12.

212. Lange's Handbook of Chemistry.
13th. John A. Dean; Norbert Adolph Lange, eds. New York, NY: McGraw-Hill; 1985. 1v. various paging, illus., index. $57.00. 0-07-016192-5.
This excellent chemical handbook covers just chemistry. It is divided into nine sections of values, formulas, facts, figures, and data: "Mathematics," "General Information and Conversion Tables," "Atomic and Molecular Structure," "Inorganic Chemistry, Analytical Chemistry," "Electrochemistry," "Organic Chemistry," "Spectroscopy, "Thermal Properties," "Physical Properties," and "Miscellaneous Chemical Information." *Grade Level:* Grades 9–12.
ARBA, 86, n.1753; WLB, May 79, p.654.

213. New Pocket Handbook of Chemistry.
Philip S. Chen; Samuel M. Chen; John Christensen. Malabar, FL: Krieger; 1984. 212p., index. $19.95. 0-89874-532-2.
This handbook, previously known as *A New Handbook of Chemistry*, is written for the student and layperson. It contains the most useful chemical and mathematical information, such as 5-place logarithms, tables of organic and inorganic compounds, and a glossary. *Grade Level:* Grades 9–12.
ARBA, 77, n.1332; SB, September 76, p.80.

214. Rapid Guide to Hazardous Chemicals in the Workplace.
N. Irving Sax; Richard J. Lewis. New York, NY: Van Nostrand Reinhold; 1986. 236p., illus., index. $19.95. 0-442-28220-6.
Sax is the authority on books covering hazardous chemicals. He has books for all levels of users, with some very comprehensive and others brief. This handbook is for the worker who needs quick information without having to search through a huge compilation. It gives basic information on hazardous chemicals, some of which may be encountered in school laboratories or places where students are employed. *Grade Level:* Grades 9–12.

EARTH SCIENCES

The term "earth sciences" is used rather than geology because geology is a more restrictive term. Earth sciences encompasses not only *geology*, which is the study of just the earth, but many other disciplines as well. Earth sciences can be defined as the study of the earth and all forces that have changed and are changing its makeup. It is, in the historical sense, related to *cosmology*, which is the study of how our universe evolved. Physical geography is a closely related discipline but normally not considered an earth science. However, *geomorphology*, which is part of physical geography, could be considered an earth science since it is the study of landforms, including description, classification, origin, history, and ongoing changes. Geomorphology has, in turn, subfields such as *glaciology, soil mechanics, remote sensing, fluvial geology, karst landscapes*, and, to some extent, *cartography*.

Other specific areas of earth science are *geochemistry*—the study of chemical processes within the geological process; *geodesy*—the science of surveying and mapping the earth's surface; *geophysics*—the study of the physical forces on and within the earth; *mineralogy*—the study of minerals found in the earth; *petrology*—the study of the three types of rocks found in and on the earth, igneous or volcanic, metamorphic or pressure changed, and sedimentary or eroded; *meteorology*—the study of the atmosphere which includes *climatology* or the study of climates; *oceanography*—the study of seas and oceans, including the shores and beaches, subsurface rocks and sediments, waves and related forces, chemistry, and all life that depends on the oceans and seas for survival; *paleontology*—the study of all fossil life, including *paleobotany, paleozoology, invertebrate paleontology*, and *micropaleontology; hydrology*—the study of the forces of water on the earth; *stratigraphy*—the study of the layers of sediments that make up the surface of the earth to the bedrock; and *economic geology*—the study of all materials that are mined from the earth.

Research reference literature in the earth sciences is as varied for the student as it is for the professional. Interest in fossils and minerals has generated a fair number of field guides, handbooks, and manuals that pertain to these topics. The *Audubon Society Field Guide to North American Fossils* and *Audubon Society Field Guide to North American Rocks and Minerals* are two excellent examples. *Challinor's Dictionary of Geology* and *The Facts on File Dictionary of Geology and Geophysics* are two very good dictionaries; there are many others that would also serve well. Some of the mineralogy books specifically cover gemstones and have outstanding color photographs. There are also the usual, good McGraw-Hill dictionaries and encyclopedias, and Macmillan and Van Nostrand Reinhold publish some excellent reference sources. Finally, the *World Atlas of Geomorphic Features* is a good example of available scientific atlases.

Atlases—Science

215. The Atlas of Natural Wonders.
Rupert O. Matthews. New York, NY: Facts on File; 1988. 240p., illus. (part in color), maps, bibliog., index. $35.00. 0-8160-1993-2.
This interesting atlas, arranged by longitude, describes 52 worldwide natural wonders. Each location has a photograph, map showing location, and a description of the natural feature. *Grade Level:* Grades 6–8. Grades 9–12.
ARBA, 89, n.1662; BL, 15 November 88, p.523; BRpt, March 89, p.46; SB, May 89, p.298; SciTech, January 89, p.15; SLJ, May 89, p.26; STARR, 90, n.320; WLB, November 88, p.121.

216. Atlas of North America: Space Age Portrait of a Continent.
Washington, DC: National Geographic Society; 1985. 264p., illus., index. $39.95, $29.95pbk. 0-87044-607-X, 0-87044-605-3pbk.
This is an atlas of North America produced through remote sensing and illustrated with photographs taken from satellites, spacecraft, and aircraft using infrared radiation. The first part is thematic and includes geology, climate, and minerals. The second part encompasses 13 broad geographic areas. The last section contains maps of major metropolitan areas and national parks. *Grade Level:* Grades 6–8. Grades 9–12.
BL, July 86, p.1590; Choice, June 86, p.1583; SLJ, May 86, p.26; S&T, May 86, p.473.

217. Atlas of the Sea.
Robert Barton. New York, NY: John Day; 1974. 128p., color illus., maps, index. $10.95. 0-381-98267-X.
This is an excellent overview of the oceans with a chapter on each of the five oceans and the major seas. The illustrations and maps are very attractive. An introductory section covers the basic concepts of physiography and currents in the sea, with special consideration given to mineral resources, fisheries, and pollution. *Grade Level:* Grades 6–8. Grades 9–12.
ARBA, 74, n.1575; BL, 1 January 75, p.455, 15 June 75, p.1091; KR, 15 December 74, p.1315; SB, May 75, p.34.

218. Atlas of World Physical Features.
Rodman E. Snead. New York, NY: Wiley; 1972. 158p., illus., maps, bibliog., index. $42.00. 0-471-80800-8.

This is a very good atlas of physical features that are visible throughout the world. Small-scale maps that show the overall distribution of the land forms indicate where the features can be found. *Grade Level:* Grades 9–12.
SB, May 73, p.59.

219. Earth Science on File.
David Lambert. Sylvia Worth, ed. New York, NY: Facts on File; 1988. 1v. various paging, illus., tables, charts, index. $145.00. 0-8160-1625-9.
Although expensive, this atlas is a compilation of 300 charts, all intended to be copied, covering the earth, astronomy, geology, tectonics, earthquakes, the atmosphere, oceans, weather, climate, erosion processes, paleontology, evolution, and earth resources. The pages are on heavy, card-stock to withstand repeated copying. *Grade Level:* Grades 3–5. Grades 6–8. Grades 9–12. Teacher's/Librarian's Resource.

220. National Geographic Atlas of the World.
5th. Washington, DC: National Geographic Society; 1981. 383p., color illus., maps, bibliog., index. $44.95. 0-87044-347-0.
This is one of the better general world atlases available at a very reasonable cost. Preceding the main series of medium and small-scale political-physical maps, arranged by region, are maps of the ocean floors and physical maps of the continents. There are brief descriptions for each nation. *Grade Level:* Grades 6–8. Grades 9–12.
ARBA, 82, n.573; ASBYP, Fall 82, p.33; BL, 1 September 83, p.44; BW, 4 December 83, p.6; Choice, April 82, p.1047; LJ, 1 April 82, p.720; SB, November 82, p.86.

221. World Atlas of Geomorphic Features.
Rodman E. Snead. Huntington, NY: Robert E. Krieger; 1980. 301p., color illus., maps, bibliog., index. $39.95. 0-88275-272-3.
This compilation of over 100 maps showing the distribution of 63 major landforms that can be seen throughout the world is divided into sections that cover general geography, structure and tectonics, oceanographic and hydrographic features, coastal features, glaciation, wind-created land forms, and water-created landforms. A brief text accompanies each map. *Grade Level:* Grades 9–12.
ARBA, 82, n.1526; BL, 1 April 82, p.1039; Choice, July 81, p.1532; LJ, 1 May 81, p.964; SB, September 81, p.29.

Bibliographies

222. Death of the Dinosaurs and Other Mass Extinctions.
David A. Tyckoson, ed. Gary Fouty, comp. Phoenix, AZ: Oryx Press; 1987. 96p., index. $18.75pbk. Oryx Science Bibliographies, v. 10. 0-89774-432-2pbk.

This unique bibliography covers the much-written-about theories of mass extinctions, with the death of the dinosaurs a major focus. Each included article has been reviewed by the compiler. All included materials are in English and readily available in libraries. Brief annotations are provided for each entry. *Grade Level:* Grades 9–12.
ARBA, 88, n.1766; Choice, January 88, p.746, December 88, p.614; STARR, 89, n.210.

Dictionaries

223. Challinor's Dictionary of Geology.
6th. John Challinor. Antony Wyatt, ed. New York, NY: Oxford University Press; 1986. 374p., index. $35.00, $15.95pbk. 0-19-520505-7, 0-19-520506-5pbk.
This is a dictionary of over 2,000 of the more commonly encountered geological terms. Each of the terms is defined in detail, many with quotations and citations to other sources. The book states that it covers geology "by examining the meaning and usage of names and terms that stand for the more significant things, facts and concepts of the science." It was previously titled *Dictionary of Geology. Grade Level:* Grades 9–12.
ARBA, 87, n.1707; SB, March 87, p.218; WLB, January 65, p.412.

224. Dictionary of Earth Sciences.
Stella E. Stiegeler, ed. Totowa, NJ: Rowmann and Allanheld; 1983 (c1976). 301p., illus. $9.95. 0-8226-0377-2.
About 3,000 words or phrases in geology, paleontology, geophysics, meteorology, and other related sciences are covered in this dictionary. *Grade Level:* Grades 9–12.
ARBA, 78, n.1352; BL, 1 November 77, p.490; Choice, December 77, p.1338; LJ, August 77, p.1625; SB, March 78, p.205.

225. Dictionary of Gemmology.
2nd. P.G. Read. Stoneham, MA: Butterworths; 1988. 166p., illus. $49.95. 0-408-02925-0.
This dictionary covers gems, the scientific terms associated with gems, and the techniques that are used in gemmology. It includes several appendices covering grading, dispersion, and other characteristics of gemstones. *Grade Level:* Grades 9–12.
ARBA, 89, n.1668.

226. Dictionary of Gems and Gemmology, Including Ornamental, Decorative and Curio Stones (Excluding Diamonds): A Glossary of Over 4,000 English and Foreign Words, Terms, and Abbreviations that May be Encountered in English Literature or in Gems, Jewelry, or Art Trades.
6th. Robert M. Shipley. Santa Monica, CA: Gemological Institute of America; 1974. 240p. $7.50. 0-87311-007-2.

This is a layperson's dictionary to gems and gemmology that covers over 4,000 English and foreign terms. *Grade Level:* Grades 9–12.

227. Dictionary of Geological Terms.
3rd. Robert L. Bates; Julia A. Jackson, eds. Garden City, NY: Anchor Press/Doubleday; 1984. 571p. $19.95. 0-385-18100-0.
This dictionary for the layperson contains a selection of terms from the *Glossary of Geology* (American Geological Institute, 1980) that are encountered in day-to-day general reading. *Grade Level:* Grades 9–12.
ARBA, 85, n.1686; BL, 1 September 84, p.36.

228. Dinosaur Dictionary.
Donald F. Glut. New York, NY: Bonanza Books; 1984 (c1972). 218p., illus., bibliog. $6.95pbk.
This general dictionary covers dinosaurs that are currently known to paleontologists. It is alphabetically arranged and includes suborder, family, description, and the skeletal evidence on which the classification is based. *Grade Level:* Grades 6–8. Grades 9–12.
ARBA, 73, n.1460; BL, 1 December 72, p.321; SB, March 73, p.324.

229. The Facts on File Dictionary of Geology and Geophysics.
Dorothy Farris Lapidus. New York, NY: Facts on Files; 1987. 347p., illus. $24.95. 0-87196-703-0.
This good general dictionary of geological terms uses concise definitions to cover many of the subfields of earth sciences, including geophysics. *Grade Level:* Grades 6–8. Grades 9–12.
ARBA, 89, n.1661; Choice, June 88, p.1538; SB, Spring 88, p.426; WLB, December 87, p.92.

230. The Facts on File Dictionary of Marine Science.
Barbara Charton. New York, NY: Facts on File; 1988. 325p., illus. $24.95. 0-8160-1031-5.
This is a good basic dictionary of terms associated with marine sciences and includes terms relating to oceans, reefs, coastlines, waves, tides, plants, animals, and chemistry. It is written for schools and the general public. *Grade Level:* Grades 6–8. Grades 9–12.
ARBA,89, n.1670; SB, May 89, p.290; STARR, 90, n.315.

231. Illustrated Dictionary of Place Names, United States and Canada.
Kelsie B. Harder, ed. New York, NY: Facts on File; 1985 (c1976). 631p., illus., bibliog. $19.95, $12.95pbk. 0-8160-1143-5, 0-8160-1048-Xpbk.
This geographical dictionary lists over 15,000 places, natural features, and historical sites located north of the Rio Grande River. Each entry includes information on general location, derivation of name, variant names, and earlier names. Biographical information is given for persons after whom a particular site was named. *Grade Level:* Grades 9–12.

ARBA, 77, n.551; BL, 15 December 76, p.627; Choice, December 76, p.1271; LJ, 15 June 76, p.1407, 15 April 77, p.877; WLB, October 76, p.186.

232. Illustrated Dinosaur Dictionary.
Helen Roney Sattler. New York, NY: Lothrop, Lee and Shepard Books/William Morrow; 1983. 315p., illus. (part in color), bibliog., index. $17.50. 0-688-00479-2.
Almost 300 descriptions of dinosaurs are presented in this illustrated dictionary. The discussions are concise and easy to read. A classification table of dinosaurs is included in the introduction. For each entry, the full name of the dinosaur is given with pronunciation, scientific classification, description, and information on the amount of evidence presently available about its existence. *Grade Level:* Grades 6–8. Grades 9–12.
ARBA, 85, n.1700; SB, September 84, p.33; SLJ, May 84, p.24.

233. McGraw-Hill Dictionary of Earth Sciences.
Sybil P. Parker, ed. New York, NY: McGraw-Hill; 1984. 837p. $36.00. 0-07-045252-0.
Most of the terms relating to all aspects of earth sciences have been taken from the *McGraw-Hill Dictionary of Scientific and Technical Terms*. The book is alphabetically arranged, and the brief definitions include synonyms, acronyms, and abbreviations. Terms from related disciplines, such as climatology, engineering geology, mapping, mineralogy, paleontology, and petrology are also included. *Grade Level:* Grades 9–12.
ARBA, 85, n.1685; BL, 15 January 85, p.703, 15 April 85, p.1188; LJ, July 84, p.1315; SB, January 85, p.142; SciTech, May 84, p.5.

234. Ocean and Marine Dictionary.
David F. Tver. Centreville, MD: Cornell Maritime Press; 1979. 358p. $18.50. 0-87033-246-5.
This is a general dictionary of terms related to sailing, ships, weather, currents, ancient terminology, seashells, marine biology, and nautical topics. Several useful tables include volume and mean depth of oceans and seas, salt present in the sea, velocity of sound in sea water, composition of sea water, mineral matter in river and sea water, and temperatures of the oceans. *Grade Level:* Grades 9–12.
ARBA, 81, n.1526; BL, 1 September 80, p.71; BL, 1 September 84, p.36; Choice, September 80, p.70; WLB, April 80, p.529.

235. Penguin Dictionary of Geography: Definitions and Explanations of Terms Used in Physical Geography.
7th. W.G. Moore. Baltimore, MD: Penguin Books; 1988. 246p., illus. $8.95pbk. 0-14-051219-5pbk.
This is a dictionary of brief but accurately defined terms encountered in physical geography, climatology, geology, astronomy, and other earth science disciplines. It was originally published as *Dictionary of Geography. Grade Level:* Grades 9–12.

ARBA, 79, n.581; LJ, 15 September 67, p.3027; WLB, September 68, p.75.

236. Penguin Dictionary of Geology.
D.G.A. Whitten. Baltimore, MD: Penguin Books; 1978 (c1972).
493p., illus. $6.95. 0-14-051049-4.
This is a small dictionary of terms in the fields of geology and physical geography. Brief biographies of prominent geologists are also included. *Grade Level:* Grades 9–12.
ARBA, 77, n.1427; Choice, March 74, p.66; WLB, May 73, p.793.

237. VNR Color Dictionary of Minerals and Gemstones.
Michael O'Donoghue. New York, NY: Van Nostrand Reinhold; 1982.
159p., color illus., bibliog., index. $12.95pbk. 0-442-37431-9pbk.
This is a dictionary for the amateur collector of minerals that gives information on how to collect and display the specimens. For each entry, the following information is given: name, chemical composition, general properties, mode of occurrence, locations where found, mode of treatment, and information on fashioning, if it can be made into jewelry or other ornamentation. *Grade Level:* Grades 9–12.
ARBA, 83, n.1414; BL, 15 September 83, p.153; SB, March 83, p.194.

Encyclopedias

238. Album of Rocks and Minerals.
Tom McGowen. New York, NY: Checkerboard Press; 1987 (c1981).
61p., illus. (part in color), index. $4.95pbk. 0-02-688504-2pbk.
This well-written encyclopedia covers 22 rocks and minerals and explains "how specific rocks and minerals were formed, why they look the way they do, and their many uses, both past and present." *Grade Level:* Grades 3–5. Grades 6–8.
ARBA, 83, n.1413; ASBYP, Spring 82, p.48; BL, 1 March 82, p.899; SB, March 82, p.213; STARR, 89, n.213.

239. Cambridge Encyclopedia of Earth Sciences.
David G. Smith, ed. New York, NY: Cambridge University Press; 1981. 496p., illus. (part in color), bibliog., index. $37.50.
0-521-23900-1.
This encyclopedia provides an excellent overview of earth sciences. Coverage of current earth science theory is especially strong. It is not arranged in the true sense of an encyclopedia but, rather, in textbook format. *Grade Level:* Grades 9–12.
ARBA, 83, n.1403; BL, 15 May 82, p.1212; Choice, July 82, p.1534; LJ, 15 May 82, p.1002; S&T, August 82, p.152, March 83, p.234; SB, November 82, p.75; SchLib, September 82, p.285.

240. Collector's Encyclopedia of Rocks and Minerals.
A.F.L. Deeson, ed. New York, NY: Exeter Books; 1983 (c1973).
288p., illus. (part in color). $15.00.

This is a good general guide to rocks and minerals arranged alphabetically by the name of the mineral or rock group. For each mineral the following is given: composition, crystal system, habit, color, luster, streak, fracture, cleavage, hardness test, specific gravity, special features, methods of identification, occurrence, environment, varieties, and synonyms and for each rock group: clan, type, grade, color, texture, structure, essential minerals, special features, occurrence, environment, varieties, and synonyms. *Grade Level:* Grades 9–12. ARBA, 75, n.1094; BL, 15 October 74, p.254; WLB, April 74, p.674.

241. Color Encyclopedia of Gemstones.
2nd. Joel E. Arem. New York, NY: Van Nostrand Reinhold; 1987. 343p., color illus., bibliog., index. $49.95. 0-442-20833-2.
This well-written encyclopedia covers over 200 gemstones, giving chemical formula, crystal structure, colors, luster, hardness, density, cleavage, optics, spectral data, luminescence, and size. The color photography is outstanding, capturing the cut and brilliance of each gem. *Grade Level:* Grades 9–12.
ARBA, 88, n.1760; STARR, 89, n.214.

242. Earthquakes, Tides, Unidentified Sounds and Related Phenomena: A Catalog of Geophysical Anomalies.
William R. Corliss, comp. Glen Arm, MD: Sourcebook Project; 1983. 214p., index. $12.95. 0-915554-11-9.
This is an interesting catalog of unexplained phenomena, such as geysers at sea, chemical differences in ocean waters, dogs howling before earthquakes, planetary or lunar alignments during earth quakes, and crackling sounds heard during auroras. References are supplied. *Grade Level:* Grades 9–12.
ARBA,84, n.1288.

243. Encyclopedia of Minerals and Gemstones.
Michael O'Donoghue, ed. New York, NY: Crescent; 1983 (c1976). 304p., illus. (part in color), bibliog., index. $22.50. 0-517-37483-8.
This encyclopedia describes over 1,000 minerals. It also presents discussions on morphology, basic and economic geology, mineral identification, gem cutting, and mineral display. *Grade Level:* Grades 6–8. Grades 9–12.
ARBA, 77, n.1437; BL, 15 May 77, p.1443; Choice, June 77, p.512; LJ, 15 November 76, p.2359; WLB, April 77, p.686.

244. Field Guide to Prehistoric Life.
David Lambert; Diagram Group. New York, NY: Facts on File; 1985. 256p., illus., bibliog., index. $17.95. 0-8160-1125-7.
This is not a field guide to be used in the field but, rather, an encyclopedic guide that describes the major forms of prehistoric life, locating them in time and place. The guide covers fossil clues, fossil plants, invertebrates, fishes, amphibians, reptiles, birds and mammals, and the records in the rocks themselves. Fossil hunting is discussed, and a roster of famous fossil hunters is given along with a list of worldwide museums. *Grade Level:* Grades 9–12.

ARBA, 86, p.1763; BL, 15 January 86, p.744; BRpt, March 86, p.46; BW, 11 May 86, p.21; SB, November 86, p.98; SLJ, May 86, p.29; VOYA, December 85, p.332.

245. Illustrated Encyclopedia of the Mineral Kingdom.
Alan R. Woolley, ed. New York, NY: Larousse; 1978. 240p., illus. (part in color), bibliog., index. Out-of-print. 0-88332-089-4.
Although out-of-print, this is still an excellent and colorful encyclopedia of minerals. It defines geological and mineralogical terms and describes over 300 of the most common minerals, giving chemical composition, crystal system, habit, twinning, specific gravity, hardness, fracture, color and transparency, streak, luster, distinguishing features, formation and occurrence, and economic value. *Grade Level:* Grades 9–12.
ARBA, 79, n.1423; BL, 1 May 79, p.1390; Choice, May 79, p.364; LJ, August 78, p.1497, 1 March 79, p.547; SB, September 79, p.83.

246. The Macmillan Illustrated Encyclopedia of Dinosaurs and Prehistoric Animals: A Visual Who's Who of Prehistoric Life.
Dougal Dixon. New York, NY: Macmillan; 1988. 312p., illus. (part in color), bibliog., index. $39.95. 0-02-580191-0.
This well-written encyclopedia details over 600 species of dinosaurs and other prehistoric animals. Each chapter covers a specific type, such as birds, reptiles, or mammal-like reptiles. The illustrations are excellent and add much to the text. *Grade Level:* Grades 9–12.
ARBA, 89, n.1669; Choice, April 89, p.1357.

247. McGraw-Hill Encyclopedia of Ocean and Atmospheric Sciences.
Sybil P. Parker, ed. New York, NY: McGraw-Hill; 1980. 580p., illus., bibliog., index. $47.50. 0-07-045267-9.
This spin-off from the *McGraw-Hill Encyclopedia of Science and Technology* covers all aspects of ocean and atmospheric sciences. It includes articles on pollution, satellites, climate modification, and sea diving. *Grade Level:* Grades 9–12.
ARBA, 81, n.1513; BL, 1 November 80, p.410; Choice, June 80, p.520; LJ, 1 February 80, p.395; SB, November 80, p.74; WLB, March 80, p.464.

248. McGraw-Hill Encyclopedia of the Geological Sciences.
2nd. Sybil P. Parker, ed. New York, NY: McGraw-Hill; 1988. 722p., illus., bibliog., index. $85.00. 0-07-045500-7.
This alphabetically arranged encyclopedia of articles on geology is taken from the *McGraw-Hill Encyclopedia of Science and Technology.* It covers geology, geochemistry, geophysics, and related aspects of oceanography and meteorology. *Grade Level:* Grades 9–12.
BL, 1 October 88, p.242; SB, January 89, p.141; SciTech, July 88, p.13.

249. Mountains of North America.
Fred Beckey. New York, NY: Bonanza Books; 1984 (c1982). 255p., color illus., bibliog. Out-of-print.

This now out-of-print book is a highly illustrated work covering some 36 separate descriptions of mountains in North America. It is interesting to read and includes practical knowledge on geology, biota, and the history of the various mountain ranges. *Grade Level:* Grades 9–12.
BL, 1 November 82, p.342; LJ, 1 March 83, p.446; PW, 17 September 82, p.102; SB, September 83, p.14.

250. Ocean World Encyclopedia.
Donald G. Groves; Lee M. Hunt. New York, NY: McGraw-Hill; 1980. 443p., illus., maps, index. $49.95. 0-07-025010-3.
This encyclopedia for the layperson covers physical, geological, chemical, and biological oceanography; oceanographic instrumentation; hurricanes; international marine science organizations; and famous oceanographers. *Grade Level:* Grades 9–12.
ARBA, 81, n.1524; BL, 15 February 81, p.841; LJ, 1 June 80, p.1292; SB, January 81, p.136; SLJ, December 80, p.22; WLB, June 80, p.670.

251. 1001 Questions Answered About Natural Land Disasters.
Barbara Tufty. New York, NY: Dodd, Mead and Co; 1969. 350p., illus., index. Out-of-print.
Although out-of-print, this is still a good question-and-answer format encyclopedia covering earthquakes, volcanos, tsunamis, floods, droughts, fires, rock avalanches, and snow slides. The text is very readable, presenting the origin or cause of the disaster, its impact, and the disaster's effect upon human life. *Grade Level:* Grades 9–12.
ARBA, 70(1), p.100; BL, 15 June 69, p.1153; Choice, September 69, p.796; SB, May 69, p.36.

252. 1001 Questions Answered About the Oceans and Oceanography.
Robert W. Taber; Harold W. Dubach. New York, NY: Dodd, Mead and Co; 1972. 269p., illus., index. Out-of-print. 0-396-06496-5.
Now out-of-print, this encyclopedia is still a good source of information on oceans and oceanography. Information presented in the form of questions and answers includes the topics of marine biology, myths, and legends. *Grade Level:* Grades 9–12.
ARBA, 73, n.1520; Choice, October 72, p.996; SB, September 72, p.132.

253. Rainbow Prehistoric Life Encyclopedia.
Mark Lambert; Adrian Sington, eds. New York, NY: Checkerboard Press; 1987 (c1981). 138p., illus. (part in color), maps, bibliog., index. $9.95. 0-026-88539-5.
The information in this book is not in encyclopedic format but, rather, in narrative. It is for grades 3 to 9 and emphasizes reptiles and mammals. The excellent illustrations help to give some information about dinosaurs, giant mammals, and cave dwellers. *Grade Level:* Grades 3–5. Grades 6–8.
ARBA, 84, n.1400.

254. Standard Encyclopedia of the World's Mountains.
Anthony Julian Huxley. New York, NY: Putnam; 1968 (c1962).
383p., illus., maps, index. Out-of-print.
Mountain ranges are the focal point for this standard reference work,
now out-of-print, giving information on geology, special fauna and
flora, historical importance, first discovery, and first explorers or
climbers. A gazetteer is included. *Grade Level:* Grades 9–12.

255. Standard Encyclopedia of the World's Oceans and Islands.
Anthony Julian Huxley. New York, NY: Putnam; 1968 (c1962).
383p., illus., bibliog., index. Out-of-print.
This standard reference work, now out-of-print, covers the world's
oceans and major islands. It includes information on their special
fauna and flora, historical importance, first discovery, and first explorers. A gazetteer is included. *Grade Level:* Grades 9–12.

256. Standard Encyclopedia of the World's Rivers and Lakes.
R. Kay Gresswell; Anthony Julian Huxley. New York, NY: Putnam;
1966 (c1965). 384p., illus., index. Out-of-print.
All major rivers and lakes of the world are included in this standard
encyclopedia, which is now out-of-print. For each entry, the river's
location, source, outlet, and length, or the lake's length, breadth, and
area are given. *Grade Level:* Grades 9–12.

257. Van Nostrand's Standard Catalog of Gems.
John Sinkankas. New York, NY: Van Nostrand Reinhold; 1976
(c1968). 286p., illus., bibliog., index. $12.95. 0-442-27621-4.
This is a catalog of cut and rough gemstones, including carvings and
other ornamental objects and pearls. It evaluates the gem, gives its
market value and supply, and explains how the gem's value is determined. *Grade Level:* Grades 9–12.
BL, 1 October 78, p.142; LJ, 15 April 69, p.1582.

Field Books

258. The Atmosphere.
Collector's Lifetime Edition. Vincent J. Schaefer; John A. Day.
Boston, MA: Houghton Mifflin; 1981. 359p., illus. (part in color),
bibliog., index. $15.95, $10.95pbk. Peterson Field Guide Series, 26.
0-395-24080-8, 0-395-33033-5pbk.
This is the fiftieth anniversary edition of a work previously entitled
Field Guide to the Atomosphere. This very interesting field guide covers
rainbows, storm systems, dust, tornados, and cloud formations. It
describes the phenomena with easy to understand text and excellent
illustrations. There is a glossary, a chapter covering simple experiments, and pointers for photographers. *Grade Level:* Grades 9–12.
ARBA, 83, n.1408; BL, 15 June 81, p.1324; Kliatt, Spring 83, p.42; LJ,
1 March 82, p.512; S&T, February 82, p.158; SB, November 81, p.76;
SLJ, August 81, p.85.

259. Audubon Society Field Guide to North American Fossils.
Ida Thompson. New York, NY: Knopf; 1982. 846p., illus. (part in color), maps, index. $13.50. Audubon Society Field Guide Series. 0-394-52412-8.
This softbound field guide to fossils is divided into a section of color photographs followed by a section of detailed descriptions. It covers 420 fossils of marine and freshwater invertebrates, insects, plants, and vertebrates that are likely to be found by the amateur. *Grade Level:* Grades 6–8. Grades 9–12.
ARBA, 83, n.1308; BL, 1 January 83, p.59, 15 September 83, p.148; BRpt, March 83, p.51; LJ, 1 March 83, p.490, 1 March 84, p.434; SLJ, April 83, p.134.

260. Audubon Society Field Guide to North American Rocks and Minerals.
Charles W. Chesterman. New York, NY: Knopf; 1978. 850p., illus. (part in color), bibliog., index. $13.50. Audubon Society Field Guide Series. 0-394-50269-8.
This well-organized field guide with excellent color photographs gives the following information for each mineral: mineralogical name, chemical name, formula, color and luster, hardness, cleavage, other data, crystals, best field marks, similar species, environment, occurrence, and color plate; and for each rock: name, texture, structure, color, luster, hardness, other data, field features, metamorphism, parent rock, mineralogy, and environment. *Grade Level:* Grades 6–8. Grades 9–12.
ARBA, 80, n.1440; BL, 15 June 80, p.1563; BW, 3 June 79, p.E2; LJ, August 79, p.1550; SB, September 80, p.14; SLJ, December 80, p.21.

261. A Field Guide to Dinosaurs.
Diagram Group. New York, NY: Avon; 1983. 256p., illus., maps, bibliog., index. $8.95pbk. 0-380-83519-3pbk.
This excellent general field guide covers over 340 dinosaurs. The book describes each dinosaur in concise text and provides general discussion about the dinosaur's demise. *Grade Level:* Grades 6–8. Grades 9–12.
ARBA, 85, n.1697; BL, July 83, p.1373; Kliatt, Fall 83, p.58; LJ, 1 September 83, p.1711; SLJ, November 83, p.90.

262. The Field Guide to Geology.
David Lambert; Diagram Group. New York, NY: Facts on File; 1988. 256p., illus., maps, bibliog., index. $22.95. 0-8160-1697-6.
This well-written introductory field guide to geology for students and the general public is well-illustrated, depicting all aspects of geology. *Grade Level:* Grades 6–8. Grades 9–12.
ARBA, 89, n.1658; BL, 15 May 88, p.1560.

263. Field Guide to Landforms in the United States.
John A. Shimer. New York, NY: Macmillan; 1972. 272p., illus., bibliog., index. Out-of-print.

This now out-of-print field guide for the physical geographer or geologist covers the major geologic provinces of the United States. The book contains excellent illustrations and descriptions of various landscape features that school children encounter on field trips. *Grade Level:* Grades 9–12.
ARBA, 73, n.1504; BL, 1 May 72, p.750; LJ, 1 March 73, p.700.

264. Field Guide to Rocks and Minerals.
4th. Frederick H. Pough. Boston, MA: Houghton Mifflin; 1987 (c1976). 480p., illus. (part in color), bibliog., index. $17.95, $12.95pbk. Peterson Field Guide Series, 7. 0-395-24047-6, 0-395-08106-8pbk.
This excellent field guide covers 270 minerals grouped according to their chemical composition. Each mineral and rock is fully described. There are also chapters describing the physical and chemical attributes of minerals, crystal classification, and home laboratory techniques. *Grade Level:* Grades 9–12.
ARBA, 77, n.1438; BL, 1 September 77, p.67; BW, 12 December 76, p.147; SB, December 77, p.158.

265. Fossils for Amateurs: A Guide to Collecting and Preparing Invertebrate Fossils.
2nd. Russell P. MacFall; Jay Collin. New York, NY: Van Nostrand Reinhold; 1983. 374p., illus., maps, bibliog., index. $19.95, $13.95pbk. 0-442-26348-1, 0-442-26350-2pbk.
This is a well-written field and laboratory guide to collecting and preparing invertebrate fossils and some fossil plants. Each fossil is described and locations for collecting are given. There are also chapters on amateur paleontological societies, fossils as art objects, and buying and selling fossils. A list of geological museums in North America is included in an appendix. *Grade Level:* Grades 9–12.
ARBA, 85, n.1698; Choice, May 84, p.1324; SB, March 85, p.200.

266. Pictorial Guide to Fossils.
Gerard R. Case. New York, NY: Van Nostrand Reinhold; 1982. 515p., illus., bibliog., index. $32.95. 0-442-22651-9.
This pictorial guide covers all fossils from protozoa to mammals other than humans. Each chapter has a general discussion of the phylum, description of classes, typical species of fossils, and the eras which they represent. A location guide for hunting that particular fossil is included. *Grade Level:* Grades 6–8. Grades 9–12.
ARBA, 83, n.1300; LJ, 15 June 82, p.1232; SB, May 83, p.256.

267. Rocks and Minerals: A Guide to Familiar Minerals, Gems, Ores, and Rocks.
Herbert S. Zim; Paul R. Shaffer. New York, NY: Golden Press; 1964 (c1957). 160p., color illus. $2.95. Golden Nature Guide. 0-307-24499-7.

This guide covers over 400 rocks and minerals, giving information about formation, structure, use, and importance. Geological information and information on how to identify and collect the rocks and minerals are also included. *Grade Level:* Grades 3–5. Grades 6–8.

268. Simon and Schuster's Guide to Fossils.
Paolo Arduini; Giorgio Teruzzi. New York, NY: Simon and Schuster; 1986. 317p., illus. (part in color). $22.95. 0-671-63219-1.
This is an excellent field guide to identifying and collecting fossils. Each fossil is described and locations of where they can be found are indicated. Notes are given on the preservation of fossil sites so that areas are not destroyed. *Grade Level:* Grades 9–12.
BL, 1 May 87, p.1321; Choice, November 87, p.451; Kliatt, Spring 87, p.51; LJ, 1 June 87, p.103.

269. Simon and Schuster's Guide to Rocks and Minerals.
Martin Prinz; George Harlow; Joseph Peters, eds. New York, NY: Simon and Schuster; 1978. 607p., illus. (part in color), index. $17.95, $9.95pbk. 0-671-24396-9, 0-671-24417-5pbk.
This guide to rocks and minerals covers identification, principles of classification, and other mineralogical topics. For each mineral entry, the chemical composition, crystal form, physical properties, rock environment, geographical distribution, major uses, and rarity are given. For each rock entry, the chemistry, origin, classification, type, grain size, environment in which formed, and pressure and temperature of formation are given. *Grade Level:* Grades 9–12.
ARBA, 80, n.1445; BL, 15 January 80, p.738; Choice, June 79, p.558; Kliatt, Winter 79, p.52; LJ, 15 January 79, p.201.

Guides

270. The Fossil Book: A Record of Prehistoric Life.
Revised and expanded. Carroll Lane Fenton; Mildred A. Fenton. Garden City, NY: Doubleday; 1989. 480p., illus. $35.00. 0-385-19327-0.
This authoritative account covers the entire range of prehistoric life except for humans. The photographs and drawings show plant and animal fossils from the earliest times to a few centuries ago, progressing from the simplest forms of life to the more complex. *Grade Level:* Grades 9–12.

271. Geology.
Frank H.T. Rhodes. New York, NY: Golden Press; 1972. 160p., illus., index. $2.95. Golden Science Guide. 0-307-24349-4.
This good elementary text discusses geological topics, such as igneous rocks, ores, mountains, earthquakes, volcanos, and oceans. The text is brief, but there are numerous photographs. *Grade Level:* Grades 3–5. Grades 6–8.
BL, 1 March 73, p.645; SB, May 73, p.37.

272. Minerals and Rocks.
Keith Lye. New York, NY: Arco; 1980 (c1979). 125p., color illus., index. $6.95. Arco Fact Guides in Color. 0-668-04847-6.
As a good introductory guide to minerals and rocks, this book gives information on the occurrence, utilization, identification, and geological formation of the minerals, as well as descriptions of 169 individual items. *Grade Level:* Grades 9–12.
ARBA, 81, n.1519; SB, January 81, p.134; SchLib, September 80, p.312; SLJ, October 80, p.173.

Handbooks

273. Gemstone Identifier.
Walter W. Greenbaum. New York, NY: Prentice-Hall; 1988. 182p., illus. (part in color), bibliog., index. $8.95pbk. 0-13-347444-5pbk.
This is a good general handbook for the layperson and gemologist. The chapters are brief but cover various ways of identifying gems, including hardness, specific gravity, refraction, magnification, fluorescence, and inclusion. Also included is information on how to determine the value of gem stones. *Grade Level:* Grades 9–12.
ARBA, 84, n.1391.

274. Gemstones of the World.
English-language. Walter Schumann. New York, NY: Sterling; 1977. 256p., illus. (part in color), bibliog., index. $21.50. 0-8069-3088-2.
This translation of *Edelsteine und Schmucksteine* is a very suitable handbook for the jeweler, layperson, and rockhound. Each type of gemstone is discussed, giving information as to where it is found, how treated, how to identify, and how and why it is synthesized. Each gem is illustrated with several examples. *Grade Level:* Grades 9–12.
ARBA, 79, n.1422; BL, 15 June 80, p.1698; LJ, 1 February 78, p.375; WLB, June 78, p.813.

275. Handbook of Gem Identification.
12th. Richard R. Liddicoat, Jr. Santa Monica, CA: Gemological Institute of America; 1989. 364p., illus., index. $39.95. 0-87311-012-9.
One of the better established handbooks for the identification of gems, this book is for the practicing gemologist but of interest to others outside that field, including hobbyists. There are full descriptions of each gem with many illustrations. *Grade Level:* Grades 9–12.

276. Handbook of Geographical Nicknames.
Harold S. Sharp. Metuchen, NJ: Scarecrow; 1980. 153p. $16.50. 0-8108-1280-0.
Nicknames of cities, rivers, mountains, islands, deserts, and countries are found in this alphabetically arranged handbook. The nickname is referred to the main entry, which is in capital letters followed by a brief explanation of location. *Grade Level:* Grades 9–12.

ARBA,81, n.622; LJ, 1 May 80, p.1070; WLB, September 80, p.65.

277. Larousse Guide to Minerals, Rocks, and Fossils.
W.R. Hamilton; Alan R. Woolley; A.C. Bishop. New York, NY: Larousse; 1978 (c1974). 320p., illus. (part in color), bibliog., index. $15.95. 0-88332-079-7.
This excellently illustrated handbook covers some 220 minerals, 90 rocks, and 300 fossils. Each entry on minerals provides information about the stone's chemical formula, crystal system, specific gravity, hardness, cleavage, fracture, color and transparency, streak, luster, distinguishing features, and occurrence. Information on rocks includes color, grain size, texture, structure, mineralogy, and field relations, while information on fossils includes geologic period, occurrence, and physical characteristics. The earlier edition was titled *Hamlyn Guide to Minerals, Rocks, and Fossils. Grade Level:* Grades 9–12.
ARBA, 78, n.1359; BL, 15 October 78, p.408; BL, 1 September 84, p.36; LJ, 15 October 77, p.2149; WLB, February 78, p.503.

278. Simon and Schuster's Guide to Gems and Precious Stones.
Curzio Cipriani; Alessandro Borelli. Kennie Lyman, ed. New York, NY: Simon and Schuster; 1986. 384p., illus. (part in color), bibliog., index. $21.95, $10.95pbk. 0-671-60116-4, 0-671-60430-9pbk.
This is a well-written and nicely illustrated guide to the many gems and precious stones found throughout the world. Each entry is fully described so that the user can easily identify the specimen at hand. *Grade Level:* Grades 6–8. Grades 9–12.

Manuals

279. Gemstone and Mineral Data Book: A Compilation of Data, Recipes, Formulas and Instructions for the Mineralogist, Gemmologist, Lapidary, Jeweler, Craftsman and Collector.
John Sinkankas. Prescott, AZ: Geoscience Press; 1988 (c1972). 352p., index. $6.95pbk.
This is a good manual for the practicing mineralogist, gemologist, jeweler, and lapidariest. It covers a wealth of information, including various formulas, chemicals, lapidary equipment, polishing tactics, jewelry data, properties, cleaning, nomenclature, optical properties, and identification. This would be a useful manual for any student in a jewelry class. *Grade Level:* Grades 9–12.
ARBA, 82, n.1525; BL, August 83, p.1551; Choice, January 73, p.1435.

Yearbooks/Annuals/Almanacs

280. Concise Marine Almanac.
Gerard J. Mangone. New York, NY: Van Nostrand Reinhold; 1986.
135p. $27.95. 0-442-26174-8.
This is a summary of facts about the seas that is brief but still informative. It covers measurements, geographic features, naval forces of the major powers, significant merchant marine forces and ports, fisheries, marine mineral resources, and marine pollution. *Grade Level:* Grades 9–12.
ARBA, 87, n.1714; Choice, December 86, p. 608.

GENERAL BIOLOGY

Biology is that part of science concerned with all life from micro-scopic animals to Sequoia trees. Since it is a broad field, it has been divided into *botany*—the study of plants, and *zoology*—the study of animals. A separate chapter has been devoted to each of these dis-ciplines. It would be impossible for any one person to have expertise in the whole field of biology. Instead biologists, botanists, and zool-ogists become specialists. They may specialize in such areas as *taxon-omy*—the systematic naming of living organisms; *morphology*—the study of the form and structure of organisms; *embryology*—the study of the early development of an organism; *physiology*—the study of all the vital functions of an organism that makes it total and unique; *cell biology*—the study of the individual cells that make up the whole; *genetics*—the study of the genes and heredity of an organism; *evolu-tion*—the study of the historical development of organisms; and *ecol-ogy*—the study of organisms in relation to their environment.

In summation, the *McGraw-Hill Concise Encyclopedia of Science and Technology* states, "The term biology embraces those principles of widest application to the origin, growth and development, struc-ture, function, evolution, and distribution of plants and animals."

The reference sources included in this general biology chapter cover information about both botany and zoology. Encyclopedias such as the *Cambridge Encyclopedia of Life Sciences, Encyclopedia of the Biological Sciences*, and the *Biology Encyclopedia* are good, all-around sources, useful to grade school, high school, and university students alike. There are many dictionaries, but the *Dictionary of Life Sciences, The Facts on File Dictionary of Biology*, and *Henderson's Dictionary of Biological Terms* stand out. Since agriculture involves both plant and animal sciences and has its roots in biology, two sources should be noted, *Black's Agricultural Dictionary* and *Farm and Garden Index*.

Biology is the study of living organisms. In the study of each organism, whether plant or animal, a name is assigned showing its relationship to all other living organisms. Therefore, one should be-come familiar with some of the taxonomic nomenclature. Each or-ganism can be classed into seven categories: (from general to specific) Kingdom, Phylum, Class, Order, Family, Genus, and Species. In larger groups of organisms where there has been a long history, more categories are used: Kingdom, Phylum, Subphylum, Superclass, Class, Subclass, Cohort, Superorder, Order, Suborder, Superfamily, Family, Subfamily, Tribe, Genus, Subgenus, Species, and Subspecies. Using the seven categories, the lion belongs to the Animalia Kingdom, Chordata Phylum, Mammalia Class, Carnivora Order, Felidae Family, *Felis* Genus, and *leo* Species, while the common house fly belongs to the Animalia Kingdom, Arthropoda Phylum, Insecta Class, Diptera Order, Muscidae Family, *Musca* Genus, and *domestica* Species. Similar procedures are followed for plants, with the white oak tree belonging to the Plantae Kingdom, Magnoliophyta Division, Magnoliopsida Class, Fogales Order, Fogaceae Family, *Quercus* Genus, and *alba* Species. There are more than 300,000 known species of plants and 1,000,000 species of animals.

Atlases—Science

281. Life Sciences on File.
Diagram Group. New York, NY: Facts on File; 1986. 1v. various paging, illus., index, loose-leaf. $145.00. 0-8160-1284-9.
This is a collection of more than 300 black-and-white diagrams pertaining to the study of biology, zoology, and botany. They are meant to be copied and are, therefore, printed on heavy card stock. There are six sections: "Unity"—biochemistry; "Continuity"—cell structure, cell reproduction, genetics, and evolution; "Diversity"—plant and animal kingdoms; "Maintenance"—nutrition, transport, secretion, respiration, excretion, coordination, locomotion, reproduction, and growth and development; "Human Biology"—life functions of humans; and "Ecology"—all aspects of ecology. Although expensive, it is very useful for teachers at all levels. *Grade Level:* Grades 3–5. Grades 6–8. Grades 9–12. Teacher's/Librarian's Resource.
BL, 1 October 86, p.210.

Dictionaries

282. Barnes and Noble Thesaurus of Biology: The Principles of Biology Explained and Illustrated.
Anne C. Gutteridge. New York, NY: Barnes and Noble; 1983. 245p., color illus., index. $13.95; $6.95pbk. 0-06-015213-3; 0-06-453581-3pbk.
This is a well-illustrated dictionary of 2,700 biological terms arranged by broad topic. The definitions are short and directed to an audience of laypersons or students. *Grade Level:* Grades 9–12.
ARBA, 85, n.1406; SB, September 85, p.23.

283. Bioscientific Terminology: Words from Latin and Greek Stems.
Donald M. Ayers. Tucson, AZ: University of Arizona Press; 1985 (c1972). 325p. $6.95. 0-8165-0305-2.

This is a good dictionary of bioscientific terms that come from Latin and Greek stems. *Grade Level:* Grades 9–12.
Choice, December 72, p.1277; SB, December 72, p.211.

284. Black's Agricultural Dictionary.
2nd. D.B. Dalal-Clayton. London, Great Britain: Adam and Charles Black; Dist. by Barnes and Noble; Totowa; NJ; 1985. 432p., illus. $35.00. 0-389-20556-7.
Although this dictionary has a British slant, it is one of the few agricultural dictionaries available today and is, therefore, useful in any library that needs agricultural information. It covers all of agriculture, including general farming. Also includes abbreviations of associations, institutions, and scientific terms. *Grade Level:* Grades 9–12.
ARBA, 83, n.1488; Choice, June 82, p.1375; LJ, 1 May 82, p.878.

285. Cambridge Illustrated Dictionary of Natural History.
R.J. Lincoln; G.A. Boxshall. New York, NY: Cambridge University Press; 1987. 413p., illus. $24.95. 0-521-30551-9.
This very good general dictionary of biological and natural history terms concerns good illustrations that add much to the definitions. *Grade Level:* Grades 9–12.
ARBA, 88, n.1511; BL, 1 March 88, p.1115; Choice, February 88, p.887; SciTech, December 87, p.14; WLB, November 87, p.87.

286. Dictionary of Biology.
Edwin B. Steen. New York, NY: Barnes and Noble; 1971. 630p. $21.50. 0-686-83546-8.
This is still one of the better general biology dictionaries even though it was published in 1971. The terms are concise, with the book's only drawback being the lack of any illustrations. *Grade Level:* Grades 9–12.
Choice, December 73, p.1534; SB, May 72, p.45; WLB, October 73, p.163..

287. Dictionary of Life Sciences.
2nd. E.A. Martin, ed. New York, NY: Pica Press; 1985 (c1983). 396p., illus. $25.00. 0-87663-740-3.
This encyclopedic dictionary covers the entire realm of biology, but emphasizes genetics, molecular biology, microbiology, and immunology. It contains many diagrams and formulas. *Grade Level:* Grades 9–12.
ARBA, 85, n.1405; BL, 1 November 77, p.490; Choice, December 77, p.1338; LJ, August 77, p.1625; SB, January 85, p.14.

288. Dictionary of the Biological Sciences.
Peter Gray. Malabar, FL: R.E.Krieger; 1986 (c1967). 602p. $44.50. 0-89874-441-5.
Gray's has been a standard biological dictionary for many years and continues to be reprinted. It contains over 40,000 terms, with words derived from the same root prefix or suffix assembled together. An abridged version is available as *Student Dictionary of Biology. Grade Level:* Grades 9–12.

Choice, January 68, p.1224; LJ, 15 December 67, p.4991; SB, December 67, p.226; WLB, December 67, p.430.

289. The Facts on File Dictionary of Biology.
Revised and expanded. Elizabeth Tootill, ed. New York, NY: Facts on File; 1988. 326p., illus. $19.95. 0-8160-1865-0.
This well-written dictionary of biological terms provides clear and understandable definitions for students and laypersons. It uses British spellings, but has cross-references from the American spellings. There are no pronunciation guides or etymological references. *Grade Level:* Grades 6–8. Grades 9–12.
ARBA, 82, n.1450; BL, 1 September 84, p.34; Choice, July 81, p.1532; LJ, 1 March 82, p.512; SB, May 89, p.287; STARR, 90, n.81.

290. Henderson's Dictionary of Biological Terms.
10th. Eleanor Lawrence, ed. New York, NY: Wiley; 1989. 637p. $49.95. 0-0-471-21446-5.
This excellent general dictionary of biology has been around for a long time. Approximately 22,500 biological terms are concisely and accurately defined for students as well as researchers. *Grade Level:* Grades 9–12.
ARBA, 87, n.1458; BL, 15 June 81, p.1364; SB, January 81, p.138; SLJ, December 80, p.22; WLB, September 80, p.63.

291. McGraw-Hill Dictionary of Biology.
Sybil P. Parker, ed. New York, NY: McGraw-Hill; 1985 (c1984). 384p., illus., bibliog., index. $15.95. 0-07-045419-1.
This small dictionary is a spin-off from the *McGraw-Hill Dictionary of Scientific and Technical Terms.* The definitions are brief and no pronunciation guide is given. Terms cover all aspects of biology from anatomy to zoology. *Grade Level:* Grades 9–12.
ARBA, 87, n.1459.

292. Minidictionary of Biology.
Revised. New York, NY: Oxford University Press; 1988. 368p., illus. $17.95. 0-19-866155-X.
This compact dictionary of biological terms for the junior high student and the nonscientist was formerly called *Concise Dictionary of Biology.* It includes all of the biological entries from the *Concise Science Dictionary* plus selected terms in geology, physics, chemistry, and medicine. The definitions are clear and concise but pronunciation is not given. *Grade Level:* Grades 9–12.
ARBA, 87, n.1457; SB, May 87, p.305; SchLib, June 86, p.197.

293. Oxford Dictionary of Natural History.
Michael Allaby, ed. New York, NY: Oxford University Press; 1985. 688p., bibliog. $45.00. 0-19-217720-6.
This impressive dictionary for the amateur naturalist contains over 12,000 entries, with brief definitions. The taxa of plants and animals are listed to the family level. *Grade Level:* Grades 9–12.

ALib, May 87, p.370; ARBA, 87, n.1460; BL, 15 October 86, p.339; Choice, July 86, p.1660; SB, November 86, p.96; SchLib, June 86, p.198.

Encyclopedias

294. Biology Data and Resource Book.
J. Hawes. Amersham, Great Britain: Hulton; Dist. by Dufour Editions; Chester Springs; PA; 1986 (c1985). 177p., illus., index. $18.95. 0-7175-1291-6.
Arranged in alphabetical order, this book for high school students presents information on biology, including the history of biology, methodology, biological theories, impact of biology on society, and biographies. It is not comprehensive and contains some minor errors, but it is very adequate for its intended use. *Grade Level:* Grades 9–12.
BL, 1 January 87, p.696.

295. Biology Encyclopedia.
Edward Ashpole; Susan Jones; David Lambert. Barbara Taylor, ed. Chicago, IL: Rand McNally; 1985. 141p., color illus., index. $12.95. 0-528-82167-9.
This well-illustrated book is arranged into five topical sections: "Life on Earth," "Animal Biology," "Plant Biology," "Survival in Nature," and "Evolution and Genetics." An excellent resource for junior high school students. *Grade Level:* Grades 6–8. Grades 9–12.
ARBA, 86, n.1483.

296. Cambridge Encyclopedia of Life Sciences.
Adrian Friday; David S. Ingram, eds. New York, NY: Cambridge University Press; 1985. 432p., illus. (part in color), index. $47.50. 0-521-25696-8.
This excellent one-volume encyclopedia of the life sciences surveys current knowledge. It is divided into three sections, with the first covering processes and organization, the second covering various environments, and the last covering evolution and paleontology. The discussions are very informative and the illustrations are excellent. *Grade Level:* Grades 9–12.
ARBA, 86, n.1479; Choice, January 86, p.729; LJ, December 85, p.90, 1 March 86, p.45; SchLib, September 85, p.286; WLB, December 85, p.62.

297. Encyclopedia of the Biological Sciences.
2nd. Peter Gray. New York, NY: Van Nostrand Reinhold; 1981 (c1970). 1,027p., illus., bibliog., index. $59.50. 0-89874-326-5.
This is a good standard reference source covering terms and topics in all areas of the biological sciences. Emphasis is on the developmental, ecological, functional, genetic, structural, and taxonomic aspects. The articles define, explain, and describe the subject and include bibliographies. *Grade Level:* Grades 9–12.

Choice, September 70, p.818; LJ, 15 May 70, p.1826; SB, September 70, p.131.

Field Books

298. Audubon Society Nature Guides.
New York, NY: Knopf; 1985. 7v., illus. (part in color), bibliog., glossary, index. $14.95 per volume.
The *Audubon Society Nature Guides* offer excellent coverage of various geographical areas of the United States. After a brief description of the particular area, there are examples of the species found there followed by a description of the individual species. A glossary is included. Excellent illustrations add to these guides, making them ideal for classroom and home use. The seven volumes in this set are: Stephen Whitney's *Western Forests* (671p., 0-394-73127-1); William A. Niering's *Wetlands* (638p., 0-394-73147-6); William Hopkins Amos's *Atlantic and Gulf Coasts* (670p., 0-394-73109-3); James A. MacMahon's *Deserts* (638p., 0-394-73139-5); Ann Sutton and Myron Sutton's *Eastern Forests* (638p., 0-394-73126-3); Lauren Brown's *Grasslands* (606p., 0-394-73121-2); and Bayard H. McConnaughey and Evelyn McConnaughey's *Pacific Coast* (633p., 0-394-73130-7). *Grade Level:* Grades 6–8. Grades 9–12.
BL, July 85, p.1486; LJ, 15 June 85, p.55, 15 April 86, p.35; SLJ, September 85, p.155, May 86, p.28; VOYA, December 85, p.341.

299. Field Guide to the Atlantic Seashore: Invertebrates and Seaweeds of the Atlantic Coast from the Bay of Fundy to Cape Hatteras.
Kenneth L. Gosner. Boston, MA: Houghton Mifflin; 1982 (c1978). 336p., illus. (part in color), index. $17.95, $12.95pbk. Peterson Field Guide Series, 24. 0-395-24379-3, 0-395-31828-9pbk.
This field guide and the following two cover in detail the invertebrate and plant life found along the Atlantic and Caribbean coasts: Eugene H. Kaplan's *A Field Guide to Coral Reefs of the Caribbean and Florida: A Guide to the Common Invertebrates and Fishes of Bermuda, the Bahamas, Southern Florida, The West Indies and the Caribbean Coast of Central and South America* (Houghton Mifflin, 1982, 256p., 0-395-31661-8, $17.95, Peterson Field Guide Series, 27) and Eugene H. Kaplan's *A Field Guide to Southeastern and Caribbean Seashores: Cape Hatteras to the Gulf Coast, Florida and the Caribbean* (Houghton Mifflin, 1988, 544p., 0-395-31321-X, 0-395-46811-6pbk, $21.95, $15.95pbk, Peterson Field Guide Series, 36). *Grade Level:* Grades 9–12.
ARBA, 80, n.1361; BL, 15 April 80, p.1227; Kliatt, Spring 82, p.55; LJ, 1 June 79, p.1240; SB, March 80, p.210.

300. Fieldbook of Natural History.
2nd. E. Lawrence Palmer. H. Seymour Fowler, ed. New York, NY: McGraw-Hill; 1975. 779p., illus., index. $42.95. 0-07-048196-2.

Approximately 2,000 plants and animals are briefly described in this field guide. In addition, there are discussions of astronomy, the atmosphere, geology, and mineralogy. It is intended to give representative examples of plants and animals that are easily identifiable in the field or at home. *Grade Level:* Grades 9–12.
ARBA, 76, n.1364; BL 15 January 76, p.706; Choice, July 75, p.664; WLB, April 75, p.595.

301. Sierra Club Naturalist's Guide to the Middle Atlantic Coast: Cape Hatteras to Cape Cod.
Bill Perry. San Francisco, CA: Sierra Club Books; 1985. 470p., illus. (part in color), bibliog., index. $25.00, $12.95pbk. 0-87156-810-1, 0-87156-816-0pbk.
This field book or handbook and Michael Berrill's *Sierra Club Naturalist's Guide to the North Atlantic Coast: Cape Cod to Newfoundland* (Sierra Club Books, 1981, 464p., 0-87156-242-1, 0-87156-243-Xpbk, $24.95, $12.95pbk) are very well organized guidebooks to the life along the sea coast. The text is easy to follow and supplemented with very good illustrations. The two books are the most comprehensive available for the Atlantic coast. *Grade Level:* Grades 9–12.
LJ, 15 October 85, p.96.

Guides

302. Biology Projects for Young Scientists.
Salvatore Tocci. New York, NY: Franklin Watts; 1987. 127p., illus., bibliog., index. $11.90. Projects for Young Scientists. 0-531-10429-X.
"This book contains ideas for biology projects that can be done either in school or at home." Each chapter begins with some background information on the topic under discussion and is followed with some ideas for projects that are designed to be done without any highly sophisticated equipment. *Grade Level:* Grades 3–5. Grades 6–8. Teacher's/Librarian's Resource.
BL, 15 December 87, p.695; BRpt, January 88, p.53; SB, September 88, p.25; SLJ, March 88, p.223; STARR, 89, n.63; VOYA, February 88, p.298.

303. Experimenting with a Microscope.
Maurice Bleifeld. New York, NY: Franklin Watts; 1988. 98p., illus., bibliog., index. $11.90. 0-531-10580-6.
This small guide to the use of the microscope includes a brief history of the microscope, biographical information, and a description of the microscope. Easy-to-understand experiments are included for grades four through nine. *Grade Level:* Grades 3–5. Grades 6–8.
BL, 15 January 89, p.866; BRpt, March 89, p.47; SB, May 89, p.300; STARR, 90, n.87; WLB, March 89, p.85.

304. Five Kingdoms: An Illustrated Guide to the Phyla of Life on Earth.
2nd. Lynn Margulis; Karlene V. Schwartz. New York, NY: W.H. Freeman; 1988. 376p., illus., bibliog., index. $35.95. 0-7167-1885-5.
After a general discussion of life based on cells, each kingdom is described and includes a phylogeny showing the possible evolutionary relationships that occur among the phyla of that kingdom. It is arranged from the simplest to the most complex. A list of the better known genera of the phylum being discussed is given and followed by an illustration and fully labeled anatomic drawing of a representative species. The most typical habitat on earth is indicated for each phylum. This is a good introductory guide. *Grade Level:* Grades 6–8. Grades 9–12.
ARBA, 83, n.1304; BWatch, March, 88, p.1; Choice, June 82, p.1427; SB, September 82, p.16.

305. Pond Life: A Guide to Common Plants and Animals of North American Ponds and Lakes.
George K. Reid. New York, NY: Golden Press; 1987. 160p., illus. $2.95. Golden Guide Series. 0-307-24017-7.
This excellent guide for students discusses the environments of ponds and lakes and shows examples of the plants, animals, insects, and fishes that can be found there. Information is given on how to collect specimens. *Grade Level:* Grades 6–8. Grades 9–12.
BL, 15 February 68, p.702; LJ, 15 February 68, p.874; PW, 8 May 67, p.60; SB, March 68, p.314.

306. Roots of Life: Layman's Guide to Genes, Evolution, and the Ways of Cells.
Mahlon B. Hoagland. Boston, MA: Houghton Mifflin; 1978 (c1977). 162p., index. $11.95. 0-395-25811-1.
This good, general guide discusses cells, evolution, and genes in terminology understandable to students. *Grade Level:* Grades 9–12.
Choice, September 78, p.902; Kliatt, Winter 80, p.55; SB, December 78, p.161; SLJ, September 78, p.172.

307. Seashores: A Guide to Animals and Plants Along the Beaches.
Herbert S. Zim; Lester Ingle. New York, NY: Golden Press; 1961 (c1955). 160p., color illus. $2.95. Golden Nature Guide. 0-307-24496-2.
This good, general guide to life as it exists along the seashore includes detailed descriptions of over 450 shells, marine plants, and sea animals. *Grade Level:* Grades 3–5. Grades 6–8.

308. Seaside Naturalist: A Guide to Nature Study at the Seashore.
Deborah A. Coulombe. Englewood Cliffs, NJ: Prentice-Hall; 1984. 246p., illus., bibliog., index. $19.95, $12.95pbk. 0-13-797259-8, 0-13-797242-3pbk.
The emphasis in this guidebook is on fauna that can be found along the beaches of the Atlantic. It includes much text that supplements the excellent descriptions of marine life from phytoplankton to whales.

There is also information on tides, currents, and marine communities, plus a glossary. *Grade Level:* Grades 9–12.
ARBA, 86, n.1764; Kliatt, Fall 84, p.61; SB, March 85, p.202.

309. Seawatch: The Seafarer's Guide to Marine Life.
Paul V. Horsman. New York, NY: Facts on File; 1985. 256p., illus. (part in color), index. $19.95. 0-8160-1191-5.
This book is "intended to enable anyone to identify any marine life they encounter" along or near the seashore. It covers plankton, invertebrates, fish, reptiles, and mammals. The descriptions are good but can be somewhat brief, and the illustrations are very good. There is also information on ecology of the sea and bioluminescence. *Grade Level:* Grades 6–8. Grades 9–12.
ARBA, 86, n.1765; SB, May 86, p.307; SchLife, September 86, p.296.

Handbooks

310. Biology Teachers' Handbook.
3rd. William V. Mayer; American Institute of Biological Sciences, Biological Sciences Curriculum Study, eds. New York, NY: Wiley; 1978. 585p., illus., index. $15.95. 0-471-01945-3.
This resource book and manual explains the Biological Sciences Curriculum Study approach to the teaching of biology and serves as a companion to the Study's textbooks. This handbook includes material on research projects, reading lists, reprints of classic papers on biology, visual aids, techniques and materials for the biology laboratory, care of laboratory animals, preparation of laboratory solutions and stains, lists of supplies, and supply houses. *Grade Level:* Grades 9–12. Teacher's/Librarian's Resource.
SB, September 70, p.132; WLB, March 72, p.605.

311. Handbook of Nature Study.
Anna Botsford Comstock. Ithaca, NY: Cornell University Press; 1987 (c1967). 887p., illus., index. $49.50, $19.50pbk. 0-8014-1913-1, 0-8014-9384-6pbk.
This reissue of a 1911 classic covers nature study as it was done early in this century, which is still a valid way of studying. The text is quaint, but the examples, lessons, and exercises are just as applicable today as they were when the book was first published. *Grade Level:* Grades 9–12. Teacher's/Librarian's Resource.
ARBA, 87, n.1463; Kliatt, Winter 87, p.50; SB, January 87, p.182.

312. Handbook on Agricultural Education in Public Schools.
5th. Lloyd J. Phipps; Edward W. Osborne. Danville, IL: The Interstate Printers & Publishers, Inc; 1988. 593p., illus., tables, charts, index. $22.95. 0-8134-2774-6.
This handbook for teachers of agriculture, teacher educators, and supervisors who are concerned about agricultural education in the public schools is both a textbook and a resource guide. Includes information

on agricultural education programs, use of microcomputers, Future Farmers of America, and adult education programs. *Grade Level:* Grades 6–8. Grades 9–12. Teacher's/Librarian's Resource.

Histories

313. History of the Life Sciences.
Lois N. Magner. New York, NY: Dekker; 1979. 489p., illus. $39.75. 0-8247-6824-8.
This readable and accurate history of the biological sciences is detailed and somewhat technical, but still a good history for students in high school and undergraduates in college. *Grade Level:* Grades 9–12.

Indexes

314. Farm and Garden Index.
Wooster, OH: Bell and Howell Microphoto; 1978–. v. 1– , index. Quarterly. $170.00. 0193-8487.
This index has excellent coverage of over 120 agricultural, popular farm, and horticultural periodicals. It is arranged alphabetically by subject and is well cross-referenced. *Grade Level:* Grades 9–12.
ARBA, 80, n.1541; Choice, June 79, p.502; LJ, 1 January 79, p.89, 1 May 80, p.1054.

315. Index to Illustrations of Living Things Outside North America: Where to Find Pictures of Flora and Fauna.
Lucile Thompson Munz; Nedra G. Slauson. Hamden, CT: Shoestring Press; 1981. 441p., bibliog. $49.50. 0-208-01857-3.
This is an index to more than 200 illustrated books about plants and fauna. The entries are alphabetical by common name with cross-references. After each common name, the scientific name is given along with a three-letter code to indicate which book has the illustration. *Grade Level:* Grades 6–8. Grades 9–12. Teacher's/Librarian's Resource.
ARBA, 83, n.1310; Choice, April 82, p.1047; LJ, 15 September 81, p.1721; SLJ, May 82, p.19; WLB, March 82, p.544.

316. Index to Illustrations of the Natural World: Where to Find Pictures of the Living Things of North America.
John W. Thompson, comp. Hamden, CT: Archon; 1983 (c1977). 265p., bibliog., index. $42.50. 0-208-02038-1.
This index to illustrations of plants and animals in books is arranged by common name of plant or animal and includes a three-letter code that indicates which book has the illustration. There are indexes to scientific names, book titles, and book code letters. *Grade Level:* Grades 6–8. Grades 9–12. Teacher's/Librarian's Resource.
ARBA, 78, n.1277; BL, 1 May 78, p.1454; Choice, January 78, p.1482; LJ, 15 September 77, p.1834; WLB, November 77, p.264.

BOTANY

Botany is the study of plants and plant life. Botany is a large and extremely important field, since life on this planet is governed by the plant life that it maintains. With environmental issues that include pollution, the greenhouse effect, and depletion of the ozone layer, research in botany has increased. New methods for growing plants without chemicals, production of hardier crops, maintenance of the rain forests, and protection of endangered species are only a few of the concerns of botanists.

Botany is not a simple science. There are many subfields, each with a full research agenda. The subfields that relate to the functions and development of plants include: *plant anatomy*—the physical make-up of the plant; *plant chemistry*—the chemical processes that occur in plants; *plant cytology*—the study of the plant cells; *plant ecology*—the study of plants in relation to the environment; *plant embryology*—the study of plant development from seeds; *plant genetics*—the evolution of plants; *plant physiology*—the study of how plants function and grow; *plant taxonomy*—the systematic naming of plants; *ethnobotany*—the study of the physical differences between plants; and *paleobotany*—the study of fossil plants.

There are also special areas of botany determined by the kind of plant: *agrostology*—the study of grasses; *algology* or *phycology*—the study of algae; *bryology*—the study of mosses; *mycology*—the study of fungi; and *pteridology*—the study of ferns. In addition to the study of botany by function and by type of plant, there are all of the areas that come from plant science in agriculture. These include *agronomy*—the study of field crops; *floriculture*—the production, marketing, and sale of bedding plants, cut flowers, potted plants, foliage plants, flower arrangements, and home gardening; *forestry*—all aspects of maintaining forests; *horticulture*—the science of growing flowers, vegetables, and fruits; *landscape architecture*—the study of the use of plants in garden architecture; and *plant breeding*—the development of better plants.

The reference literature of botany for research purposes is varied and large. The most important area with the greatest amount of reference material for young people is in plant identification. Identifications are made utilizing field guides, of which there are hundreds, from general ones covering an entire country to special ones for a small geographical area. Included in this chapter are many field guides covering wide geographical areas. The *Peterson Field Guide Series* is the best known and includes guides to flowers, trees, grasses, shrubs, and other types of plants. The Audubon Society also has a series of guides noted for their excellent photographs. A general series published by W.C. Brown, titled *Pictured Key Nature Series*, is good for beginners. Good botany dictionaries include *Facts on File Dictionary of Botany* and the *Timber Press Dictionary of Plant Names*. Since horticulture and gardening are of interest to a great many people, especially with the decrease in the use of chemicals, several gardening books have been included, such as *Knott's Handbook for Vegetable Growers* and *Wyman's Gardening Encyclopedia*.

Dictionaries

317. Complete Book of Mushrooms: Over 1,000 Species and Varieties of American, European, and Asiatic Mushrooms with 460 illustrations in Black and White and in Color.
Augusto Rinaldi; Vassili Tyndalo. New York, NY: Crescent Books; 1985 (c1974). 332p., illus. (part in color), bibliog., index. $14.98. 0-517-51493-1.
This dictionary of mushrooms is a translation of *L'Atlante dei Funghi*. It describes over 1,000 species and varieties, giving all of their characteristics, including whether or not they are poisonous. There is also a general discussion on hunting, eating, and cultivating mushrooms, with information on nutrients, cooking, and preserving. *Grade Level:* Grades 9–12.
BL, 15 April 75, p.876; Choice, February 75, p.1758; LJ, 15 January 75, p.112; WLB, April 75, p.596.

318. Facts on File Dictionary of Botany.
Elizabeth Tootill, ed. New York, NY: Facts on File; 1984. 390p., illus. $21.95. 0-87196-861-4.
This is a dictionary of botany for the layperson and student. Definitions are short to lengthy, depending on the term being considered. Only about 3,000 terms are covered, but they are the terms that one would encounter in day-to-day reading. *Grade Level:* Grades 6–8. Grades 9–12.
ARBA, 84, n.1408; BL, 15 January 85, p.698; Choice, October 84, p.246.

319. Glossary of Botanic Terms with Their Derivation and Accent.
4th. Benjamin D. Jackson. New York, NY: Hafner; 1971 (c1928). 481p., bibliog. $27.50. 0-02-847110-5.
Although this is a 1928 publication, it is still the standard source for the derivation and accent of some 10,000 botanic terms. For each term, the Latin equivalent, derivation, pronunciation, and definition are given. *Grade Level:* Grades 9–12.

320. Timber Press Dictionary of Plant Names.
Allen J. Coombes. Portland, OR: Timber Press; 1985. 207p., bibliog.
$9.95. 0-88192-023-1.
This is a concise guide to the pronunciation, derivation, and meaning
of cultivated plant names. Common names are referred to the scienti-
fic name for full information. *Grade Level:* Grades 9–12.
ARBA, 87, n.1466; Choice, February 86, p.888.

Directories

321. Gardening by Mail: A Source Book.
2nd revised and enlarged. Barbara J. Barton. San Francisco, CA:
Tusker Press; 1988. 1v. various paging, illus., bibliog., index.
$16.00pbk. 0-937633-02-Xpbk.
This is a directory of seed companies, nurseries, garden supplies,
associations, societies, horticulture libraries, periodicals, and books.
For each entry, the specialties are listed along with the usual directory
information of addresses, telephone numbers, and business hours.
Grade Level: Grades 6–8. Grades 9–12. Teacher's/Librarian's Resource.
BL, 15 April 88, p.1399, 15 May 89, p.1619.

Encyclopedias

322. Audubon Society Book of Trees.
Les Line; Ann Sutton; Myron Sutton. New York, NY: Abrams; 1981.
263p., color illus. $50.00. 0-8109-0673-2.
The excellent color photographs are the key to this book on trees.
Grouped by geographical region and botanical family, the book covers
trees from the tropics to the deserts. The text fully describes the
various families of trees. *Grade Level:* Grades 6–8. Grades 9–12.
BL, 1 November 81, p.361; LJ, 1 November 81, p.2145.

323. Audubon Society Book of Wildflowers.
Les Line; Walter Henricks Hodge. New York, NY: Abrams; 1978.
259p. color illus. $50.00. 0-8109-0671-6.
The most important part of this excellent encyclopedia is the striking
color photographs of the wildflowers of the world. The book covers the
flowers of the pine forests, tropics, Arctic tundra, plains, and the
deserts. The text is brief but informative. *Grade Level:* Grades 6–8.
Grades 9–12.
BL, 1 January 79, p.726; Choice, July 79, p.691; LJ, 1 December 78,
p.2434; PW, 2 October 78, p.125; SB, December 79, p.150.

324. Encyclopedia of Organic Gardening.
Newly revised. *Organic Gardening* (magazine). Emmaus, PA: Rodale
Press; 1978. 1,236p., illus. $24.95. 0-87857-225-2.

This is an encyclopedia of over 2,000 fruits, grains, nuts, vegetables, and ornamentals, giving identification, cultivation, and use. Plants are listed by their common names, with the Latin name also given. There is additional information on companion planting, composting, greenhouse construction and maintenance, insect control, and soil testing and improvement. *Grade Level:* Grades 9–12.
ARBA, 79, n.1539; LJ, 1 October 78, p.1997; PW, 18 September 78, p.159; SB, December 79, p.160.

325. Flowering Plants of the World.
Vernon H. Heywood, ed. Englewood Cliffs, NJ: Prentice-Hall; 1985. 335p., illus. (part in color), maps, index. $39.95. 0-13-322405-8.
This is a comprehensive survey of some 250,000 species of flowering plants in 300 flowering plant groups. Each family gives characteristics, distribution, diagnostic features, classification, and economic uses of the plants in that family. There are over 200 locator-distribution maps and a glossary plus an index of English and Latin names. *Grade Level:* Grades 9–12.
ARBA, 86, n.1497; BL, 1 June 86, p.1446.

326. Oxford Encyclopedia of Trees of the World.
Bayard Hora, ed. New York, NY: Oxford University Press; 1981. 288p., illus. (part in color), bibliog., index. $27.50. 0-19-217712-5.
This is a general encyclopedic book of trees of the world, with a special section on the native and exotic trees of North America. Each plant description includes a summary of the distribution, characteristics, economic importance, and diseases. Includes excellent photographs and a glossary. *Grade Level:* Grades 9–12.
ARBA, 83, n.1335; BL, 15 June 81, p.1324, 1 November 82, p.404; BW, 6 December 81, p.18; LJ, 1 June 81, p.1208; SB, November 81, p.79; WLB, June 81, p.779.

327. Popular Encyclopedia of Plants.
Vernon H. Heywood, ed. New York, NY: Cambridge University Press; 1982. 368p., color illus., bibliog., index. $34.50. 0-521-24611-3.
This concise encyclopedia is actually an abridgement of a larger work, *Plants and Man.* It contains 2,200 entries alphabetically arranged by scientific name or popular name. The articles are for the layperson, with no botany background needed. A brief glossary is included. *Grade Level:* Grades 9–12.
ARBA, 83, n.1212; BL, 1 September 84, p.34; Choice, October 82, p.246; LJ, 15 June 82, p.1210, 15 May 83, p.963; SchLib, September 82, p.292.

328. 10,000 Garden Questions Answered by 20 Experts.
4th. Marjorie J. Dietz, ed. New York, NY: Doubleday; 1982. 1,507p., illus., index. $19.95. 0-385-18509-X.
This encyclopedia for the amateur gardener uses a question and answer format. It covers all topics from soils and fertilizers to pests and their control. There is also a chapter on types of plants and plant groups. Although some of the information may be dated, there is still useful

material on books, state agricultural experiment stations, plant societies, botanical gardens, arboreta, and public gardens. *Grade Level:* Grades 9–12.
ARBA, 84, n.1476; BL, 15 May 82, p.1215; LJ, 1 June 82, p.1087; PW, 19 February 82, p.59.

329. Trees of North America.
Alan Mitchell. New York, NY: Facts on File; 1987. 208p., illus. (part in color), maps, index. $24.95. 0-8160-1806-5.
This well-illustrated encyclopedia covers over 500 species and 250 varieties of trees growing in North America, giving common name; scientific name; origin; description of general characteristics, such as size, flowering pat terns, leaf colors, fruit types, and seasons; and geographical range. *Grade Level:* Grades 6–8. Grades 9–12.
ARBA, 88, n.1541.

330. Wyman's Gardening Encyclopedia.
2nd new and expanded. Donald Wyman, ed. New York, NY: Macmillan; 1986. 1,221p., illus. (part in color), index. $29.95. 0-02-632070-3.
This popular gardening encyclopedia covers most horticultural practices, providing information on individual plant species. It is well-written and easy to use, with a wealth of information for the amateur. *Grade Level:* Grades 9–12.
ALib, April 73, p.212; ARBA, 88, n.1478; BL, 15 September 71, p.65, 15 September 77, p.238; SciTech, May 87, p.29.

Field Books

331. Audubon Society Field Guide to North American Mushrooms.
Gary H. Lincoff; Carol Nehring. New York, NY: Knopf; 1981. 926p., illus. (part in color), index. $13.50. The Audubon Society Field Guide Series. 0-394-51992-2.
This is a field guide to over 700 types of mushrooms. The guide is divided into a color photograph section that is followed by text fully describing the mushrooms and giving their habitat, range, edibility, and season. There are also notes on the preparation of edible species and comments on mushroom poisoning. See also *A Field Guide to Mushrooms of North America. Grade Level:* Grades 6–8. Grades 9–12.
BL, 15 March 82, p.930; BW, 10 January 82, p.12; LJ, 15 February 82, p.443; SLJ, May 83, p.25.

332. Audubon Society Field Guide to North American Trees: Western Region.
Elbert L. Little. New York, NY: Knopf; 1980. 639p., illus. (part in color), maps, index. $9.95pbk. 0-394-50761-4pbk.
This book and Elbert L. Little's *Audubon Society Field Guide to North American Trees: Eastern Region* (Knopf, 1980, 714p., 0-394-50760-6pbk, $9.95pbk) are excellent guides to the trees of North America.

The photographs are exceptional, with nontechnical descriptions, clear drawings, and color guides enabling one to identify the trees when only the leaf type and/or type of flower or fruit are in hand. The plates are arranged into four groups: leaves, flowers, fruit and cones, and autumn leaves. Descriptions also include information on the uses of the tree, its possible toxicity, and its rarity. See also *A Field Guide to Eastern Trees* and *Complete Trees of North America*. *Grade Level:* Grades 6–8. Grades 9–12.
ARBA, 81, n.1453–1454; BL, 1 October 80, p.186; LJ, 15 October 80, p.2220, 1 May 81, p.941; SLJ, November 80, p.96.

333. Audubon Society Field Guide to North American Wildflowers: Western Region.
Richard Spellenberg. New York, NY: Knopf; 1979. 862p., illus. (part in color), index. $13.50. 0-394-50431-3.
This guide and William A. Niering and Nancy C. Olmstead's *Audubon Society Field Guide to North American Wildflowers: Eastern Region* (Knopf, 1979, 863p., 0-394-50432-1, $13.50) are excellent field guides to the wildflowers of North America. The first part of each guide contains color photographs arranged by color, and the second part contains the descriptive text arranged by family. For each entry, the vernacular and scientific name, description, flowering dates, habitat, range, comments, origin of name, historical facts, plant lore, and poisonous and edible qualities are given. See also *A Field Guide to Pacific States Wildflowers*. *Grade Level:* Grades 6–8. Grades 9–12.
ARBA, 80, no. 1381, 1383; BL 1 December 80, p.529.

334. Book of Flowers.
2nd. Kathleen N. Daly. Durham, NC: Sacrum Press; 1986 (c1976). 44p., illus. $10.00. 0-937543-00-4.
This field book was formerly titled *A Child's Book of Flowers*. It is a book on flower identification for young children and covers such common flowers as dandelions, daisies, buttercups, and violets. *Grade Level:* Grades 3–5.

335. Complete Trees of North America: Field Guide and Natural History.
Thomas S. Elias. New York, NY: Gramercy Publishing; 1987 (c1980). 948p., illus., index. $9.98. 0-517-64104-6.
The main part of this field guide contains the description of individual species of trees. Information is arranged in a series of dichotomous keys, guiding the user first to major groups of trees, then to families, to genera, and finally to species. The keys are usually based on leaves, but fruits and flowers are also considered. See also *A Field Guide to Eastern Trees* and *Audubon Society Field Guide to North American Trees*. *Grade Level:* Grades 9–12.
ARBA, 82, n.1469; BL, 15 October 80, p.292; LJ, 15 October 80, p.2220; LJ, March 81, p.524; SB, May 81, p.202.

336. Familiar Flowers of North America: Western Region.
Ann H. Whitman, ed. New York, NY: Knopf; 1987. 192p., illus. (part
in color). $4.95. Audubon Society Pocket Guides. 0-394-74844-1.
This pocket field guide and Ann H. Whitman's *Familiar Flowers of
North America: Eastern Region* (Knopf, 1987, 192p., 0-394-74843-3,
$4.95) are excellent beginner's guides. They cover the most familiar
flowers that one would encounter while on nature hikes. The descrip-
tions are concise and the color keys make these two books easy to use.
See also *Peterson's First Guide to Wildflowers of Northeastern and
North-Central North America. Grade Level:* Grades 9–12.

337. Familiar Trees of North America: Western Region.
Ann H. Whitman, ed. New York, NY: Knopf; 1986. 192p., illus. (part
in color). $4.95. Audubon Society Pocket Guides. 0-394-74852-2.
This field guide and Ann H. Whitman's *Familiar Trees of North America: Eastern Region* (Knopf, 1986, 191p., 0-394-74851-4, $4.95) help
the layperson and student identify the most common trees that one
sees in North America. The descriptions, excellent photographs, and
color keys are an outstanding feature of all Audubon field guides.
Grade Level: Grades 9–12.
ARBA, 88, n.1544–1545.

338. Field Guide to Berries and Berrylike Fruits.
Madeline Angell. New York, NY: Bobbs-Merrill; 1981. 250p., illus.
(part in color). $10.95, $6.95pbk. 0-672-52676-X, 0-672-52695-6pbk.
This book is an aid in identifying large numbers of wild berries. It is
arranged by the color of the mature fruit and subarranged by growth
form, such as herb, shrub, vine, or tree. For each entry, common and
scientific names, family, description, habitat, remarks, notes on use,
and a drawing are included. Uses other than for food are also noted.
Grade Level: Grades 9–12.
ARBA, 83, n.1317; Kliatt, Winter 82, p.63.

**339. Field Guide to Eastern Trees: Eastern United States and
Canada.**
George A. Petrides. Boston, MA: Houghton Mifflin; 1988. 272p.,
illus. $19.95. Peterson Field Guide Series, 11. 0-395-46730-6.
Formerly called *Field Guide to Trees and Shrubs*, this guide includes
descriptions of 455 species of trees organized into six groups according
to leaf, twig, and flower or fruit. Excellent colored plates are included.
See also *Audubon Society Field Guide to North American Trees* and
Complete Trees of North America. Grade Level: Grades 9–12.
ARBA, 89, n.1437.

340. A Field Guide to Mushrooms of North America.
Kent M. McKnight; Vera B. McKnight. Boston, MA: Houghton Miff-
lin; 1987. 448p., illus. (part in color). $19.95, $13.94pbk. Peterson
Field Guide Series, 34. 0-395-42101-2, 0-395-42102-0pbk.

This is one of the standard field guides for identifying mushrooms. The typical Peterson keys and excellent photographs make it a very useful field guide. See also *Audubon Society Field Guide to North American Mushrooms*. *Grade Level:* Grades 9–12. ARBA 88, n.1530.

341. Field Guide to North American Edible Wild Plants.
Thomas S. Elias; Peter A. Dykeman. New York, NY: Outdoor Life Books; 1982. 286p., illus. (part in color), maps, index. $19.95pbk. 0-442-22254-8pbk.
This handy little guide describes more than 200 common, edible wild plants, excluding mushrooms. It is arranged by edible season and then plant type, giving a full description with photographs. Lee Allen Peterson's *Field Guide to Edible Wild Plants of Eastern and Central North America* (Houghton Mifflin, 1978, 336p., 0-395-20445-3, 0-395-31870-Xpbk, $17.95, $12.95pbk, The Peterson Field Guide Series, 23) is another field guide that describes about 400 species. *Grade Level:* Grades 9–12.
ARBA, 84, n.1312; BL, 1 April 83, p.1003; LJ, 1 May 83, p.912.

342. A Field Guide to Pacific State Wildflowers: Field Marks of Species Found in Washington, Oregon, California, and Adjacent Areas; a Visual Approach Arranged by Color, Form and Detail.
Theodore F. Niehaus; Charles L. Ripper. Boston, MA: Houghton Mifflin; 1976. 432p., color illus., index. $17.95, $12.95pbk. The Peterson Field Guide Series, 22. 0-395-21624-9, 0-395-31662-6pbk.
This field guide and the following three cover the wildflowers of the United States, using standard keys of color, form, and detail: John J. Craighead, Frank C. Craighead, Jr., and Ray J. Davis's *A Field Guide to Rocky Mountain Wildflowers from Northern Arizona and New Mexico to British Columbia* (Houghton Mifflin, 1963, 288p., 0-395-07578-5, 0-395-18324-3pbk, $17.95, $12.95pbk, The Peterson Field Guide Series, 14); Theodore F. Niehaus's *A Field Guide to Southwestern and Texas Wildflowers* (Houghton Mifflin, 1984, 464p., 0-395-32876-4, 0-395-36640-2pbk, $18.95, $12.95pbk, The Peterson Field Guide Series, 31); and Roger Tory Peterson and Margaret McKenny's *A Field Guide to Wildflowers of Northeastern and North Central North America* (Houghton Mifflin, 1987, 480p., 0-395-08086-X, 0-395-18325-1pbk, $17.95, $12.95pbk, The Peterson Field Guide Series, 17). All four books are in the typical Peterson format, providing good descriptions, arrangment by color, and excellent illustrations. See also *Audubon Society Field Guide to North American Wildflowers*. *Grade Level:* Grades 9–12.

343. A Field Guide to Poisonous Plants and Mushrooms of North America.
Charles Kingsley Levy; Richard B. Primack. Brattleboro, VT: Stephen Greene Press; 1984. 178p., illus. (part in color), bibliog., index. $16.95, $9.95pbk. 0-8289-0531-2, 0-8289-0530-4pbk.

This is a popular guide to the identification of those plants that are poisonous. It includes some 250 species divided into five sections: "Plants that cause dermatitis," "Hallucinogenic plants," "Toxic plants of the home and garden," "Wild poisonous plants," and "Poisonous mushrooms." Each entry includes popular and scientific names, a description of physical characteristics, an explanation of the active toxins and their symptoms, and a guide to first aid and treatment. *Grade Level:* Grades 9–12.
ARBA, 85, n.1426.

344. Field Manual of the Ferns and Fern-Allies of the United States and Canada.
David B. Lellinger. Washington, DC: Smithsonian Institution Press; 1985. 389p., illus. (part in color), bibliog., index. $45.00, $29.95pbk. 0-87474-602-7, 0-87474-603-5pbk.
This excellent guide covers ferns, club- mosses, spike-mosses, quillworts, and horse tails. The 406 species are described in moderate detail for the amateur. There is a glossary as well as an introduction to the biology, evolution, cultivation and study of ferns. Also useful in the identification of ferns is Boughton Cobb's *Field Guide to the Ferns and Their Related Families of Northeastern and Central North America with a Section on Species also Found in the British Isles and Western Europe* (Houghton Mifflin, 1956, 288p., 0-395-07560-2, 0-395-19431-8pbk, $17.95, $12.95pbk, The Peterson Field Guide Series, 10). *Grade Level:* Grades 9–12.
ARBA, 86, n.1493; Choice, February 86, p.888; LJ, 15 February 86, p.173; SciTech, December 85, p.14.

345. A Guide to Field Identification: Wildflowers of North America.
Frank D. Venning. Racine, WI: Golden Press/Western Publishing; 1984. 340p., color illus., bibliog., index. $10.95, $7.95pbk. 0-307-47007-5, 0-307-13664-7pbk.
This field guide covers 1,553 species of wildflowers. Each is described fully and has an excellent color illustration. It is arranged by taxonomic order, but there is no key, thus making it somewhat difficult to use. However, the excellent illustrations and the reasonable price make it a recommended book. *Grade Level:* Grades 6–8. Grades 9–12.
ARBA, 85, n.1421; BL, 1 October 84, p.179; SB, September 85, p.24.

346. How to Know the Aquatic Plants.
2nd. G.W. Prescott. Dubuque, IA: William C. Brown; 1980. 171p., illus., bibliog., index. $14.95. Pictured Key Nature Series. 0-697-04774-1.
This is a field guide to identifying the various water plants that grow in the United States. Flowering plants are given special emphasis, but the guide includes information on algae, bryophytes, and pteridophytes. Fresh-water plants are distinguished from those in salt marshes and other saline areas. The descriptions are concise and at the generic level, with a species described only if it is a large and diverse one. *Grade Level:* Grades 6–8.
ARBA, 81, n.1425.

347. How to Know the Cacti: Pictured Keys for Determining the Native Cacti of the U.S. and Many of the Introduced Species.
E. Yale Dawson. Dubuque, IA: William C. Brown; 1963. 158p., illus, index. $2.75. Pictured Key Nature Series.
This is a good elementary field guide to identifying cacti. The descriptions are concise and easy to follow with good illustrations. *Grade Level:* Grades 9–12.

348. How to Know the Ferns and Fern Allies.
John T. Mickel. Dubuque, IA: William C. Brown; 1979. 229p., illus. index. $7.95, $5.95 spiralbound. Pictured Key Nature Series. 0-697-04770-9, 0-697-04771-7 spiralbound.
This is an excellent beginner's guide to identifying 57 of the most important ferns found in the eastern and central United States. *Grade Level:* Grades 6–8.
ARBA 81, n.1426.

349. How to Know the Gilled Mushrooms.
Alexander H. Smith; Helen V. Smigh; Nancy S. Weber. Dubuque, IA: William C. Brown; 1979. 334p., illus., index. $11.85, $9.70pbk. Pictured Key Nature Series. 0-697-04772-0, 0-697-04773-3pbk.
This book and Alexander H. Smith's *How to Know the Non-Gilled Mushrooms* (2nd ed., William C. Brown, 1981, 324p., 0-697-04778-4, $11.85, Pictured Key Nature Series) cover all aspects of collecting and preserving mushrooms, terminology, and identification. *Grade Level:* Grades 6–8.
ARBA, 81, n.1447.

350. How to Know the Grasses.
3rd. Richard W. Pohl. Dubuque, IA: William C. Brown; 1978. 200p., illus., bibliog., index. $13.95. Pictured Key Nature Series. 0-697-04877-2.
Keys and pictures of 324 species of American grasses are covered in this beginner's guide. Distribution maps for each species are included and forage value, flowering, and fruiting seasons are indicated. *Grade Level:* Grades 6–8.
ARBA, 79, n.1350.

351. How to Know the Lichens.
2nd. Mason E. Hale. Dubuque, IA: William C. Brown; 1979. 246p., illus., bibliog., index. $13.95. Pictured Key Nature Series. 0-697-04762-8.
This field guide covers and fully describes 427 species of lichens. It is divided into five keys and also includes a list of synonyms, phylogenetic list of genera and families, and a glossary. *Grade Level:* Grades 6–8.

352. How to Know the Mosses and Liverworts.
2nd. Henry S. Conrad; Paul L. Refearn, Jr. Dubuque, IA: William C. Brown; 1979. 302p., illus., index. $10.75. Pictured Key Nature Series. 0-697-04769-5.
Some prior knowledge of mosses, liverworts, and bryophytes is assumed in order to use this guide. It is an excellent field guide, with good illustrations and descriptions for these small plants. One does need good eyesight and access to a microscope to make positive identification of these plants. *Grade Level:* Grades 6–8.
ARBA, 81, n.1444.

353. How to Know the Spring Flowers.
2nd. Susan Verhoek; Mabel Jacques Cuthbert. Dubuque, IA: William C. Brown; 1982. 245p., illus., maps, index. $7.45 spiralbound. Pictured Key Nature Series. 0-697-04782-2 spiralbound.
This well-written guide covers 505 species and varieties of spring flowering herbaceous plants in North America east of the Rocky Mountains (exclusive of tropical Florida). Descriptions of each plant are given with flowering dates. *Grade Level:* Grades 6–8.
ARBA, 83, n.1320.

354. How to Know the Trees.
3rd. H.A. Miller; H.E. Jaques. Dubuque, IA: William C. Brown; 1978. 263p., illus., bibliog., index. $13.95. Pictured Key Nature Series. 0-697-04896-9.
This field guide and Harry J. Baerg's *How to Know the Western Trees* (William C. Brown, 1973, 179p., 0-697-04801-2, $13.95, Pictured Key Nature Series) covers all the major species of trees in the United States and Canada. They describe the trees as individual entities and as part of a forest ecosystem. *Grade Level:* Grades 6–8.

355. Mushrooms: A Quick Reference Guide to Mushrooms of North America.
Alan Bessette; Walter J. Sundberg. New York, NY: Macmillan; 1987. 173p., color illus., bibliog., index. $24.95. Macmillan Field Guides. 0-02-615260-6.
This small field guide describes only 200 of the most common species of mushrooms. It has concise descriptions and exceptional pictures that aid in identification. *Grade Level:* Grades 9–12.
ARBA, 89, n.1429; BL, 1 February 88, p.896; SB, September 88, p.25.

356. Mushrooms and Toadstools: A Color Field Guide.
U. Nonis. New York, NY: Hippocrene Books; 1982. 229p., illus. (part in color), bibliog., index. $12.95. 0-88254-755-0.
Although this book was originally published in Europe, it is an excellent and well-written guide to mushrooms of both Europe and the United States. The color illustrations are beautiful, and the descriptions are both complete and entertaining. It covers some 168 common species. *Grade Level:* Grades 9–12.
ARBA, 84, n.1314; BL, August 83, p.1434; Choice, October 83, p.254.

357. Mushrooms of North America.
Revised. Orson K. Miller, Jr. New York, NY: Dutton; 1985. 368p., illus. (part in color). $14.50pbk. 0-525-48226-1pbk.
This is probably the best of all of the field guides to mushrooms. In addition to the mushroom, it includes bracket fungi, puffballs, earthstars, tongue fungi, and many other less familiar groups. It has excellent photographs associated with the keys, and a glossary is included. Each of the species is fully described and includes information on edibility, toxicity, geographic range and habitat, and cooking suggestions. *Grade Level:* Grades 6–8. Grades 9–12.
ARBA, 78, n.1302; BL, 15 February 73, p.544, 15 June 78, p.1638; BW, 29 August 76, p.M9; Choice, April 73, p.312; LJ, 1 March 73, p.695; SB, September 78, p.94; WLB, December 77, p.348.

358. North American Trees (Exclusive of Mexico and Tropical United States).
4th. Richard J. Preson, Jr. Ames, IA: Iowa State University Press; 1989. 430p., illus., maps, index. $34.95, $19.95pbk. 0-8138-1171-6, 0-8138-1172-4pbk.
This is a good field book for tree identification. The descriptions of each species include an enumeration of habit, leaf form, floral, fruit, twig, and bark characteristics and silvicultural value. Most descriptions are accompanied by line drawings of the flower, leaf, fruit, and occasionally twig of the tree in question, and a map of its distribution in North America. *Grade Level:* Grades 9–12.
ARBA, 77, n.1370.

359. Peterson First Guide to Wildflowers of Northeastern and North Central North America.
Roger Tory Peterson. Boston, MA: Houghton Mifflin; 1986. 128p., illus. $3.95pbk. 0-395-40777-Xpbk.
This is a simplified version of the more extensive field guides covering wildflowers in the United States. See also *Familiar Flowers of North America*. *Grade Level:* Grades 3–5. Grades 6–8.

360. Seed Identification Manual.
Alexander Campbell Martin; William D. Barkley. Berkeley, CA: University of California Press; 1973 (c1961). 221p., illus., index. $35.00. 0-520-00814-6.
This field guide to various seeds is arranged by general location of farmlands, wetlands, and woodlands, with a full photograph of the seed accompanied by identification clues. *Grade Level:* Grades 9–12.

361. Trees: A Quick Reference Guide to Trees of North America.
Robert H. Mohlenbrock; John W. Thieret. New York, NY: Macmillan; 1987. 155p., illus. (part in color), bibliog., index. $24.95. Macmillan Field Guides. 0-02-063430-7.
This guide covers the more common trees of North America north of Mexico, listing 232 species. The common name, scientific name, field marks, and habitat are given for each tree, and for some, variation within species and similar species are described. Range maps are

included, and each tree species is illustrated in color, showing leaves, twig, flower, or fruit. *Grade Level:* Grades 9–12.
ARBA, 89, n.1436; STARR, 89, n.79.

362. Wildflowers of North America.
George S. Fichter. New York, NY: Random House; 1982. 96p., illus. (part in color), index. $3.95pbk. An Audubon Society Beginner Guide. 0-394-84770-9pbk.
This is a field book for young children. The nomenclature is simplified yet accurate, with references made to the common names and arrangement of flowers by color. *Grade Level:* Grades 3–5. Grades 6–8.
ARBA, 84, n.1307; ASBYP, Winter 83, p.58; BL, 15 October 83, p.311; SLJ, November 82, p.82.

Glossaries

363. The Names of Plants.
D. Gledhill. New York, NY: Cambridge Unviersity Press; 1985. 159p., illus., bibliog. $34.50, $9.95pbk. 0-521-30549-7, 0-521-31562-Xpbk.
The first part of this glossary includes a history of plant naming with information on the changes to plant names and the International Code of Nomenclature for Cultivated Plants. The rules of botanical Latin are included. The second part is a glossary of Latin and Greek terms with their corresponding English translations. *Grade Level:* Grades 9–12.
ARBA, 87, n.1467; Choice, June 86, p.1560; SciTech, July 86, p.18.

Guides

364. The Complete Guide to Water Plants: A Reference Book.
Revised. Helmut Mühlberg. East Ardsley, Great Britain: EP Publishing; Dist. by Sterling; New York; NY; 1982. 391p., illus. (part in color), bibliog., index. $14.95. 0-7158-0789-7.
Two hundred species of aquatic grasses and plants are described in this guide, giving descriptions that include scientific name, distribution, characteristics, cultivation, and propagation. A discussion on the biology of aquatic plants is included. *Grade Level:* Grades 9–12.
ARBA, 83, n.1316.

365. Edible Mushrooms.
2nd revised. Clyde M. Christensen. Minneapolis, MN: University of Minnesota Press; 1981. 118p., illus. (part in color), bibliog., index. $12.95, $8.95pbk. 0-8166-1049-5, 0-8166-1050-9pbk.
This is a guide to some 60 species of edible mushrooms. Each species is fully described, and many cautions are given against eating mushrooms depicted in this guide. The color photographs are excellent. *Grade Level:* Grades 9–12.
ARBA, 82, n.1464; LJ, 1 September 81, p.1622.

366. The Everest House Complete Book of Gardening.
Jack Kramer. New York, NY: Everest House; 1982. 382p., illus. (part in color), index. $29.95. 0-89696-041-2.
This gardening book for the layperson contains a wealth of information about designing gardens, from the small patio garden to the rose garden. It also gives descriptive information on annuals, perennials, trees, shrubs, vines, bulbs, herbs, lawns, and ground cover. The book discusses plants and cultivation by region, giving specific pointers for growing plants in that region. *Grade Level:* Grades 6-8. Grades 9-12. ARBA, 84, n.1478; BL, 15 January 83, p.649, 1 September 83, p.64; PW, 19 November 83, p.71; SB, September 83, p.26.

367. Flowers for All Seasons: A Guide to Colorful Trees, Shrubs and Vines.
Jeff Cox; Marilyn Cox. Emmaus, PA: Rodale Press; 1987. 312p., illus. (part in color), index. $24.95. 0-87857-726-2.
This book concentrates on woody perennial flowering trees, shrubs, and vines that may be evergreen or deciduous but, unlike herbaceous perennials that die back to the roots each year, keep their wood stems, branches, and trunks alive all year. It guides the reader through the creation of a flowering garden for any size yard and for any taste. *Grade Level:* Grades 9-12.
LJ, 1 February 88, p.70; PW, 22 January 88, p.100; STARR, 89, n.33.

368. Non-Flowering Plants.
Floyd S. Shuttleworth; Herbert S. Zim. New York, NY: Golden Press; 1967. 160p., color illus., index. $2.95pbk. Golden Nature Guide. 0-307-24014-2pbk.
Over 400 species of nonflowering plants, such as algae, fungi, lichens, mosses, liverworts and hornworts, ferns and fern allies, and gymnosperms are covered in this small guide for young people. It has good illustrations and provides the scientific names. *Grade Level:* Grades 3-5. Grades 6-8.
BL, 15 September 67, p.132; PW, 28 November 66, p.65; SB, December 67, p.234.

369. Simon and Schuster's Guide to Garden Flowers.
Guido Moggi; Luciano Giugnolini. Stanley Schuler, ed. New York, NY: Simon and Schuster; 1983. 511p., color illus., bibliog., index. $19.95, $9.95pbk. 0-671-46674-7, 0-671-46678-Xpbk.
The beautiful photographs in this guide to garden flowers make it an excellent book for anyone who is interested in growing flowers. It covers, in addition to descriptions of individual flowers, cultivation, climatic suitability, food requirements, history and origin of the plants, and other small tidbits of information. *Grade Level:* Grades 9-12.
ARBA, 85, n.1371; BL, 1 September 83, p.14, 1 December 84, p.510.

370. Simon and Schuster's Guide to Trees.
New York, NY: Simon and Schuster; 1978. 1v. various paging, illus.
(part in color), index. $19.95. 0-671-24124-9.
This is another of the excellent guides published by Simon and
Schuster. It is a general guide to trees that includes good descriptions,
excellent photographs, and the etymology of various tree names. *Grade
Level:* Grades 9–12.
ARBA, 79, n.1365; BL, 15 March 79, p.1183; Choice, December 78,
p.1399; LJ, 1 October 78, p.1997, 15 April 79, p.888; SB, September
79, p.88; WLB, November 78, p.279.

371. Tom Brown's Guide to Wild Edible and Medicinal Plants.
Tom Brown, Jr. New York, NY: Berkley Books; 1985. 241p., illus.,
index. $7.95pbk. 0-425-08452-3pbk.
This guide, written in narrative style, describes 44 different plants, and
details the nutritional and medicinal aspects of each. The author
stresses proper plant management to prevent their destruction by pollution. Only the most common types of plants are included, such as
cattails, mint, violets, and thistle. *Grade Level:* Grades 9–12.
ARBA, 87, n.1479.

Handbooks

372. Carnivorous Plants of the World.
James Pietropaolo; Patricia Pietropaolo. Portland, OR: Timber Press;
1986. 206p., illus. (part in color), maps, bibliog., index. $24.95.
0-88192-066-5.
This colorful handbook covers 125 species of carnivorous plants. The
first part gives information on each group or genus, including history
of the plant, natural environment, trapping mechanism, species that
comprise the genus, botanical description, specific cultural requirements, and propagating techniques. The second part covers the cultural
data for growing the plants. *Grade Level:* Grades 9–12.
ARBA, 87, n.1470; BL 1 April 87, p.1164; Choice, May 87, p.1428;
SciTech, May 87, p.28.

373. Complete Guide to Basic Gardening.
Michael MacCaskey, ed. Tucson, AZ: HP Books; 1986. 240p., illus.
(part in color), maps, index. $12.95pbk. 0-89586-325-1pbk.
This small, compact handbook contains information on growing many
of the common flowering annuals and perennials, as well as fruits,
vegetables, and nuts. It covers planning the garden, mowing heights for
grasses, pesticides, landscaping, and selecting ornamental plants. Addresses of mail-order retailers and state extension services are included.
Grade Level: Grades 9–12.
ARBA, 87, n.1425; BL, 1 February 86, p.786; PW, 21 February 86,
p.164.

374. The Complete Handbook of Garden Plants.
Michael Wright; Sue Minter; Brian Carter. New York, NY: Facts on
File; 1984. 544p., color illus., maps, index. $18.95. 0-87196-632-8.
This comprehensive handbook covers outdoor garden plants, excluding
fruits and vegetables. Over 9,000 species are detailed, with the entries
arranged by plant type—trees and shrubs, perennial climbers, border
and bedding perennials, bulbs, corms and tubers, rock plants, annuals
and biennials, and water plants. Within each described type, the plants
are listed in alphabetical order by botanical name, with information on
sizes of the plants, leaf sizes, color descriptions of varieties, hardiness
and soil needs, how and when to propagate, pruning, and the best
varieties of each species. *Grade Level:* Grades 6–8. Grades 9–12.
ARBA, 86, n.1462; BL, 15 June 84, p.1426; Choice, July 84, p.1594;
LJ, 15 May 84, p.955.

375. Diseases and Pests of Ornamental Plants.
5th. Pascal P. Pirone. New York, NY: Wiley; 1978. 566p., illus.,
bibliog., index. $32.50. 0-471-07249-4.
This handbook is in two parts, with part one giving a summary of
plant diseases, pests, and control and part two, arranged by botanical
name of host plant, listing the diseases and pests of that host. The
diseases and pests are fully described with recommended methods of
control. *Grade Level:* Grades 9–12.
ARBA, 80, n.1570; Choice, June 71, p.534; LJ, 15 April 72, p.1388.

376. The Encyclopedia of Wood.
Revised. U.S. Department of Forestry Staff. New York, NY: Sterling
Publishing Co., Inc; 1989. 464p., illus., tables, charts, bibliog., index.
$19.95pbk. 0-8069-6994-6pbk.
This heavily illustrated handbook contains information on the structure of wood, physical and mechanical properties of wood, lumber
stress grades, fasteners, wood bonding, glued members, plywood, sand-
wich construction, control of moisture content, fire safety, wood
finishing, protection of wood from pests, preservation of wood, lami-
nates, and particle panels. *Grade Level:* Grades 9–12.

377. The Gardener's Handbook of Edible Plants.
Rosalind Creasy. San Francisco, CA: Sierra Club Books; 1986. 420p.,
illus., bibliog., index. $25.00, $12.95pbk. 0-87156-758-X,
0-87156-759-8pbk.
This book is an adaptation of *The Complete Book of Edible
Landscaping*, also by Rosalind Creasy. For each vegetable, herb, fruit
and nut, tree, shrub, and vine, a complete description is given with an
illustration. The handbook also includes information on how to pur-
chase, grow, and use each of the plants, plus pointers on soil preparation, watering, and disease and pest control. *Grade Level:* Grades 9–12.
ARBA, 87, n.1426; BL, 15 October 86, p.315; LJ, December 86, p.124.

378. The Healthy Garden Book: How to Control Plant Diseases, Insects, and Injuries.
Tom Riker. New York, NY: Stein and Day; 1979. 224p., illus., maps, index. $7.95pbk. 0-8128-6009-8pbk.
This small, inexpensive guide covers plant pests, diseases, and controls. It discusses the various major pests and the damages that they can cause to garden plants. One chapter covers the control of pests without chemical pesticides. *Grade Level:* Grades 9–12.
ARBA, 80, n.1571; BL, 1 January 79, p.726; BL, 1 December 79, p.530; LJ, 15 October 78, p.2125; PW, 18 September 78, p.164.

379. Knott's Handbook for Vegetable Growers.
3rd. Oscar A. Lorenz; Donald N. Maynard. New York, NY: Wiley; 1988. 456p., illus., index. $17.00. 0-471-85240-6.
This handbook covers all aspects of the vegetable growing industry, including plant growing, planting, soil, fertilizers, water and irrigation, pests, weed control, harvesting, storage, seed production, and other aspects of the industry. Numerous tables are included in the appendices, such as the nutritional composition of vegetables, crops and air pollutants, distance travelled at various tractor speeds, and the relative life expectancy of vegetable seeds. *Grade Level:* Grades 9–12.
ARBA, 82, n.1613; SciTech, July 88, p.27.

380. New York Times Book of House Plants.
Joan Lee Faust. New York, NY: Times Books; 1983 (c1973). 266p., illus. (part in color), index. $9.95pbk. 0-8129-6230-2pbk.
For those who have a collection of some of the more common house plants, this book is a good source of information on 150 of the better known ones. It gives information on light, water, air temperature, humidity, soil, fertilizer, potting and pruning, tender loving care, trouble signs, pests, indoor gardens, office plants, bottle gardens, terrariums, and hanging plants. *Grade Level:* Grades 9–12.
ARBA, 74, n.1727; BL, 15 June 73, p.964, 15 July 73, p.1017, 1 April 76, p.1134.

Manuals

381. Exotic Plant Manual: Fascinating Plants to Live With—Their Requirements, Propagation, and Use.
5th. Alfred Byrd Graf. East Rutherford, NJ: Roehrs; 1978. 840p., illus. (part in color), index. $37.50. 0-911266-13-5.
This is a manual of over 4,200 exotic plants that are cultivated in the United States. For each entry, the description covers native habitat, synonym, family relationship, and details on growth habit, foliage, inflorescence, and features of peculiar interest. This is a condensed version of *Exotica. Grade Level:* Grades 9–12.
ARBA, 72, n.1536; BL, 15 November 72, p.249; Choice, September 71, p.808; LJ, 1 May 71, p.1597, 15 April 72, p.1388; SB, September 71, p.147.

382. Manual of the Grasses of the United States.
2nd revised. Agnes Chase; A.S. Hitchcock. New York, NY: Dover;
1971. 2v., illus., index. $8.50. 0-486-22717-0, v.1; 0-486-22718-9, v.2.
This is a reprint of a government document that includes 2,000 line
drawings of common grasses of the United States, giving complete
identification keys, descriptions, and distribution ranges. It includes a
comprehensive glossary of synonyms of grasses that have appeared in
the botanical literature. *Grade Level:* Grades 9–12.
ARBA, 72, n.1532; Choice, June 72, p.527..

ZOOLOGY

Zoology is that part of biology which covers all living animal organisms from the microscopic to the mammoth whales. The study of zoology is based upon the structure and function of the animal, including *physiology*—the living processes that make up the whole animal; *embryology*—the development and new life of animals; *genetics*—the area of heredity and variation; *parasitology*—animals living in or on other animals; *natural history*—behavior of animals in nature; *ecology*—relation of animals to their environment; *evolution*—origin and differentiation of animal life; and *taxonomy*—classification and naming of animals. Many zoologists become experts on a particular class of animals, including *entomology*—the study of insects; *ichthyology*—the study of fishes; *ornithology*—the study of birds; *mammalogy*—the study of mammals; and *herpetology*—the study of snakes, lizards, crocodiles, turtles, dinosaurs, frogs, toads, and salamanders.

This chapter contains a large number of field guides. For young people, field guides are the key to learning about and understanding animals. They are excellent textbooks that encourage young people to study animals. The *Peterson Field Guide Series* is a standard and well-known series that covers virtually all animals in various volumes. The Audubon Society has some excellent field guides noted for their illustrations. W.C. Brown publishes a beginner's series called *Pictured Key Nature Series* and Simon and Schuster has several publications that are a cross between a field guide and an encyclopedia.

The *Dictionary of Animals*, *A Dictionary of Birds*, and *Dictionary of Zoology* are all recommended. Facts on File has published many encyclopedic reference sources on animals, including *The Encyclopedia of Birds*, *The Encyclopedia of Insects*, and *The Encyclopedia of Mammals*. Since all pets are animals, there are reference sources in this chapter covering cats, dogs, horses, and aquarium animals. Also included are two veterinary works: *Merck Veterinary Manual: Handbook of Diagnosis, Therapy and Disease Prevention and Control* and *Black's Veterinary Dictionary*.

Atlases—Science

383. Dr. Axelrod's Mini-Atlas of Freshwater Aquarium Fishes.
Mini-edition. Neptune, NJ: T.F.H; 1987. 992p., illus. (part in color), index. $19.95. 0-86622-385-1.
This is an outstanding atlas of all the fish any hobbyist would want. The excellent photographs, over 1,800, descriptions, and guide to owning make this a unique book. *Grade Level:* Grades 6–8. Grades 9–12.
ARBA, 89, n.1456; STARR, 90, n.147.

Dictionaries

384. Birdwatcher's Dictionary.
Peter Weaver. Calton, Great Britain: Privately published; Dist. by Buteo Books; Vermillion; SD; 1981. 155p., illus., maps. $17.50. 0-85661-028-3.
This handy, little book lists and briefly defines, in alphabetical order, those terms that birdwatchers may encounter. It is somewhat technical but still useful for the beginner. *Grade Level:* Grades 6–8. Grades 9–12.
ARBA, 83, n.1350; Choice, June 82, p.1385.

385. Black's Veterinary Dictionary.
15th. Geoffrey P. West, ed. Totowa, NJ: Barnes and Noble; 1985. 896p., illus. $35.00. 0-389-20555-9.
This is probably the most comprehensive veterinary dictionary available. It was first published in 1928 and has become a standard reference source. The book includes diseases, conditions, symptoms, and any other terminology associated with veterinary science. The definitions are concise. *Grade Level:* Grades 9–12.
ARBA, 84, n.1481; BL, 1 September 84, p.32; Choice, January 81, p.642.

386. Collegiate Dictionary of Zoology.
Robert William Pennak. Malabar, FL: Krieger; 1987 (c1964). 566p. $24.50. 0-89874-921-2.
This good, standard general dictionary of zoology gives brief definitions. *Grade Level:* Grades 9–12.
BL, 1 September 84, p.32.

387. Common Names of Insects and Related Organisms.
College Park, MD: Entomological Society of America; 1982. 132p. $15.00. 0-938522-18-3.

This handy little dictionary contains listings of common names for over 1,900 insects and other invertebrates that have been approved by the Entomological Society of America. Listings are by both common name and scientific name. *Grade Level:* Grades 9–12.

388. The Dictionary of American Bird Names.
Revised. Ernest A. Choate; Raymond A. Paynter, Jr. Boston, MA: Harvard Common Press; 1985. 226p., illus., bibliog. $17.95, $9.95pbk. 0-87645-121-0, 0-87645-117-2pbk.
This is a dictionary of the scientific and common names of North American birds, with information on the origins and the past meanings of the names of each. It conforms to the American Ornithologists' Union's checklist. *Grade Level:* Grades 9–12.
ARBA, 86, n.1514; BL, July 85, p.1524.

389. Dictionary of Animals.
Michael Chinery, ed. New York, NY: Arco; 1984. 379p., color illus., index. $17.95. 0-668-06155-3.
This book for young people gives brief information about all animals from mammals to one-celled organisms. It is arranged alphabetically by common name. There are some errors, but they can be overlooked in favor of the illustrations. *Grade Level:* Grades 6–8. Grades 9–12.
ARBA, 86, n.1507; BL, 1 April 85, p.1118, 15 June 85, p.1441; SB, May 85, p.308; SLJ, May 85, p.39; WLB, January 85, p.355.

390. A Dictionary of Birds.
Bruce Campbell; Elizabeth Lack, eds. Vermillion, SD: Buteo Books; 1985. 670p., illus. $75.00. 0-931130-12-3.
Although expensive, this dictionary is still a good one and should be considered. It has been written by over 280 specialists. The articles range in length from brief to major discussions of topics and taxonomic groups. The book includes all aspects of ornithology and covers taxa down to the family level. Individual species are not covered. *Grade Level:* Grades 9–12.
ARBA,86, n.7513; Choice, January 86, p.725; LJ, July 85, p.58, 15 April 86, p.36; SciTech, August 85, p.10.

391. Dictionary of Herpetology: A Brief and Meaningful Definition of Words and Terms Used in Herpetology.
James Arthur Peters. New York, NY: Hafner; 1982 (c1964). 392p., illus. $16.25. 0-02-850230-2.
This is one of the best comprehensive dictionaries explaining the scientific terminology associated with snakes. The definitions are brief, with conflicting meanings considered. *Grade Level:* Grades 9–12.

392. Dictionary of Zoology.
3rd. A.W. Leftwich. London, Great Britain: Constable and Co; Dist. by Crane, Russak; New York; NY; 1973. 478p., bibliog. $27.50. 0-8448-0845-8.

This well-known student's dictionary covers about 5,500 terms in the field of zoology. The definitions are brief and concise. Also included is a classification and nomenclature discussion, translation of Greek words, and a short bibliography. *Grade Level:* Grades 9–12. Choice, November 67, p.966; SB, December 67, p.236.

393. Glossary of Entomology: Smith's "an Explanation of Terms Used in Entomology."
Completely revised and rewritten. Jose Rollin De La Torre-Bueno. New York, NY: New York Entomological Society; 1985. 336p., illus., bibliog. $19.00. 0-934454-44-2.
This standard dictionary contains over 10,000 terms, with brief definitions covering insects. *Grade Level:* Grades 9–12.

Directories

394. Lions and Tigers and Bears: A Guide to Zoological Parks, Visitor Farms, Nature Centers, and Marine Life Displays in the United States and Canada.
Jefferson G. Ulmer; Susan Gower. New York, NY: Garland; 1985. 230p., illus., index. $20.00. 0-8240-8770-4.
This directory contains 835 entries, including governmental, private nonprofit, and commercial establishments. It is arranged geographically by state or province, then by city. Each entry contains name, address, telephone number, season and hours of operation, fees, a concise description of the facility and its exhibits, a list of special programs, and an indication of wheelchair access. *Grade Level:* Grades 6–8. Grades 9–12.
ARBA, 86, n.1537; Choice, May 85, p.1312; SciTech, April 85, p.15.

Encyclopedias

395. Aquarium Encyclopedia.
Gunther Sterba. Dick Mills, ed. Cambridge, MA: MIT Press; 1983 (c1978). 605p., illus. (part in color). $42.50. 0-262-19207-1.
This is a translation of *Lexikon der Aquaristik und Ichthyologie.* The book is alphabetically arranged, with animal names listed under their scientific names. The explanations are concise and clear but do presume some biological knowledge. *Grade Level:* Grades 6–8. Grades 9–12.
BL, 15 August 84, p.1168; Choice, July 83, p.157; LJ, 15 May 83, p.992; SB, November 83, p.92.

396. The Audubon Society Book of Insects.
Les Line; Lorus Milne; Margery Milne. New York, NY: Abrams; 1983. 260p., color illus., index. $50.00. 0-8109-1806-4.

Excellent photographs are the highlight of this encyclopedia. This book is a general survey of insects for the layperson, giving brief but accurate information on the insects, including basic concepts of insect anatomy, reproduction, and classification. *Grade Level:* Grades 6–8. Grades 9–12.
ARBA, 85, n.1459; BL, July 83, p.1374; LJ, July 83, p.1370; PW, 13 May 83, p.46.

397. Audubon Society Encyclopedia of Animal Life.
Ralph Buchsbaum. New York, NY: Portland House; 1987 (c1982). 606p., illus. (part in color), index. $45.00. 0-517-54657-4.
This well-written encyclopedia with excellent photographs provides brief descriptions of both vertebrates and invertebrates, with the majority of entries covering vertebrates. English or common names and scientific names are used. *Grade Level:* Grades 6–8. Grades 9–12.
ARBA, 83, n.1337; BL, 15 December 82, p.542; LJ, 15 December 82, p.2329.

398. Audubon Society Encyclopedia of North American Birds.
John K. Terres. New York, NY: Knopf; 1980. 1,109p., illus. (part in color), bibliog. $75.00. 0-394-46651-9.
This outstanding, but somewhat expensive, work covers Baja California, Canada, Greenland, Bermuda and all states except Hawaii. This encyclopedic reference is arranged alphabetically and contains almost 6,000 entries detailing the life histories of 847 species of birds, biographical sketches of over 120 people after whom American birds have been named, 625 major articles on ornithological subjects, and over 700 definitions of ornithological terms. *Grade Level:* Grades 6–8. Grades 9–12.
ARBA, 82, n.1484; BL, 1 June 82, p.1325; BW, 7 December 80, p.10; Choice, April 81, p.1078; LJ, 15 January 81, p.137, 15 May 82, p.960; WLB, June 81, p.782.

399. Bird Families of the World.
C.J.O. Harrison, ed. New York, NY: Abrams; 1978. 264p., color illus. $25.00. 0-8109-0706-2.
This beautifully illustrated encyclopedia of birds covers both living and extinct families, and discusses the topics of distribution, behavior, feeding, courtship, nesting and the young, and economic importance. *Grade Level:* Grades 9–12.
ARBA, 81, n.1462; BL, 1 February 80, p.786; Choice, June 79, p.554; LJ, 15 February 79, p.50; SB, December 79, p.153.

400. Butterflies of the World.
H.L. Lewis. New York, NY: Harrison House; 1987 (c1973). 312p., illus. (part in color), index. $29.95. 0-51748-165-0.
This encyclopedic guide to the butterflies of the world contains plates arranged geographically, with the butterflies grouped together by family and then by genera and species. Generic and specific names, author of the name, and the locality where most frequently seen are given for each family. The color photographs are from the collection of the

British museum. For a briefer coverage, see Rod Preston-Mafham's *Butterflies of the World.* *Grade Level:* Grades 9–12.
ARBA, 74, n.1559; BL, 15 July 74, p.1208; Choice, May 74, p.464; LJ, 15 March 74, p.745, 1 March 75, p.446.

401. Charlie Brown's Super Book of Questions and Answers: About All Kinds of Animals. . .from Snails to People.
Hedda Nussbaum, ed. New York, NY: Random House; 1978. 152p., index. $10.95. 0-394-83249-3.
This excellent reference book covers all animals in a question and answer format. The explanations are clear and accurate and cover such topics as animals with no bones, reptiles of long ago, reptiles of today, you and how you grow, your brain and nervous system, and the food you eat. *Grade Level:* Grades 3–5. Grades 6–8.

402. The Collector's Encyclopedia of Shells.
2nd. S. Peter Dance. New York, NY: McGraw-Hill; 1976. 288p., illus. $24.95. 0-07-015292-6.
The shells or mollusks are arranged by class, superfamily, family, sub-family, and genus and indicate habitat, inhabitant, form, and geographic range. This is a photographically well-illustrated encyclopedia. *Grade Level:* Grades 9–12.
ARBA, 78, n.857; BL, 15 June 75, p.1092; Choice, March 75, p.46; LJ, 15 January 75, p.110; WLB, January 75, p.353.

403. Complete Dog Book: The Photograph, History and Official Standard of Every Breed Admitted to AKC Registration, and the Selection, Training, Breeding, Care and Feeding of Pure-Bred Dogs.
17th. New York, NY: Howell Book House; 1985. 768p., color illus., index. $16.95. 0-87605-463-7.
This is the only authoritative and complete reference to nearly all breeds of dogs. It has excellent color photographs, a chapter on dog sports and a list of available AKC films and services. It covers 124 recognized breeds, giving their histories and standards in detail. See also *Harper's Illustrated Handbook of Dogs,* which contains the same kind of information but also has information on mongrels, mixed-breeds, mutts, and random-bred dogs. *Grade Level:* Grades 6–8. Grades 9–12.
ARBA, 80, n.1547.

404. Complete Encyclopedia of Horses.
M.E. Ensminger. Cranbury, NJ: A.S. Barnes; 1977. 487p., illus. (part in color), bibliog. $29.50. 0-498-01508-4.
This book covers almost everything there is to know about the horse. It includes anatomy, diseases, riding and hunting terms, equipment, clothing, breeds, colors, feed, stabling, and racing. *Grade Level:* Grades 9–12.
ARBA, 78, n.1463; BL, 15 January 79, p.824; Choice, August 78, p.372; LJ, 15 March 78, p.675; WLB, April 78, p.648.

405. Crocodiles and Alligators.
Charles A. Ross; Stephen Garnett, eds. New York, NY: Facts on File; 1989. 240p., color illus., maps, tables, charts, bibliog., index. $35.00. 0-8160-2174-0.
This beautifully illustrated encyclopedia contains information about crocodiles and alligators, with 22 species described in detail. Three broad topics are covered: evolution and biology, behavior and environment, and crocodilians and humans. *Grade Level:* Grades 6–8. Grades 9–12.

406. Dolphins and Porpoises.
Richard Ellis. New York, NY: Random House; 1982. 270p., illus. (part in color), bibliog., index. $25.00. 0-394-51800-4.
The excellent illustrations distinguish this encyclopedia covering 43 species of dolphins and porpoises. It explains dolphin and porpoise behavior, anatomy, ecology, natural history, and mythology. See also *A Field Guide to the Whales, Porpoises and Seals of the Gulf of Maine and Eastern Canada: Cape Cod to Newfoundland. Grade Level:* Grades 9–12.
ARBA, 84, n.1347; BL, 1 October 82, p.173p.; BW, 19 December 82, p.11; Choice, March 83, p.1014; LJ, 1 October 82, p.1886; PW, 10 September 82, p.71; SB, November 83, p.82.

407. The Encyclopedia of Animal Evolution.
R.J. Berry; A. Hallam, eds. New York, NY: Facts on File; 1987. 144p., illus. (part in color), bibliog., glossary, index. $24.95. The Encyclopedia of Animals. 0-8160-1819-7.
This is a good encyclopedic treatment of animal evolution. It is divided into six major sections: "The Prehistoric World," "The Background of Evolution," "The Course of Evolution," "The Consequences of Evolution," "The Mechanisms of Evolution," and "Man and Evolution." *Grade Level:* Grades 6–8. Grades 9–12.
BL, 15 November 87, p.520; Choice, December 87, p.598; R&RBkN, February 88, p.18; SB, May 88, p.301; STARR, 89, n.100.

408. Encyclopedia of Aquatic Life.
Keith Banister; Andrew Campbell, eds. New York, NY: Facts on File; 1985. 349p., illus. (part in color), maps, bibliog., index. $40.00. 0-8160-1257-1.
This encyclopedia covers mammals, fishes, and aquatic invertebrates. The articles are all signed and information is accurate and current, with scientific terminology kept to a minimum. The photographs are good and are of living animals. Even though the title states that this is aquatic life, it does not cover plants and aquatic insects. *Grade Level:* Grades 6–8. Grades 9–12.
ALib, May 86, p.313; ARBA, 86, n.1508; BL, 1 February 86, p.784; Choice, April 86, p.1192; LJ, 1 March 86, p.87, 15 April 86, p.36; SciTech, January 86, p.17; WLB, February 86, p.61.

409. The Encyclopedia of Birds.
Christopher M. Perrins; Alex L.A. Middleton, eds. New York, NY:
Facts on File; 1985. 445p., illus. (part in color), maps, bibliog., index.
$45.00. 0-8160-1150-8.
This well-written book with excellent photographs covers the 180 bird
families of the world. In addition to the illustrations, there are general-
ized silhouettes and size indicators relative to the human foot, head, or
leg. This is an accurate book with information about the birds plus
brief mention of topics, such as lead poisoning in waterfowl, sexual
dimorphism in birds of prey, and water transport by sand grouse.
Grade Level: Grades 6–8. Grades 9–12.
ARBA, 87, n.1519; BL, August 85, p.1609; Choice, October 85, p.270;
LJ, 15 September 85, p.72; WLB, October 85, p.65.

410. The Encyclopedia of Insects.
Christopher O'Toole, ed. New York, NY: Facts on File; 1986. 141p.,
illus., (part in color), bibliog., index. $24.95. 0-8160-1458-6.
The excellent photographs and the well-written text help to make this a
very useful and entertaining encyclopedia. The book includes descriptions of insect morphology, behavior, and ecology, as well as descriptions of some of the insects themselves. *Grade Level:* Grades 6–8.
Grades 9–12.
ARBA, 87, n.1524; BL, 1 June 86, p.1423; Choice, July 86, p.1696; LJ,
July 86, p.72; SciTech, June 86, p.13; SLJ, May 83, p.22; WLB, June
86, p.80.

411. The Encyclopedia of Mammals.
David Macdonald, ed. New York, NY: Facts on File; 1984. 895p.,
illus., (part in color), maps, bibliog., index. $50.00. 0-87196-871-1.
The 700 entries in this beautifully written encyclopedia cover all of the
major species, giving basic evolutionary facts, appearance, social patterns, and environmental concerns. The unique charts show the relative size of each animal compared to man. Other information includes
the average body size, gestation period, longevity, and distribution.
Grade Level: Grades 6–8. Grades 9–12.
ALib, May 85, p.291; ARBA, 85, n.1465; BL, 1 November 84, p.349,
15 May 85, p.1318; BW, 2 December 84, p.10; Choice, January 85,
p.658; LJ, January 85, p.74, 15 April 85, p.38; VOYA, August 85,
p.206; WLB, February 85, p.422.

412. Encyclopedia of Marine Invertebrates.
Jerry G. Walls, ed. Neptune, NJ: T.F.H; 1982. 736p., illus., (part in
color), bibliog., index. $49.95. 0-87666-495-8.
This encyclopedic reference on marine invertebrates is suitable for salt
water aquariums. This book describes each species in terms for the
nonspecialist, and the illustrations are outstanding. *Grade Level:*
Grades 9–12.
ARBA, 84, n.1359; Choice, March 83, p.955; LJ, 1 March 83, p.490.

413. Encyclopedia of North American Wildlife.
Stanley Klein. New York, NY: Facts on File; 1983. 315p., color illus., bibliog., index. $35.00. 0-87196-758-8.
This beautifully illustrated book contains entries for 105 mammals, 111 birds, 51 reptiles, 23 amphibians, and 34 fish. It is arranged alphabetically by common name, giving the common name, Latin name, range and habitat, size and other physical characteristics, behavior patterns, diet, breeding habits and family life, social characteristics, a notation of animals that are similar, and human use of or effect on the animal. *Grade Level:* Grades 6–8. Grades 9–12.
ARBA, 84, n.1324; BL 15 February 84, p.834, 15 September 84, p.117; BW, 4 December 83, p.18; Choice, March 84, p.954; LJ, January 84, p.76; WLB, January 84, p.372.

414. The Encyclopedia of Reptiles and Amphibians.
Tim R. Halliday; Kraig Adler, eds. New York, NY: Facts on File; 1986. 143p., illus. (part in color), maps, bibliog., index. $24.95. 0-8160-1359-4.
This encyclopedia includes entries for representative species of all the families in Reptilia and Amphibia. The descriptions are very accurate and concise, with excellent illustrations. Range maps are included. *Grade Level:* Grades 6–8. Grades 9–12.
ARBA, 87, n.1536; BL, 1 June 86, p.1423; Choice, September 86, p.158; LJ, July 86, p.72; SB, November 86, p.100; SciTech, June 86, p.13; SLJ, May 87, p.22; WLB, June 86, p.80.

415. Encyclopedia of the Animal World.
New York, NY: Facts on File; 1988. 4v., illus. (part in color), maps, glossary, index. $17.95 per volume.
This beautifully illustrated book covers the mammals of the world, giving descriptions and brief information about range, habitat, diet, behavior, and other pertinent facts. Each book covers a particular type of mammal: primates, insect-eaters and baleen whales; hunters; large plant-eaters; and small plant-eaters. *Grade Level:* Grades 6–8. Grades 9–12.

416. Fishes of the World.
2nd. Joseph S. Nelson. New York, NY: Wiley; 1984. 523p., illus., maps, bibliog., index. $48.95. 0-471-86475-7.
This comprehensive encyclopedia covers all of the main species of fishes, worldwide, giving clear and concise descriptions, indication of range, and illustrations. The large bibliography permits the user to consult other sources for more detailed discussions of specific fishes. *Grade Level:* Grades 9–12.
Choice, March 77, p.88; SB, September 77, p.83.

417. International Encyclopedia of Horse Breeds.
Jane Kidd. Tucson, AZ: HP Books; 1986. 208p., color illus., index. $14.95pbk. 0-89586-393-6pbk.

This encyclopedia covers all horse breeds worldwide. After an introductory chapter on the evolution of the horse, the various types of horses are described, giving scale of height, the country of origin, typical colors and features of the breed, a history of the breed's development, and a description of present uses. *Grade Level:* Grades 9–12.
ARBA, 87, n.1515.

418. Lizards of the World.
Chris Mattison. New York, NY: Facts on File; 1989. 192p., illus. (part in color), bibliog., index. $23.95. 0-8160-1900-2.
This beautifully illustrated encyclopedia contains information that the layperson would want to know about lizards. It includes a historical essay on lizards and chapters on interaction with the environment, feeding, defense, reproduction, and world distribution. Detailed descriptions of the lizards of the world are included as well as information on the amphisbaenian, a wormlike reptile. *Grade Level:* Grades 6–8. Grades 9–12.

419. The Macmillan Illustrated Encyclopedia of Birds: A Visual Who's Who in the World of Birds.
Philip Whitfield, ed. New York, NY: Collier Books/Macmillan; 1988. 224p., color illus., index. $19.95pbk. 0-02-044462-1pbk.
Each of the more than 700 entries in this encyclopedia has an excellent color illustration; scientific, family, and common name; range; habitat; size; and a brief description of the physiology, breeding, and feeding habits of the bird. The status of threatened species is indicated by symbols representing endangered, vulnerable, rare, and indeterminate. *Grade Level:* Grades 9–12.
STARR, 90, n.136.

420. Marine Mammals of Eastern North Pacific and Arctic Waters.
2nd. Delphine Haley, ed. Seattle, WA: Pacific Search Press; 1986. 295p., illus. (part in color), maps, bibliog., index. $22.95pbk. 0-931397-11-1pbk.
This encyclopedia of marine mammals is written in the form of essays, each covering a specific mammal. Each essay contains some of the same kinds of information but each is also unique. Topics that may be covered include origins and evolution, behavior patterns, role of the mammal in human history and culture, hunting, and pollution. *Grade Level:* Grades 9–12.
ARBA, 87, n.1529; SciTech, April 87, p.16.

421. The Oxford Companion to Animal Behavior.
David McFarland, ed. New York, NY: Oxford University Press; 1982. 657p., illus., index. $19.95. 0-19-281990-9.
This collection of articles discusses animal behavior. It is in the form of an encyclopedia with long, signed articles. There is an index to scientific and English names but no subject index. *Grade Level:* Grades 9–12.

ARBA, 83, n.1339; BL, July 82, p.1406, 1 March 84, p.961, 1 September 84, p.34; Choice, September 82, p.121; LJ, July 82, p.1326; SB, January 83, p.135.

422. Simon and Schuster's Guide to Horses and Ponies of the World.
Maurizio Bongianni. Jane Kidd, ed. New York, NY: Simon and Schuster; 1988. 255p., color illus., bibliog., index. $19.95, $9.95pbk. 0-671-66067-5, 0-671-66068-3pbk.
This beautifully illustrated pocket encyclopedia of the world's horses and ponies gives information on 173 popular and rare breeds of American and international interest. It has clear line-drawings and photographs illustrating conformation, coloration, markings, and gait. *Grade Level:* Grades 6–8. Grades 9–12.
STARR, 90, n.3.

423. Snake Discovery Library.
Vero Beach, FL: Rourke Enterprises; 1986–87. 12v., color illus., glossary, index. $11.66 per volume.
This excellent set of books covers 12 different types of snakes. Each volume is well-illustrated, contains 27 pages, and gives the same following information: habitat, appearance, senses, head and mouth, babies, prey, defenses, and relationships to humans. The 12 volumes are: *Cobras* (0-86592-955-6), *Boa* (0-86592-959-9, *Copperheads* (0-86592-957-2), *Cotton* (0-86592-958-0), *Mambas* (0-86592-960-2), *Rattlers* (0-86592-956-4), *Anacondas* (0-86592-249-7), *Coral* (0-86592-246-2), *Kingsnakes* (0-86592-248-9), *Pythons* (0-86592-244-6), *Rat* (0-86592-247-0), and *Tree* (0-86592-245-4). *Grade Level:* Grades 6–8. Grades 9–12.
STARR, 89, n.99, 102–03.

424. Spiders of the World.
Rod Preston-Mafham; Ken Preston-Mafham. New York, NY: Facts on File; 1984. 191p., illus. (part in color), bibliog., index. $17.95. 0-87196-996-3.
This is a good encyclopedia of the spiders of the world. Photographs showing spiders in their natural habitat add to the well-written, descriptive text. *Grade Level:* Grades 6–8. Grades 9–12.
ARBA, 85, n.1462; BL, 15 October 84, p.271; Choice, November 84, p.449; LJ, 1 November 84, p.2072.

425. Turtles and Tortoises of the World.
David Alderton. New York, NY: Facts on File; 1988. 191p., color illus., bibliog., index. $24.95. 0-8160-1733-6.
This encyclopedia is an easy-to-read introduction to the natural history of the world's turtles and tortoises. It provides overviews to the main topics students generally need to cover when writing a high school term paper. The text is easy to understand and not overwhelmed with technical data. The book includes excellent photographs. *Grade Level:* Grades 6–8. Grades 9–12.
STARR 90, n.137.

426. Whales, Dolphins and Porpoises.
Richard Harrison; M.M. Bryden, eds. New York, NY: Facts on File;
1988. 240p., color illus., bibliog., index. $35.00. 0-8160-1977-0.
This work documents the current state of scientific knowledge of
whales, dolphins, and porpoises, as well as their place in literature and
art. The text is clearly written in language understandable to the
layperson. The narrative and color illustrations convey the sense of
wonder, mystery, and excitement the contributors feel for these aquatic
animals. See also *Sierra Club Handbook of Whales and Dolphins.*
Grade Level: Grades 6–8. Grades 9–12.
STARR, 90, n.138.

Field Books

427. Amphibians of North America: A Guide to Field Identification.
Hobart M. Smith. New York, NY: Golden Press; 1978. 160p., color
illus., bibliog., index. $7.95. Golden Field Guide Series.
0-307-13662-0.
Nearly 180 species of amphibians found in North America are identified and described in this field guide. The book includes frogs, toads,
salamanders, newts, a list of subspecies, range maps, and illustrations.
There is a brief discussion of the biology of amphibians and their
conservation. *Grade Level:* Grades 3–5. Grades 6–8.
ARBA, 80, n.1415; BL, 1 February 79, p.861; SLJ, March 79, p.156.

**428. Audubon Society Field Guide to North American Birds: Western
Region.**
Milos D.F. Udvardy. New York, NY: Knopf; 1977. 855p., illus. (part
in color), index. $12.50. 0-394-41410-1.
This guide and John Bull and John Farrand, Jr.'s *Audubon Society
Field Guide to North American Birds: Eastern Region* (Knopf, 1977,
775p., 0-394-41405-5, $12.50) cover the entire United States. The first
half of each book consists of colored photographs, while the second
half is devoted to species accounts, including descriptions, voice, habitat, range, nesting, and miscellaneous information. There are many
field guides to birds, each with its own unique qualities. See also *How
to Know the Land Birds* and *A Field Guide to Birds. Grade Level:*
Grades 6–8. Grades 9–12.
ARBA, 78, n.1323; BL, 15 October 78, p.403; BW, 16 October 77,
p.E1; Choice, March 78, p.51; LJ, 15 April 78, p.818.

429. The Audubon Society Field Guide to North American Butterflies.
Robert Michael Pyle. New York, NY: Knopf; 1981. 916p., illus. (part
in color), index. $13.50. 0-394-51914-0.
Over 1,000 color photographs make this field guide a beautiful one to
read and use. The book contains sections on description, similar species, life cycle, flight, habitat, range, and a general section with comments on behavior, conservation, and other biological aspects of the
butterfly for each species. It covers all 670 species found in the United

States. There is also an index of host plants that are eaten by the caterpillars. *Grade Level:* Grades 6–8. Grades 9–12.
ARBA, 83, n.1360; BL, 15 October 81, p.273; Choice, November 81, p.400; LJ, 15 September 81, p.1718.

430. Audubon Society Field Guide to North American Fishes, Whales, and Dolphins.
Herbert T. Boschung, Jr. New York, NY: Knopf; 1983. 848p., color illus., index. $13.50. The Audubon Society Field Guide Series. 0-394-53405-0.
The excellent illustrations in this field guide are grouped together by body type, with the text arranged in taxonomic order, providing complete descriptions of the fishes, whales, and dolphins. See also *A Field Guide to Atlantic Coast Fishes of North America. Grade Level:* Grades 6–8. Grades 9–12.
BL, 15 February 84, p.833; BRpt, May 84, p.48; Choice, May 84, p.946; Kliatt, Winter 84, p.63; LJ, 1 February 84, p.172; VOYA, June 84, p.107.

431. Audubon Society Field Guide to North American Insects and Spiders.
Lorus Milne; Margery Milne. New York, NY: Knopf; 1980. 989p., illus. (part in color), index. $13.50. The Audubon Society Field Guide Series. 0-394-50763-0.
Excellent color photographs are arranged by the shape of the insect or spider and are followed by descriptive text that gives the physical description, habitat, range, food, and life cycle. There is a glossary of terms. See also *Field Guide to the Insects of America North of Mexico, Simon and Schuster's Guide to Insects, How to Know the Spiders,* and *Insects: A Guide to Familiar American Insects. Grade Level:* Grades 6–8. Grades 9–12.
ARBA, 82, n.1493; BL, 15 January 81, p.657; Choice, March 81, p.926; LJ, 15 February 81, p.462.

432. Audubon Society Field Guide to North American Mammals.
John O. Whitaker, Jr. New York, NY: Knopf; 1980. 745p., illus. (part in color), index. $12.50. The Audubon Society Field Guide Series. 0-394-50762-2.
Another of the excellent field guides arranged by the shape, size, and color of the mammal. Information for each animal includes its classification, common name, common measurements, color, markings, anatomy, similar species, sign (tracks, scat, etc.), breeding, habitat type, range, behavior, natural history, and conservation status. There is a key to the tracks of the animals arranged by shape similarities. See also *Field Guide to the Mammals. Grade Level:* Grades 6–8. Grades 9–12.
ARBA, 82, n.1497; BL, 15 January 81, p.657; Choice, April 81, p.1125; LJ, 1 February 81, p.362, 1 March 82, p.515.

433. Audubon Society Field Guide to North American Reptiles and Amphibians.
John L. Behler; F. Wayne King. New York, NY: Knopf; 1979. 719p.,

illus. (part in color), maps, index. $13.50. The Audubon Society Field Guide Series. 0-394-50824-6.

Photographs of the reptiles and amphibians are arranged in six main groups: salamanders, frogs and toads, crocodilians, turtles, lizards, and snakes, then sub-arranged by color. The marine turtles of coastal waters are also included. The text describes each of the species and gives common and scientific names, description, voice, breeding, habitat, subspecies, range, and descriptive comments. See also the much briefer *How to Know the Amphibians and Reptiles. Grade Level:* Grades 6–8. Grades 9–12.

ARBA, 81, n.1487; Choice, April 80, p.243; LJ, 1 March 80, p.623.

434. Audubon Society Field Guide to North American Seashells.
Harrold Rehder. New York, NY: Knopf; 1981. 894p., illus. (part in color), index. The Audubon Society Field Guide Series. 0-394-51913-2.

Over 671 species of North American seashells are included in this field guide. Color photographs are placed at the beginning of the guide with arrangement based on the shape and color of the shell. The text that follows gives description, habitat, range, and general comments. See also *Field Guide to Pacific Coast Shells. Grade Level:* Grades 6–8. Grades 9–12.

ARBA, 82, n.1489; BL, 1 November 81, p.361; BW, 10 January 82, p.12; LJ, 1 November 81, p.2128, 1 March 82, p.515; SB, September 82, p.20.

435. Audubon Society Field Guide to North American Seashore Creatures.
Norman A. Meinkoth. New York, NY: Knopf; 1981. 799p., illus. (part in color), maps, index. $13.50. The Audubon Society Field Guide Series. 0-394-51993-0.

This very good, unique field guide covers some 850 marine invertebrate animals living in or around the shallow waters of the temperate seacoasts of the United States and Canada. Excellent color photographs are grouped at the beginning of the book, followed by text that gives, for each animal, a short description, common and scientific names, habitat, range, and comments. *Grade Level:* Grades 6–8. Grades 9–12.

ARBA, 83, n.1371; BL 1 March 82, p.837; BW, 10 January 82, p.12; LJ, 15 February 82, p.443, 1 May 82, p.853, 1 March 83, p.448; SLJ, May 82, p.93.

436. Birds: A Guide to the Most Familiar American Birds.
Herbert S. Zim; Ira N. Gabrielson; Chandler S. Robbins. New York, NY: Golden Press; 1987. 160p., illus. $7.95. Golden Nature Guide. 0-307-24053-3.

This small field guide is for preteens and covers 120 American birds. It includes full descriptions, with additional information on migration, eggs, nests, food, parts of birds, history of birds, photography of birds, bird watching, and collecting. See also two other small pocket guides: *Familiar Birds of North America: Eastern Region* and *Familiar Birds of North America: Western Region. Grade Level:* Grades 3–5. Grades 6–8.

437. Birds of North America.
George S. Fichter. New York, NY: Random House; 1982. 96p., illus.
(part in color), index. $3.95pbk. An Audubon Society Beginner
Guide. 0-394-84771-7pbk.
This introductory field guide for children and laypeople explains how
to identify birds, where to look, and how to look, with some information on bird anatomy and behavior. *Grade Level:* Grades 3–5. Grades
6–8.
ARBA, 84, n.1329; ASBYP, Winter 83, p.58; BL, 15 October 82,
p.311; SLJ, November 82, p.82.

**438. Birds of North America, Eastern Region: A Quick Identification
Guide to Common Birds.**
John Bull. New York, NY: Macmillan; 1985. 157p., illus., index.
$16.95, $9.95pbk. Macmillan Field Guides. 0-02-518230-7,
0-02-079660-9pbk.
This handy little field guide covers the birds of the eastern United
States. Identifications can be made quickly and easily. *Grade Level:*
Grades 9–12.
BL, August 85, p.1608.

**439. The Butterflies of North America: A Natural History and Field
Guide.**
James A. Scott. Stanford, CA: Stanford University Press; 1986. 583p.,
illus. (part in color), maps, bibliog., index. $49.50. 0-8047-1205-0.
This is both an encyclopedia and a field guide written for the amateur.
All 679 species of butterflies are covered, with keys to identification,
distribution, ecology, and behavior. Numerous shaded maps show
where the species reside and there is a "Hostplant Catalogue" that
indicates which species frequent which plants. *Grade Level:* Grades
9–12.
ARBA, 87, n.1525; BL, 15 November 86, p.458; Choice, February 87,
p.867; LJ, 1 April 87, p.140, 15 April 87, p.37; SB, March 87, p.221;
SciTech, December 86, p.14.

440. Collector's Guide to Seashells of the World.
Jerome M. Eisenberg; William E. Old, Jr. New York, NY: McGraw-
Hill; 1981. 237p., illus. (part in color), bibliog., index. $26.95.
0-07-019140-9.
This is a good field book with excellent photographs of nearly 4,000
specimens from the families of Gastropoda, Pelecypoda,
Polyplacophora, Scaphopoda, and Cephalopoda. There is a brief de-
scription for each shell. See also the encyclopedic guide *The Collector's
Encyclopedia of Shells. Grade Level:* Grades 9–12.
ARBA, 82, n.1498; BL, 1 May 81, p.1178.

441. Dangerous Marine Animals of the Pacific Coast.
Christina Parsons. San Luis Obispo, CA: Helm Publishing; 1986.
96p., illus., bibliog., index. $4.95pbk. 0-930118-11-1pbk.

This is a small easy-to-use handbook of practical information about dangerous marine life along the Pacific coast. It is intended for field use by skin-divers, surfers, fishermen, swimmers, and beach combers. *Grade Level:* Grades 9–12.
ARBA, 87, n.1518.

442. Eastern Birds.
John Farrand, Jr. New York, NY: McGraw-Hill; 1988. 484p., illus. (part in color), index. $13.50. Audubon Handbook. 0-07-019976-0.
This book is intended to replace the *Audubon Society Field Guide to North American Birds: Eastern Region*. The pictures and text appear on the same page. The text is clear and very readable, and the photographs are outstanding. *Grade Level:* Grades 6–8. Grades 9–12.
ARBA, 89, n.1442; BL, 15 November 87, p.520; Choice, March 88, p.1064; LJ, 15 November 87, p.72.

443. Easy Identification Guide to North American Snakes.
Hilda Simon. New York, NY: Dodd, Mead; 1979. 128p., color illus., maps, index. $12.95. 0-396-07771-4.
This is a guide for the amateur arranged by the color and shape of the snake. It has good illustrations, clear range maps, and a descriptive text that should make it easy to identify the snake. *Grade Level:* Grades 9–12.
ARBA, 81, n.1490; LJ, 15 February 80, p.150; SB, November 80, p.78; WLB, April 80, p.528.

444. Familiar Birds of North America: Eastern Region.
Ann H. Whitman, ed. New York, NY: Knopf; 1986. 192p., illus. $4.95. Audubon Society Pocket Guides. 0-394-74839-5.
This book and Whitman's *Familiar Birds of North America: Western Region* (Knopf, 1986, 192p., 0-394-74842-5, $4.95, *Audubon Society Pocket Guides*) are two small field guides that are excellent for the beginner. As with all Audubon books, they are easy to use and illustrated with excellent photographs. *Grade Level:* Grades 6–8. Grades 9–12.
ARBA, 88, 1558–1559; VOYA, August 87, p.135.

445. A Field Guide to Animal Tracks.
2nd. Olaus J. Murie. Boston, MA: Houghton Mifflin; 1975. 400p., illus, index. $17.95, $12.95pbk. Peterson Field Guide Series, 9. 0-395-19978-6, 0-395-18323-5pbk.
This is one of the well-known Peterson books covering animal tracks. Each animal track is illustrated and followed with identification notes. See also *A Field Guide to Mammal Tracking in Western America*. *Grade Level:* Grades 9–12.

446. A Field Guide to Atlantic Coast Fishes of North America.
C. Richard Robins; G. Carleton Ray. Boston, MA: Houghton Mifflin; 1986. 354p., illus. (part in color), maps, bibliog., index. $20.95, $14.95pbk. Peterson Field Guide Series, 32. 0-395-31852-1, 0-395-39198-9pbk.

This field guide and William N. Eschmeyer and Earl S. Heralds's *A Field Guide to Pacific Coast Fishes of North America from the Gulf of Alaska to Baja, California* (Houghton Mifflin, 1983, 336p., 0-395-26873-7, 0-395-33188-9pbk, $20.95, $12.95pbk, *Peterson Field Guide Series, 28*) cover the Atlantic and Pacific coast fishes. It does not include freshwater fishes, deepwater species, and open sea fishes. A brief description gives scientific and common names, identification characteristics, range, habitat, and size. The illustrations are excellent. See also *Audubon Society Field Guide to North American Fishes, Whales, and Dolphins*. *Grade Level:* Grades 9–12.
ARBA, 87, n.1519; BL, 1 June 82, p.1424; LJ, 1 September 86, p.190.

447. A Field Guide to Bird Songs of Eastern and Central North America.
2nd. Roger Tory Peterson. Boston, MA: Houghton Mifflin; 1983. 2 records. $19.95. 0-395-34677-0 cassettes, 0-395-34674-6 records.
This two-record or two-cassette set of bird songs is to be used with the *Field Guide to the Birds*. It is a collection of unique songs for 250 species of birds and enables the user to identify the birds from their songs. *Grade Level:* Grades 9–12.

448. A Field Guide to Dangerous Animals of North America: Including Central America.
Charles Kingsley Levy. Lexington, MA: Stephen Green Press; 1983. 164p., illus. (part in color), bibliog., index. $9.95pbk. 0-8289-0503-7pbk.
This field guide covers animals that are dangerous in the lethal sense, as well as those that can just cause injuries. It is divided into six sections: "Animals dangerous to eat," "Animals that bite," "Venomous reptiles," "Venomous fishes," "Venomous arthropods," and "Dangerous lower invertebrates." Each animal is fully described and information on habitat, distribution, avoidance and control, nature of the injury, first aid, and medical treatment is given. A very good book for the nature lover. *Grade Level:* Grades 9–12.
ARBA, 84, n.1323.

449. A Field Guide to Hawks of North America.
William S. Clark. Boston, MA: Houghton Mifflin; 1987. 198p., illus. (part in color), maps, bibliog., index. $19.95, $13.95pbk. Peterson Field Guide Series, 35. 0-395-36001-3, 0-395-44112-9pbk.
This specialized field guide covers one order of birds, hawks or diurnal raptors. It covers 39 native North American hawks with good descriptions and excellent detailed color plates. *Grade Level:* Grades 9–12.
ARBA, 89, n.1441; BL, 1 October 87, p.194; Choice, December 87, p.596; LJ, 15 April 88, p.31.

450. A Field Guide to Mammal Tracking in Western America.
James Halfpenny. Boulder, CO: Johnson Books; 1986. 161p., illus. (part in color), bibliog., index. $11.95pbk. 0-933472-98-6pbk.

This field guide covers mammal tracks in the broadest sense: foot prints, scat, feeding signs, and special marks, such as clawmarks on trees, rocks, and the ground. It covers mostly the larger mammals and treats the smaller animals only briefly. By far, the biggest coverage is on footprints; each footprint is illustrated and described for identification. See also *Field Guide to Animal Tracks*. *Grade Level:* Grades 9–12. ARBA, 87, n.1530; BL, July 86, p.1568.

451. Field Guide to Reptiles and Amphibians of Eastern and Central North America.
2nd. Roger Conant. Boston, MA: Houghton Mifflin; 1975. 448p., illus. (part in color), index. $17.95, $12.95pbk. Peterson Field Guide Series, 12. 0-395-19979-4, 0-395-19977-8pbk.
This field guide and Robert C. Stebbins's *Field Guide to Western Reptiles and Amphibians: Field Marks of All Species in Western North America, Including Baja, California* (2nd rev. ed., Houghton Mifflin, 1985, 448p., 0-395-38254-8, 0-395-38253-Xpbk, $17.95, $12.95pbk, *Peterson Field Guide Series, 16*) cover the entire spectrum of snakes, lizards, frogs, turtles, etc., found in North America. These books have excellent illustrations and good text. *Grade Level:* Grades 9–12. ARBA, 76, n.1448; BL, 1 May 76, p.1291; Choice, May 76, p.83; SB, March 76, p.197.

452. A Field Guide to the Beetles of North America.
Richard E. White. Boston, MA: Houghton Mifflin; 1983. 368p., illus. (part in color), bibliog., index. $15.95, $10.95pbk. Peterson Field Guide Series, 29. 0-395-31808-4, 0-395-33953-7pbk.
This is a typical field guide, giving descriptions of just beetles and information on their structure, growth, development, and scientific classification. There is also information on collecting and preparing the specimens for display. *Grade Level:* Grades 9–12. BL, 1 November 83, p.385; SB, March 84, p.205.

453. A Field Guide to the Birds: A Completely New Guide to All the Birds of Eastern Central North America.
4th. Roger Tory Peterson. Boston, MA: Houghton Mifflin; 1980. 384p., illus. (part in color), maps, index. $17.95, $12.95pbk. Peterson Field Guide Series, 1. 0-395-26621-2, 0-395-26619-Xpbk.
This excellent standard field guide on birds of eastern and central North America contains clear descriptions, good illustrations, and range maps. The birds are grouped according to body form and habitat. Since birdwatching is so popular, there are many field guides. Three others by Roger Tory Peterson that cover birds are: *Field Guide to Mexican Birds: Field Marks of All Species Found in Mexico, Guatemala, Belize (British Honduras), El Salvador* (Houghton Mifflin, 1973, 304p., 0-395-17129-6, $17.95, *Peterson Field Guide Series, 20*); *Field Guide to the Birds of Texas and Adjacent States* (Houghton Mifflin, 1963, 304p., 0-395-08087-8, 0-395-26252-6pbk, $18.95, $12.95pbk, *Peterson Field Guide Series, 13*); and *Field Guide to Western Birds: Field Marks of All Species Found in North America West of the 100th Meridian with a Section on Birds of the Hawaiian Islands*

(2nd ed., Houghton Mifflin, 1972 (c1969), 320p., 0-395-08085-1, 0-395-13692-Xpbk, $17.95, $12.95pbk, *Peterson Field Guide Series, 2*). See also *Field Guide to Bird Songs of Eastern and Central North America*, which is considered a companion set of records to this field guide, *How to Know the Land Birds*, and *Audubon Society Field Guide to North American Birds*. *Grade Level:* Grades 9–12. ARBA, 82, n.1483; BL, 1 December 80, p.492; BW, 28 September 80, p.4; LJ, 1 October 80, p.2070; WLB March 81, p.543.

454. Field Guide to the Birds of North America.
Shirley L. Scott, ed. Washington, DC: National Geographic Society; 1983. 464p., color illus., maps, index. $13.95pbk. 0-87044-472-7pbk. This field guide is part of *The Wonder of Birds* and also includes four 9-inch records with 200 bird calls and songs, which are keyed to the field guide. The illustrations and descriptions are excellent, especially of young and immature birds. *Grade Level:* Grades 6–8. Grades 9–12. ARBA, 85, n.1438; BL, 15 May 84, p.1280; Choice, June 84, p.1442.

455. Field Guide to the Butterflies of North America East of the Great Plains.
Alexander B. Klots. Boston, MA: Houghton Mifflin; 1977 (c1951). 349p., illus. (part in color), bibliog., index. $17.95, $12.95pbk. Peterson Field Guide Series, 4. 0-395-07865-2, 0-395-25859-6pbk. The *Peterson Field Guide Series* includes three excellent field guides covering butterflies and moths of North America; this one and the following two: James W. Tilden and Arthur Clayton Smith's *A Field Guide to Western Butterflies* (Houghton Mifflin, 1986, 370p., 0-395-35407-2, 0-395-41654-Xpbk, $19.95, $12.95, *Peterson Field Guide Series, 33*) and Charles V. Covel, Jr.'s *A Field Guide to the Moths of Eastern United States* (Houghton Mifflin, 1984, 512p., 0-395-26056-6, 0-395-36100-1pbk, $18.95, $13.95, *Peterson Field Guide Series, 30*). Together, these three field guides cover all major butterflies and moths that one would encounter in North America. Habits, life histories, range, larval food plants, classification, and collecting are covered. *Grade Level:* Grades 9–12. ARBA, 78, n.1330.

456. Field Guide to the Insects of America North of Mexico.
Donald J. Borror; Richard E. White. Boston, MA: Houghton Mifflin; 1970. 404p., illus. (part in color), bibliog., index. $17.95, $12.95pbk. Peterson Field Guide Series, 19. 0-395-07435-3, 0-395-18523-8pbk. This field guide covers some 579 families of insects, with factual descriptions of each species that is included. There is information on collecting, preservation, and insect physiology. See also *Simon and Schuster's Guide to Insects, How to Know the Insects,* and *The Audubon Society Field Guide to North American Insects and Spiders. Grade Level:* Grades 9–12. BL, 15 September 70, p.72; Choice, July 70, p.669; KR, 15 February 70, p.236; LJ, July 70, p.2502; SB, September 70, p.144.

457. Field Guide to the Mammals: North America North of Mexico.
3rd. William H. Burt; Richard P. Grossenheider. Boston, MA:
Houghton Mifflin; 1987. 320p., illus. (part in color), bibliog., index.
$17.95, $12.95pbk. Peterson Field Guide Series, 5. 0-395-24082-4,
0-395-24084-0pbk.
This field guide covers 380 species of mammals, including whales,
dolphins, and porpoises. Each one is described in detail and most are
depicted in color photographs and additional black-and-white sketches.
Range maps are included. The description includes information on
distinguishing marks, habitat, litter size, appearance of young, specimen tracks, and representations of nests. See also *Audubon Society
Field Guide to North American Mammals. Grade Level:* Grades 9–12.
ARBA, 77, n.1392; BL, 15 January 77, p.746; BW, 12 December 76,
p.47; Choice, February 77, p.1568; SB, December 77, p.147.

**458. Field Guide to the Nests, Eggs, and Nestlings of North
American Birds.**
Brattleboro, VT: Stephen Greene Press; 1984 (c1978). 416p., illus.
(part in color), index. $19.95. 0-8289-0532-0.
This excellent field guide helps to identify the eggs, nests, and nestlings
of North American birds. The color photographs are very clear, and
the descriptive text is well-written. This field guide, together with the
following two by Hal H. Harrison, give comprehensive coverage of
birds' nests in the United States: *Field Guide to Birds Nests of 285
Species Found Breeding in the U.S. East of the Mississippi River*
(Houghton Mifflin, 1975, 247p., 0-395-20434-8, $15.95, *Peterson Field
Guide Series, 21*) and *Field Guide to Western Birds' Nests of 520
Species Found Breeding in the United States West of the Mississippi
River* (Houghton Mifflin, 1979, 288p., 0-395-27629-2, $11.95, *Peterson
Field Guide Series, 25*). *Grade Level:* Grades 9–12.
ARBA, 80, n.1401.

**459. Field Guide to the Pacific Coast Shells: Including Shells of
Hawaii and the Gulf of California.**
2nd. Percy A. Morris. Boston, MA: Houghton Mifflin; 1974 (c1966).
304p., illus. (part in color), bibliog., index. $15.95, $10.95pbk.
Peterson Field Guide Series, 8. 0-395-08029-0, 0-395-18322-7pbk.
This field guide, formerly called *Field Guide to Shells of the Pacific
Coast and Hawaii*, and Percy A. Morris's *Field Guide to the Shells of
the Atlantic and Gulf Coasts and the West Indies* (3rd ed., Houghton
Mifflin, 1973, 320p., 0-395-16809-0, 0-395-17170-9pbk, $17.95,
$12.95pbk, *Peterson Field Guide Series, 3*) are two well-known field
guides covering shells. Together they give excellent coverage of all
shells that can be found on both coasts of North America, the Gulf
Coast, and Hawaii. Excellent illustrations and good descriptive text are
trademarks of this series. See also *Audubon Society Field Guide to
North American Seashells. Grade Level:* Grades 9–12.

**460. A Field Guide to the Whales, Porpoises and Seals of the Gulf of
Maine and Eastern Canada: Cape Cod to Newfoundland.**
Steven K. Katona; Valerie Rough; David T. Richardson. New York,

NY: Scribner's; 1983. 255p., illus., bibliog., index. $19.95, $12.95pbk. 0-684-17901-6, 0-684-17902-4pbk.
This excellent small guidebook covers 22 species of whales and porpoises and six seals found near the northeastern North American coast. There are good tips on whale and seal watching. See also *Dolphins and Porpoises*. *Grade Level:* Grades 9–12.
ARBA, 84, n.1350; BW, 18 September 83, p.12; Kliatt, Winter 84, p.64; SB, March 84, p.204.

461. Fishes: A Guide to Fresh and Salt-Water Species.
Herbert S. Zim; Hurst H. Shoemaker. New York, NY: Golden Press; 1987 (c1956). 160p., color illus. $2.95. Golden Nature Guide. 0-307-24059-2.
This is an excellent identification guide to 278 species of fresh-water and salt-water fishes. For each entry, physical characteristics, habitat, size, adaptability, and compatibility are given together with full color drawings. *Grade Level:* Grades 3–5. Grades 6–8.

462. A Guide to Animal Tracking and Behavior.
Donald W. Stokes; Lillian Q. Stokes. Boston, MA: Little, Brown; 1986. 418p., illus., maps, bibliog., index. $18.95. 0-316-81730-9.
This field book gives information on how to identify animals through their tracks, trails, scats, and signs. The first part is a guide to mammal tracks, scats, and other signs while the second part contains descriptions of each mammal. *Grade Level:* Grades 6–8. Grades 9–12.
ARBA, 88, n.1579; R&RBkN, Winter 87, p.22; SB, March 87, p.233; Kliatt, January 88, p.46.

463. A Guide to Bird Behavior.
Donald W. Stokes; Lillian Q. Stokes. Boston, MA: Little, Brown; 1983. 2v., illus., bibliog., index. $16.45 per volume. 0-316-81722-8, v.1; 0-316-81726-0, v.2.
This field guide to bird behavior includes 25 birds in each volume. For each bird, there is a behavior calendar that charts the months in which the following activities take place: definition of territory, courtship, nest building, breeding, plumage, seasonal movement, flock behavior, and feeding behavior. It is an excellent supplement to the many field guides for bird identification. *Grade Level:* Grades 9–12.
ARBA, 85, n.1442; BL, 1 March 84, p.930.

464. How to Know the Amphibians and Reptiles.
Royce E. Ballinger; John D. Lynch. Dubuque, IA: W. G. Brown; 1983. 229p., illus. $10.75. Pictured Key Nature Series. 0-697-04786-5.
This is a very good field guide to the snakes, lizards, frogs, and other amphibians and reptiles in the United States. Descriptions are clear and illustrations are well done. See also the much larger and more comprehensive *The Audubon Society Field Guide to North American Reptiles and Amphibians, Reptiles and Amphibians of North America,* or *Reptiles of North America*. *Grade Level:* Grades 6–8.

465. How to Know the Beetles.
2nd. Ross H. Arnett, Jr.; N.M. Downie; H.E. Jaques. Dubuque, IA:
W. C. Brown; 1980. 416p.,illus., bibliog., index. $10.95. Pictured Key
Nature Series. 0-697-04776-8.
Since one-fifth of all living animal species are beetles, this field guide
is very useful. It covers more than 1,500 common species, giving good
keys to identification and excellent photographs. See also *A Field
Guide to the Beetles of North America. Grade Level:* Grades 6–8.
ARBA, 82, n.1489.

**466. How to Know the Butterflies: Illustrated Keys for Determining
the Species of All Butterflies Found in North America, North of
Mexico, with Notes on Their Distribution, Habits, and Larval Food,
and Suggestions for Collecting and Studying Them.**
Paul R. Ehrlich; Ann H. Ehrlich. Dubuque, IA: W.C. Brown; 1961.
262p., illus., bibliog., index. $3.25. Pictured Key Nature Series.
This well-written, small field guide covers butterflies found in North
America. The descriptions and identification aids are well done, and
the illustrations add much to the work. See also *Audubon Society Field
Guide to North American Butterflies. Grade Level:* Grades 6–8.

467. How to Know the Freshwater Crustacea.
Joseph F. Fitzpatrick, Jr.; J.C. Underhill. Dubuque, IA: W.C. Brown;
1983. 227p., illus., bibliog., index. $8.95. Pictured Key Nature Series.
0-697-04783-0.
This is a simple, easy-to-use field guide to various shells and other
crustaceans that are found in the fresh-waters of the United States. See
also *Fresh-Water Invertebrates of the United States. Grade Level:*
Grades 6–8.

468. How to Know the Freshwater Fishes.
3rd. Samuel Eddy, ed. Dubuque, IA: W.C. Brown; 1978. 215p., illus.,
bibliog., index. $5.95. Pictured Key Nature Series. 0-697-04750-4.
There are many guides that cover the fish along the coasts of the
United States but few that cover the fresh-water fish. This guide gives
good descriptions and identifications of these fish, supplemented with
well-drawn illustrations. *Grade Level:* Grades 6–8.
Choice, January 70, p.1556.

469. How to Know the Insects.
3rd. Roger G. Bland; H.E. Jaques. Dubuque, IA: W.C. Brown; 1978.
409p., illus., bibliog., index. $13.95. Pictured Key Nature Series.
0-697-04753-9.
This excellent field book covers insects in general, giving information
about study, identification, collecting, and mounting. With the following three guides from the *Pictured Key Nature Series,* identification of
insects should be easy: Jacques R. Helfer's *How to Know the Grass-
hoppers, Crickets, Cockroaches, and Their Allies* (W. C. Brown, 1963,
359p., $4.25); H. F. Chu's *How to Know the Immature Insects: An
Illustrated Key for Identifying the Orders and Families of Many of the
Immature Insects with Suggestions for Collecting, Rearing and Studying*

Them (W.C. Brown, 1949, 234p., $3.00); and D.M. Lehmkuhl's *How to Know the Aquatic Insects* (W.C. Brown, 1979, 168p., 0-697-04766-0, $13.95). See also *Field Guide to the Insects of America North of Mexico, Simon and Schuster's Guide to Insects,* and *The Audubon Society Field Guide to North American Insects and Spiders. Grade Level:* Grades 6–8.

470. How to Know the Land Birds: Pictured-Keys for Determining All of the Land Birds of the Entire U.S. and Southern Canada, with Maps Showing Their Geographic Distribution and Other Helpful Features.
Garr E. Jaques; Mabel J. Cuthbert. Dubuque, IA: W.C. Brown; 1947. 196p., illus., bibliog., index. $2.50. Pictured Key Nature Series.
This volume in the *Pictured Key Nature Series* and Harry E. Jaques and Mabel J. Cuthbert's *How to Know the Water Birds: Pictured-Keys for Determining the Water Birds of the U.S. and Canada, with Maps Showing Their Geographic Distribution, and with Other Helpful Features* (W.C. Brown, 1960, 159p., $3.75) are good general field guides to the birds of the U.S. and Canada. They are not as comprehensive as other field guides but are still very well done and useful for beginners. See also *Audubon Society Field Guide to North American Birds* and *A Field Guide to Birds. Grade Level:* Grades 6–8.

471. How to Know the Mammals.
4th. Ernest S. Booth. Dubuque, IA: W.C. Brown; 1982. 198p., illus., maps, index. $7.45pbk. Pictured Key Nature Series. 0-697-04781-4pbk.
This field guide covers some 1,500 varieties of mammals in the United States and Canada. After an introductory section on the science of mammalogy, there is information on what is needed and how to study mammals. The main part of the book is the description of the mammals, with keys for identification, black-and-white line drawings, and map locations. See also *Mammals: A Guide to Familiar American Species, Audubon Society Field Guide to North American Mammals,* and *Field Guide to Mammals. Grade Level:* Grades 6–8.
ARBA, 83, n.1363.

472. How to Know the Mites and Ticks.
Burruss McDaniel. Dubuque, IA: W.C. Brown; 1979. 335p., illus., bibliog., index. $13.95pbk. Pictured Key Nature Series. 0-697-04757-1pbk.
Mites and ticks are difficult animals to identify and study because of their size. They are, however, very important to know about because of the diseases they can cause. This book discusses collecting and mounting techniques, morphology, and why one needs to know about them. The descriptions are good. *Grade Level:* Grades 6–8.
ARBA, 80, n.1411.

473. How to Know the Protozoa.
2nd. Theodore Louis Jahn; Eugene Cleveland Bovee; Frances Floed Jahn. Dubuque, IA: W.C. Brown; 1979. 279p., illus., bibliog., index. $10.75. Pictured Key Nature Series. 0-697-04758-X.

The four groups of protozoa, mastigophora, sarcodina, sporozoa, and ciliophora are described in detail for identification. There is also information on studying, collection procedures, sizes of the one-celled creatures, movement, and use. *Grade Level:* Grades 6–8. ARBA, 81, n.1413.

474. How to Know the Spiders.
3rd. B.J. Kaston. Dubuque, IA: W.C. Brown; 1978. 272p., illus., bibliog., index. $13.95. Pictured Key Nature Series. 0-697-04899-3.
This field guide covers 55 families, 223 genera, and 519 species of spiders. It gives complete keys for their identification and instructions for finding, collecting, and rearing common spiders. See also *Audubon Society Field Guide to North American Insects and Spiders. Grade Level:* Grades 6–8.

475. How to Know the True Bugs: (Hemiptera-Heteroptera).
James A. Slater; Richard M. Baranowski. Dubuque, IA: W.C. Brown; 1978. 256p., illus., bibliog., index. $13.95. Pictured Key Nature Series. 0-697-04893-4.
This well-written field guide helps to identify the common species of 41 families of Hemiptera-Heteroptera or true bugs. For each bug, there is a description, distribution keys, and common and scientific names. Information is also given on collecting and preserving techniques. *Grade Level:* Grades 6–8.

476. Insects: A Guide to Familiar American Insects.
Herbert S. Zim; Clarence Cottam. New York, NY: Golden Press; 1987. 160p., color illus., index. $29.95pbk. Golden Nature Series. 0-307-24055-Xpbk.
This field guide for young people covers some 225 insect species that are commonly found in the wild. Each species is fully described and colorfully illustrated for easy identification. See also *Field Guide to the Insects of America North of Mexico, How to Know the Insects, Audubon Society Field Guide to North American Insects and Spiders,* and *Simon and Schuster's Guide to Insects. Grade Level:* Grades 3–5. Grades 6–8.

477. Mammals: A Guide to Familiar American Species.
Revised. Herbert S. Zim; Donald F. Hoffmeister. New York, NY: Golden Press; 160p., illus. (part in color), maps, bibliog., index. $3.95pbk. 0-307-24058-4pbk.
This small field book gives information on seeing, observing, and photographing mammals. The well-written descriptions give size and color and have good illustrations and range maps. See also *How to Know the Mammals, Audubon Society Field Guide to North American Mammals,* and *Field Guide to the Mammals. Grade Level:* Grades 3–5. Grades 6–8.
ARBA, 89, n.1463.

478. Peterson First Guide to Birds of North America.
Roger Tory Peterson. Boston, MA: Houghton Mifflin; 1986. 128p., color illus. $3.95pbk. 0-395-40684-6pbk.

This first guide and the following two guides are simplified versions of the more comprehensive field guides and are intended for younger children, who are just developing an interest in studying animals: Christopher Lehy's *Peterson First Guide to Insects of North America* (Houghton Mifflin, 1987, 96p., 0-395-35640-7pbk, $3.95pbk) and Peter Alden's *Peterson First Guide to Mammals of North America* (Houghton Mifflin, 1987, 0-395-42767-3pbk, $3.95pbk). *Grade Level:* Grades 9–12.

479. Peterson First Guide to Fishes of North America.
Michael Filisky. Boston, MA: Houghton Mifflin Co; 1989. 128p., color illus., index. $4.95pbk. Peterson First Guides, Fishes. 0-395-50219-5pbk.
This is a small field guide for school children, giving information on the basic features of fishes and how to identify them. Each description includes range of the fish, habitat, and distinctive features, plus a color illustration. *Grade Level:* Grades 3–5. Grades 6–8.

480. Reptiles of North America: A Guide to Field Identification.
Hobart M. Smith; Edmund D. Brodie, Jr. Racine, WI: Western Publishing; 1982. 240p., illus. (part in color), bibliog., index. $7.95pbk. Golden Field Guides. 0-307-13666-3pbk.
This well-written and illustrated field book covers turtles, lizards, snakes, amphibians, and crocodiles of North America. Each animal is fully described, with additional information given on when to look for reptiles, collecting, first aid for snake bite, reptile names and kinds of variations, and special features of reptiles. See also *How to Know the Amphibians and Reptiles* and *Reptiles and Amphibians of North America. Grade Level:* Grades 3–5.
ARBA, 84, n.1362; ASBYP, Spring 83, p.49; BL, 15 December 82, p.543; Choice, December 82, p.604; SB, May 83, p.260.

481. Rodale's Garden Insect, Disease and Weed Identification Guide.
Miranda Smith; Anna Carr. Emmaus, PA: Rodale Press; 1988. 328p., illus. (part in color), bibliog., glossary, index. $21.95, $15.95pbk. 0-87857-758-0, 0-87857-759-9pbk.
The purpose of this field book is to educate those who have gardens and farms so that they understand the value of all garden insects and weeds, recognizing life cycles, growth habit, and the ecological role. The book is divided into three sections: insects, diseases, and weeds. There is also a short section on non-insects that covers centipedes, millipedes, mites, slugs, and snails. Each section has an overview followed with one-page descriptions of each entry, giving such information as common name, scientific name, larva size, type of organism, and type of damage. *Grade Level:* Grades 9–12.
STARR, 90, n.43.

482. Sea Mammals of the World.
Bernard Stonehouse. New York, NY: Viking Penguin; 1985. 158p., color illus., maps, bibliog., index. $7.95. 0-14-007081-8.

This interesting little field book covers all marine mammals, including the bears and otters, seals, sea lions and walruses, sirenians, and whales. It has excellent illustrations with well-written descriptions. *Grade Level:* Grades 9–12.
ARBA, 87, n.1533; BL, 15 February 86, p.839.

483. Shorebirds: An Identification Guide to the Waders of the World.
Peter Hayman; John Marchant; Tony Prater. Boston, MA: Houghton Mifflin; 1986. 412p., illus. (part in color), maps, bibliog., index. $34.95. 0-395-37903-2.
This is an excellent field guide to the shore birds or waders of the world. The color photographs are outstanding, and the descriptions cover all aspects of the birds: plumage, voice, habits, movements, and measurements. Distribution maps are well done. *Grade Level:* Grades 9–12.
ARBA, 87, n.1508.

484. Simon and Schuster's Guide to Insects.
Ross H. Arnett, Jr.; R.L. Jacques. New York, NY: Simon and Schuster; 1981. 511p., color illus., glossary, index. $19.95, $9.95pbk. 0-671-25913-2, 0-671-25014-0pbk.
This authoritative field guide covers 350 of the more commonly found insects in North America. It has good descriptions of the individual insects. See also *Field Guide to the Insects of America North of Mexico, How to Know the Insects, Audubon Society Field Guide to North American Insects and Spiders,* and *Insects: A Guide to Familiar American Insects. Grade Level:* Grades 9–12.

485. Simon and Schuster's Guide to Shells.
Bruno Sabelli; Harold S. Feinberg. New York, NY: Simon and Schuster; 1980. 512p., color illus., maps, index. $9.95pbk. 0-671-25370-4pbk.
This excellent field guide, divided into five parts, covers soft surface mollusks, firm surface mollusks, coral dwellers, land and fresh water mollusks, and other marine mollusks. Each page depicts a separate shell, with a half-page color illustration and a half-page description. *Grade Level:* Grades 9–12.
ARBA, 81, n.1485; BL, 15 July 80, p.1644; Choice, December 80, p.548; LJ, August 80, p.1648.

Glossaries

486. It's Easy to Say Crepidula (kreh PID'ul luh): A Phonetic Guide to Pronunciation of the Scientific Names of Sea Shells and a Glossary of Terms Frequently Used in Malacology.
Jean M. Cate; Selma Raskin. Santa Monica, CA: Pretty Penn Press; 1986. 155p., illus., bibliog., glossary. $19.95pbk. 0-938509-00-4pbk.

This unique little glossary gives the pronunciation of the many sea shells that both collectors and scientists encounter. Terms are phonetically listed and the book also includes a glossary of terms associated with the study of mollusks. *Grade Level:* Grades 9–12. STARR, 89, n.93.

Guides

487. American Insects: A Handbook of the Insects of America North of Mexico.
Ross H. Arnett, Jr. New York, NY: Van Nostrand Reinhold; 1985. 850p., illus., index. $84.95.
This is a comprehensive, pictorial guide to the insects that are found north of Mexico. The descriptions are well-prepared, and the introductory materials are useful for the novice as well as the professional. Although a little expensive for the school library, it should be considered, especially in the larger school districts. *Grade Level:* Grades 9–12. ARBA, 87, n.1520; BL, 1 March 86, p.962; Choice, December 85, p.623.

488. American Spiders.
2nd. Willis J. Gertsch. New York, NY: Van Nostrand Reinhold; 1979. 274p., illus. (part in color), bibliog., index. $38.95. 0-442-22649-7.
This very comprehensive encyclopedia of Araneae, commonly known as spiders, presents morphology, life histories, behavior, diversity, and historical attitudes towards spiders as related in literature and mythology. *Grade Level:* Grades 9–12.
BL, 1 July 79, p.1568; SB, December 79, p.151.

489. Amphibians.
Giuseppe Minelli. New York, NY: Facts on File; 1987. 57p., color illus. $12.95. History of Life on Earth. 0-8160-1557-0.
This fine guide is amply illustrated with color drawings and diagrams, presenting an impressive amount of information in an interesting and accessible manner. The physical characteristics of living amphibians are described in the context of their evolutionary history. *Grade Level:* Grades 6–8. Grades 9–12.
ASBYP, Spring 88, p.40; KR, 15 August 87, p.1243; SB, September 88, p.26; SLJ, February 88, p.90; STARR, 89, n.98.

490. Butterflies of the World.
Rod Preston-Mafham; Ken Preston-Mafham. New York, NY: Facts on File; 1988. 192p., illus. (part in color), bibliog., glossary, index. $22.95. Animals of the World. 0-8160-1601-1.
This basic introduction to the world's butterflies provides an excellent overview. The book presents well-documented background information of a scientific nature "seasoned" with original anecdotal material contributed by personal observations. See also H.L. Lewis's *Butterflies of*

the World for a more comprehensive coverage. *Grade Level:* Grades
6-8. Grades 9-12.
STARR, 90, n.166.

491. Close Encounters with Insects and Spiders.
James B. Nardi. Ames, IA: Iowa State University Press; 1988. 185p.,
illus., bibliog., index. $12.95. 0-8138-1978-4.
This book provides an introduction to some of the more common
small creatures that are likely to be encountered in our homes, lawns,
gardens, and the nearby countryside. The author provides numerous
suggestions for capturing insects and observing them in glass jars,
terrariums, and aquariums, in addition to watching them as they go
about their business in their natural surroundings. An introduction
provides some general information about arthropods and their classification. At the end of each chapter, the scientific names are provided and explained for the insects discussed in that chapter. *Grade
Level:* Grades 9-12.
BWatch, July 88, p.3; SB, January 89, p.168; SciTech, June 88, p.14;
STARR, 89, n.109.

**492. Compendium of Seashells: A Color Guide to More than 4,200 of
the World's Marine Shells.**
Revised. R. Tucker Abbott; S. Peter Dance. New York, NY: Dutton;
1986. 411p., illus. (part in color), index. $49.95. 0-915826-17-8.
This very well done guide to shells contains excellent photographs and
is arranged taxonomically, with accurate descriptions and ecological,
geographical, and natural history information given. *Grade Level:*
Grades 9-12.
ARBA, 84, n.1355.

493. A Complete Guide to Monkeys, Apes and Other Primates.
Michael Kavanagh. New York, NY: Viking Press; 1983. 224p., color
illus., maps, bibliog., index. $19.95. 0-670-43543-0.
This book for the general reader gives information about monkeys,
apes, and other primates, including primate biology, evolution, and
classification. There is a list of species with a description of each.
Conservation measures are also discussed. *Grade Level:* Grades 9-12.
ARBA, 85, n.1464; BL, 1 May 84, p.1214; Choice, October 84, p.300;
LJ, 1 March 85, p.36, 15 April 85, p.39; PW, 1 March 84, p.81; SB,
March 85, p.203.

494. Frogs and Toads of the World.
Chris Mattison. New York, NY: Facts on File; 1987. 191p., illus.
(part in color), bibliog., index. $22.95. 0-8160-1602-X.
This excellent guide with color and line-drawn illustrations covers the
physiology and behavior of toads and frogs. A bibliography of record-
ings of toad and frog sounds is included. *Grade Level:* Grades 6-8.
Grades 9-12.
BL, 15 April 88, p.1377; BRpt, March 88, p.47; Choice, July 88,
p.1717; SB, September 88, p.26; STARR, 89, n.101; VOYA, October
88, p.204.

495. Mammals of the American North.
Adrian Forsyth. Camden East, Ontario: Camden House; 1985. 351p., color illus., maps, bibliog., index. $29.95. 0-920656-42-0.
This layperson's guide to mammals is divided according to the type of mammal: cloven-hoofed mammals, whales, dolphins and porpoises, seals and sea lions, meat eaters, rabbits, hares and pikas, bats, and insectivores and marsupials. The following information is given for each: scientific name, meaning of the name, description of the animal, total length, tail length, weight, habitat, major predators of the animal, and dental formula. Range maps are included. *Grade Level:* Grades 9–12.
ARBA, 87, n.1528; BL, 1 February 86, p.784; Choice, March 86, p.1092; SB, November 86, p.99; SciTech, January 86, p.18.

496. The Pocket Guide to Aquarium Fishes.
Gwynne Vevers. New York, NY: Simon and Schuster; 1980. 180p., color illus., maps, index. $6.95pbk. 0-671-25451-0pbk.
This good, brief guide to aquarium fishes gives advice on how to set up both fresh-water and marine aquariums and information on anatomy, diseases, plants, feeding, and breeding. See also *Freshwater Aquarium Fish and Color Guide. Grade Level:* Grades 6–8. Grades 9–12.
ARBA, 81, n.1624.

497. Reptiles and Amphibians of North America.
George S. Fichter. New York, NY: Random House; 1982. 96p., illus. (part in color), index. $2.95pbk. An Audubon Society Beginner Guide. 0-394-84769-5pbk.
This beginner's guide for small children gives information on field observation, collecting, and care of specimens. The book covers the more common reptiles and amphibians in North America. See also *How to Know the Amphibians and Reptiles. Grade Level:* Grades 3–5.
ARBA, 84, n.1361; ASBYP, Winter 83, p.58; BL 15 October 82, p.311; SLJ, November 82, p.82.

498. Simon and Schuster's Guide to Cats.
U.S. edition. Gino Pugnetti. New York, NY: Simon and Schuster; 1983. 255p., illus. (part in color), bibliog., index. $23.95, $8.95pbk. 0-671-49167-9, 0-671-49170-9pbk.
This beautifully illustrated guide to cats gives the history of the cat and descriptions of 40 cat breeds. The following information is given for each breed: origin, specific physical characteristics, character, ideal owner, environment to which best suited, diet, special care requirements, breeding facts, faults, and varieties. *Grade Level:* Grades 9–12.
ARBA, 84, n.1447; BL 1 February 84, p.779.

499. Wild Animals of North America.
Revised. Washington, DC: National Geographic Society; 1987. 406p., illus. (part in color), index. $26.90. 0-686-66211-3.

This excellent general guide to the wild animals of North America is divided into six sections: "Animals in fur," "The hoofed mammals," "The meat eaters," "Gnawing mammals," "Survivors of ancient orders," and "Ocean dwellers." *Grade Level:* Grades 9–12. R&RBkN, February 88, p.19.

Handbooks

500. The Audubon Society Handbook for Birders.
Stephen W. Kress. New York, NY: Scribner's; 1981. 322p., illus., bibliog., index. $17.95. 0-684-16838-3.
This manual and source book for the bird watcher covers field trip techniques, using binoculars and spotting scopes, observing birds, photographing and recording birds, educational programs, research programs, periodicals and organizations, and building a bird-watchers's library. This latter chapter is an extensive annotated listing of bird field guides and other materials of interest to the birdwatcher. *Grade Level:* Grades 6–8. Grades 9–12.
BL, 15 April 81, p.1131; Choice, October 81, p.222; KR, 1 March 81, p.348; LJ, 1 April 81, p.804, 1 May 82, p.853, 15 May 82, p.960.

501. The Audubon Society Handbook for Butterfly Watchers.
Robert Michael Pyle. New York, NY: Scribner's; 1984. 274p., illus., bibliog., index. $17.95. 0-684-18151-7.
This handbook for those who watch butterflies covers butterfly biology, how and where to find butterflies, nomenclature and taxonomy, record keeping, mapping and censusing butterflies, butterfly behavior, gardening to attract butterflies, photographing butterflies, conservation, and locations for butterfly watching. It is intended to help in using the field guides. *Grade Level:* Grades 6–8. Grades 9–12.
ARBA, 86, n.1535; LJ, 15 June 84, p.1233.

502. The Birder's Handbook: A Field Guide to the Natural History of North American Birds, Including All Species that Regularly Breed North of Mexico.
Paul R. Ehrlich; David S. Dobkin; Darryl Sheye. New York, NY: Simon and Schuster; 1988. 785p., illus., bibliog., index. $24.45. 0-671-62133-5.
This is not a guide to the identification of birds but a book to lead one to further information about the birds that have been identified. The main part of the handbook contains descriptions of 650 species followed by essays on aspects of natural history tied to the individual species accounts. *Grade Level:* Grades 9–12.
STARR, 90, n.155.

503. Butterflies and Moths: A Companion to Your Field Guide.
Jo Brewer; Dave Winter. New York, NY: Prentice-Hall; 1986. 194p., illus. (part in color), bibliog., index. $14.95pbk. 0-13-108846-7.

This introductory handbook for amateur butterfly watchers who want to understand the biology of butterflies and moths covers five broad areas: "People and Lepidoptera" (observing butterflies and months), "Habits, Habitats and Hazards" (life cycles, behavior, ecology, diseases, predators, and defense mechanisms), "On the Matter of Names" (naming and classifying Lepidoptera), "To Collect or Not to Collect" (conservation and ethics), and "Tricks and Tools" (methodology and equipment). *Grade Level:* Grades 9–12.
ARBA, 87, n.1521; SB, May 87, p.314.

504. The Complete Book of Cat Health.
William J. Kay; Elizabeth Randolph. New York, NY: Macmillan; 1985. 258p., illus., bibliog., index. $19.95. 0-02-502350-0.
This well-written guide to cat health covers all aspects, including who should own a cat, cat structure and function, cat diets, behavior, and behavior modification. A glossary and an encyclopedia of diseases are included. See also *The Complete Book of Questions and Answers Cat Owners Ask Their Vet. Grade Level:* Grades 6–8. Grades 9–12.
ARBA, 86, n.1528; BL, 1 January 86, p.648; KR, 1 December 85, p.1326; LJ, January 86, p.93.

505. The Complete Book of Dog Health.
William J. Kay; Elizabeth Randolph. New York, NY: Macmillan; 1985. 253p., illus., bibliog., index. $19.95. 0-02-600930-7.
This guide to the health of your dog, written in the same style as the one for cats, covers all aspects of the dog's health, diet, behavior, and behavior modification. See also *The Complete Book of Questions and Answers Dog Owners Ask Their Vet. Grade Level:* Grades 6–8. Grades 9–12.
BL, 1 June 85, p.1359; KR, 15 April 85, p.371; LJ, 1 June 85, p.135; PW, 17 May 85, p.107.

506. The Complete Book of Questions and Answers Cat Owners Ask Their Vet.
Susan McDonough; Bryna Lawson. Philadelphia, PA: Running Press; 1980. 126p., illus., index. $12.90, $4.95pbk. 0-89471-074-5; 0-89471-073-7pbk.
In a question and answer format, facts about cats are presented. The six parts cover "Caring for Your Cat," "Understanding Your Cat," "General Medical Care," "Breeding," "Accidents and Ailments," and "Serious Illnesses." See also *The Complete Book of Cat Health. Grade Level:* Grades 9–12.
ARBA, 81, n.1656; KR, 15 May 80, p.707; Kliatt, Fall 80, p.53; LJ, August 80, p.1648; SLJ, September 80, p.100.

507. The Complete Book of Questions and Answers Dog Owners Ask Their Vet.
Steven Radbill; Morris Kennedy. Philadelphia, PA: Running Press; 1980. 159p., illus., index. $12.90, $4.95pbk. 0-89471-084-2, 0-89471-081-8pbk.

Similar to the same book on cats, questions and answers cover all aspects of caring for a dog, including the older dog, emergencies, puppies, and discipline. See also *The Complete Book of Dog Health. Grade Level:* Grades 9–12.
ARBA, 81, n.1657; KR, 15 May 80, p.708; LJ, August 80, p.1648; SLJ, September 80, p.100.

508. The Complete Book of the Dog.
David MacDonald. New York, NY: Holt, Rinehart and Winston; 1985. 224p., illus. (part in color), index. $18.95. 0-03-006019-2.
This good book on the care and training of a dog covers canine evolution and genetics, relationships between dogs and humans, selecting and training a dog, dog anatomy, health and fitness, and a catalog of dog breeds. *Grade Level:* Grades 9–12.
ALib, May 87, p.337; ARBA, 86, n.1524; BL, 15 October 85, p.296; SchLib, March 86, p.88; SLJ, April 86, p.107; VOYA, February 86, p.400.

509. Freshwater Aquarium Fish and Color Guide.
J.P. Gosse. New York, NY: Hippocrene Books; 1982. 184p., color illus., bibliog., index. $12.95. 0-88254-759-3.
Each page of this handbook and guide covers a specific fish, giving name and pictograms indicating volume of the tank, water pH, lighting, water temperature, maximum size, ease of rearing, position in the tank, sociability, reproduction, and diet and feeding. See also *The Pocket Guide to Aquarium Fishes. Grade Level:* Grades 6–8. Grades 9–12.
ARBA, 84, n.1341; BL, August 83, p.1434; Choice, October 83, p.250.

510. Fresh-Water Invertebrates of the United States.
2nd. Robert William Pennak. New York, NY: Wiley; 1978. 803p., illus., bibliog., index. $42.50. 0-471-04249-8.
This comprehensive handbook describes the fresh-water invertebrates of the United States. For a simple identification guide, one should also see *How to Know the Freshwater Crustacea. Grade Level:* Grades 9–12.
SB, September 79, p.90.

511. Harper's Illustrated Handbook of Cats: A Guide to Every Breed Recognized in America.
Roger Caras, ed. New York, NY: Harper and Row; 1985. 191p., illus. (part in color). $9.95pbk. 0-06-091199-9pbk.
This handbook covers 39 recognized breeds of cats in North America. Information is given on the anatomy of the cat followed by an article on each of the 39 breeds. The articles cover personality, appearance, potential health problems, and care and grooming. There is a helpful section on cat health. See also *Simon and Schuster's Guide to Cats. Grade Level:* Grades 6–8. Grades 9–12.
ARBA, 86, n.1526; BL, 1 December 85, p.519; Kliatt, Winter 86, p.62.

512. Harper's Illustrated Handbook of Dogs.
Roger Caras, ed. New York, NY: Harper and Row; 1985. 319p., illus. (part in color), index. $9.95pbk. 0-06-091198-0pbk.
This handbook not only gives information about American Kennel Club and other "pure" breeds, but also covers mongrels, mixed-breeds, mutts, or random-bred dogs. It gives such information as temperament and physical characteristics. Not as comprehensive as *Complete Dog Book*. *Grade Level:* Grades 6–8. Grades 9–12.
ARBA, 86, n.1527; BL, 1 December 85, p.519; Kliatt, Winter 86, p.62.

513. The Marine Aquarium Reference: Systems and Invertebrates.
Martin A. Moe, Jr. Plantation, FL: Green Turtle Publications; 1989. 510p., illus., tables, charts, bibliog., index. $21.95pbk. 0-939960-05-2pbk.
This useful handbook contains information for the person interested in marine aquariums. It includes a description of the natural marine environment from the aquarist's perspective; composition of seawater; the physical environment of the aquarium; techniques and technology in setting up the aquarium; and the foods and feeding of marine invertebrates. *Grade Level:* Grades 9–12.

514. Merck Veterinary Manual: Handbook of Diagnosis, Therapy and Disease Prevention and Control.
6th. Clarence M. Fraser, ed. Rahway, NJ: Merck; 1986. 1,677p., illus. $19.00. 0-911910-53-0.
The various Merck manuals have withstood the test of time. This handbook for the veterinarian is no exception. It covers all aspects of veterinary medicine, giving methods of diagnosis and therapy. *Grade Level:* Grades 9–12.

515. Sierra Club Handbook of Whales and Dolphins.
Stephen Leatherwood; Randall Reeves. San Francisco, CA: Sierra Club Books; 1983. 302p., illus. (part in color), bibliog., index. $25.00, $12.95pbk. 0-87156-341-1, 0-87156-340-1pbk.
The excellent photographs and short, concise text make this a very useful handbook to whales and dolphins. It covers, for each entry, the biology, natural history, behavior, distribution, and current status of the animals. See also *The World's Whales* and *Whales, Dolphins and Porpoises*. *Grade Level:* Grades 9–12.
ARBA, 84, n.1351; BL, 1 November 83, p.384; Choice, February 84, p.806; Kliatt, Winter 84, p.64; LJ, 15 November 83, p.2152; SB, March 84, p.204; SLJ, March 84, p.180.

516. Turtles of the United States.
Carl H. Ernst; Roger W. Barbour. Lexington, KY: University Press of Kentucky; 1973. 347p., illus. (part in color), maps, bibliog., index. $45.00. 0-8131-1272-9.
This good handbook covers the turtles of the United States. It discusses characteristics and detailed accounts of each species, giving behavior, ecology, and conservation. *Grade Level:* Grades 9–12.

ARBA, 74, n.1562; BL, 1 September 73, p.17; Choice, February 74, p.1891; LJ, July 73, p.2127, 15 April 74, p.1099.

TECHNOLOGY/ ENGINEERING

The terms "technology" and "engineering" are more or less inter-changeable in today's language. There is a difference, however, in the definition of the two terms. Engineering is the application of all physical knowledge and research to developing products that make our lives easier. Technology, on the other hand, is concerned with the actual tools and techniques that help to bring about the development of engineering products. Together they form a massive and growing area that is producing large amounts of literature. According to the *McGraw-Hill Concise Encyclopedia of Science and Technology*, "engineering involves people, money, materials, machines, and energy" and "requires imagination to innovate useful applications of natural phenomena" by seeking "newer, cheaper, better means of using natural sources of energy and materials."

An engineer or technologist must have a formal education in the sciences, especially physics, but also more and more, chemistry and biology. These individuals need to understand the "hows and whys" before being able to apply this knowledge in the development of products. Early on in their education, engineers specialize in one or maybe two specific areas of engineering. One new phrase that is being attached to the areas of computer, telecommunications, and robotics is "new technologies." The development of these products fits nicely within the definition of technology, which, as stated above, concerns itself with tools and techniques.

The broad field of technology/engineering can be subdivided into any number of subfields based on the specific application. These subfields can, in many cases, be further subdivided. *Agricultural engineering* is a growing field that is concerned with developing better ways to produce food and fibers. It includes machinery, plant engineering, genetic engineering, and soil engineering and works closely with other areas of science, such as chemistry, medicine, nutrition, botany, zoology, and environmental science. *Chemical engineering* is a discipline that covers a large area where basic raw materials, such as ores, salts, sulfur, limestone, coal, natural gas, petroleum, air, and water are converted into a variety of products through various chemical processes. These products include aluminum, magnesium, and titanium metals; fuels; solvents; synthetic fertilizers; resins; plastics; antibiotics; paper; and petrochemicals. *Civil engineering* is a field familiar to many. It is basically concerned with the planning, design, construction, and management of any work project or facility, including buildings, structures, transportation facilities, water resource projects, dams, bridges, power generation plants, roads, harbors, river management, canals, wastewater facilities, sanitation facilities, soil mechanics, and foundations. Specialized areas within civil engineering include building engineering, structural engineering, highway engineering, traffic engineering, transportation engineering, bridge engineering, tunnel engineering, coastal engineering, harbor and river engineering, dam engineering, hydraulics engineering, sanitary engineering, engineering geology, and soils engineering.

Electrical engineering is concerned with the development of electric power through any number of processes, including generators, wind, solar, water, and nuclear means. It is closely related to *electronics*, which is the control and use of electricity. *Engineering design* covers the initial creation of systems, devices, and processes. It is actually a part of all areas of engineering, with each engineer practicing engineering design. *Environmental engineering* is a fast expanding field concerned with all aspects of the environment and how to protect it. It includes such concerns as pollution, pesticide control, cleaner air, waste, ecology, and nuclear safety. These engineers work closely with those in all areas of engineering to help ensure the best environmental conditions possible.

Industrial engineering uses mathematics, physics, and chemistry to design, improve, and install integrated systems that involve people, materials, equipment, and energy. In other words, it is the branch of engineering that seeks to improve efficiency. It is concerned with machines, robotics, materials, energy, and management. *Mechanical engineering* is a large field with many subspecialties. This field of engineering is the application of physics in the development of any useful product. There is a little bit of mechanical engineering in all fields of engineering, including engineering graphics, robotics, engineering instruments, mechanics, strains and stresses, strength of materials, and testing. *Mining engineering* is concerned with all aspects of mining for minerals and hard fuels, such as coal. Liquid fuels are covered in the field of *petroleum engineering*, and nuclear fuels are categorized under *nuclear engineering*. These are a few of the many subfields of engineering. There are numerous other smaller, more specialized fields including *bioengineering, ergonomics, systems*, and *HVAC* (heating, ventilation, and air conditioning).

The reference literature in technology/engineering is voluminous. Every subfield has its own collection of encyclopedias, dictionaries, and handbooks, and most of these are highly technical and useful only at the research or practicing level. Those more general, and in most cases, less specific reference sources have been included in this chapter. Handbooks are the most important reference type for the engineer. Engineers are usually pressed for time and space and prefer to have one-volume sources of information. Such titles as *Student's Shop Reference Handbook, TAB Handbook of Hand and Power Tools*, and *Weekend Mechanic's Handbook: Complete Guide to Do-*

It-Yourself Repairs are good examples of practical handbooks that young people will find useful. The McGraw-Hill dictionaries and encyclopedias are very good and include *McGraw-Hill Dictionary of Engineering, McGraw-Hill Encyclopedia of Electronics and Computers,* and *McGraw-Hill Encyclopedia of Engineering.* If the parent volumes of *McGraw-Hill Encyclopedia of Science and Technology* and *McGraw-Hill Dictionary of Scientific and Technical Terms* are owned, these individual volumes would be unnecessary. For young people, reference books on cars, motorcycles, airplanes, and ham radios are of great interest, and this chapter reflects that interest. Finally, for a good historical account, consult *History of Technology and Invention: Progress Through the Ages.*

Biographical Sources

517. Famous Names in Engineering.
James Carvill. Woburn, MA: Butterworths; 1981. 93p., illus., bibliog., index. $14.95pbk. 0-408-00540-8pbk.
This interesting biography of 83 famous engineers gives birth, death, contemporaries, historical setting, achievements, and the impact of the person's work on events. *Grade Level:* Grades 9–12.
ARBA, 83, n.1578; Choice, January 82, p.646; SB, September 82, p.25.

518. Heroes in Space: From Gagarin to Challenger.
Peter Bond. New York, NY: Basil Blackwell; 1987. 467p., illus., index. $24.95. 0-631-15349-7.
This is an interesting narrative of the astronauts who have traveled into space, giving an insight on their personalities, experiences, and thoughts on the importance of their missions. The illustrations are good, and each account is well documented. *Grade Level:* Grades 6–8. Grades 9–12.
ARBA, 89, n.1470; BL, 1 October 87, p.194; Choice, December 87, p.642; LJ, 15 June 87, p.80, 1 March 88, p.33; R&RBkN, Fall 87, p.38; SB, January 88, p.166; SciTech, September 87, p.34.

519. Who's Who in Space: The First 25 Years.
Michael Cassutt. Boston, MA: G.K. Hall; 1987. 326p., illus., index. $35.00. 0-8161-8801-7.
This excellent book contains introductory essays on the American, Soviet, and international space programs, biographical data on over 380 astronauts, cosmonauts, back-up crew members, payload specialists, and X-15 and X-20 test pilots; 360 individual photographs, plus other group photos and equipment photos; all the NASA mission patches; a list of space-related acronyms and abbreviations with their meanings; and, chronological logs of space missions and X-plane test flights. *Grade Level:* Grades 9–12.
ARBA, 88, n.1587; BL, 15 June 87, p.1584; R&RBkN, Fall 87, p.38; SB, November 87, p.96; Sci Tech, September 87, p.34; SLJ, May 88, p.32; STARR, 89, n.565; WLB, September 87, p.97.

Dictionaries

520. Automotive Reference: A New Approach to the World of Auto/ Related Information.
G. J. Davis. Boise, ID: Whitehorse; 1987. 460p. $29.95, $19.95pbk. 0-937591-01-7, 0-937591-00-9pbk.
Automotive Reference is a thorough glossary of automobile-related terms. The book contains definitions (but no diagrams) of numerous auto-related terms from "AAMCO," and "con game" (eight pages of shady practices which could be encountered by almost any driver), to "Z-car." *Grade Level:* Grades 6–8. Grades 9–12.
ARBA, 88, n.1803; BL, 15 February 88, p.980; R&RBkN, April 88, p.25; STARR, 89, n.575.

521. Gerrish's Technical Dictionary: Technical Terms Simplified.
Howard H. Gerrish. South Holland, IL: Goodheart-Willcox; 1982. 368p., illus. $10.00. 0-87006-400-2.
This good basic dictionary of some 7,250 technical terms used in industry includes many of the slang expressions, acronyms, and other expressions that are unique to the industrial professions. *Grade Level:* Grades 9–12.
ARBA, 83, n.1515.

522. Illustrated Dictionary of Electronics.
4th. Rufus P. Turner; Stan Gibilisco. Blue Ridge Summit, PA: TAB; 1988. 648p., illus. $36.95, $23.60pbk. 0-8306-0900-8, 0-8306-2900-9pbk.
This dictionary deals with a broad terminology, covering computers, cyclotrons, microcircuitry, audio electronics, physics, and chemistry. The definitions are concise and precise, but they do not provide background information or context for the terms. It includes abbreviations and acronyms and has excellent circuit diagrams, line drawings, and tables. Appended tables give a resistor color code chart, a table of electronic symbols, wire gauges, various conversion factors, standard abbreviations, mathematics symbols, and the Greek alphabet. *Grade Level:* Grades 9–12.
ARBA, 89, n.1490; BL, 15 December 88, p.691; BRpt, November 88, p.49.

523. Illustrated Encyclopedic Dictionary of Electronics.
2nd. John Douglas-Young. Englewood Cliffs, NJ: Prentice Hall; 1987. 692p., illus. $42.95, $16.95pbk. 0-13-450701-0, 0-13-451006-2pbk.
This alphabetically arranged dictionary of electronics terms gives brief definitions and encyclopedic coverage of comprehensive terminology and concepts. There are numerous illustrations, schematics, and tables to aid in defining the terms. *Grade Level:* Grades 9–12.
ARBA, 89, n.1487; SciTech, October 87, p.40.

524. McGraw-Hill Dictionary of Engineering.
Sybil P. Parker, ed. New York, NY: McGraw-Hill; 1984. 659p.
$32.50. 0-07-045412-4.
This good dictionary of more than 16,000 engineering terms, with concise definitions covers the engineering fields of aerospace, civil, design, industrial, mechanical, metallurgical, mining, petroleum, systems, and materials science. As with all of the smaller McGraw-Hill dictionaries, this one is a spin-off from the *McGraw-Hill Dictionary of Scientific and Technical Terms*. *Grade Level:* Grades 9–12.
ARBA, 85, n.1471; BL, August 85, p.1648; Choice, January 85, p.662; LJ, January 85, p.76; SB, May 85, p.302; SciTech, March 85, p.20; WLB, January 85, p.358.

525. Modern Dictionary of Electronics.
6th. Rudolf F. Graf. Indianapolis, IN: Howard W. Sams; 1984.
1,152p., illus. $39.95. 0-672-22041-5.
This excellent dictionary of over 25,000 terms gives concise definitions covering the fields of communications, microelectronics, fiber optics, semiconductors, reliability, computers, and medical electronics. Also indicates terms in related areas. *Grade Level:* Grades 9–12.
ARBA, 86, n.1570; SLJ, February 81, p.37.

526. The Parts of a House.
Graham Blackburn. New York, NY: Richard Marek; 1980. 191p., illus. $15.00. 0-389-90074-8.
This very well-written description of the parts of a house is presented by means of a glossary of definitions of terms. The book is arranged in alphabetical order, and is entertaining, as well as informative, to read.
Grade Level: Grades 6–8. Grades 9–12.
ARBA, 81, n.1674; BL, 15 July 80, p.1644; LU, July 80, p.1504; SLJ, September 80, p.103.

527. Railway Age's Comprehensive Railroad Dictionary.
Robert G. Lewis, ed. Omaha, NE: Simmons-Boardman Books; 1984.
160p. $17.95. 0-911382-00-3.
This is a dictionary of brief definitions, covering terms dealing with railroad communications, signaling, track, structures, operations, and administration, as well as cars and locomotives. *Grade Level:* Grades 9–12.
ARBA, 86, n.1782.

528. Road and Track Illustrated Auto Dictionary.
John Dinkel. New York, NY: W. W. Norton; 1981 (c1977). 92p., illus. $6.95, $3.90pbk. 0-393-08777-8, 0-393-00028-1pbk.
This useful, small dictionary gives definitions of terms related to the automobile, including basic mechanical concepts of the modern internal combustion engine. *Grade Level:* Grades 6–8. Grades 9–12.
ARBA, 78, n.1511; BL, 15 September 77, p.154; Kliatt, Spring 81, p.34.

529. VNR Dictionary of Ships and the Sea.
John V. Noel, Jr. New York, NY: Van Nostrand Reinhold; 1981.
393p., illus. (part in color). $19.95. 0-442-25631-0.
This is a simple dictionary of terms and phrases that are encountered
when reading about ships and the sea. The entries are brief. *Grade Level:* Grades 9–12.
ARBA, 82, n.1647; BL, 15 September 81, p.134; Choice, February 81,
p.777; WLB, January 81, p.380.

Encyclopedias

530. Airplanes of the World 1940–1976.
Revised and enlarged. William Winter; William Byshyn; Hank Clark.
New York, NY: Simon & Schuster; 1978. 482p., illus., index. $11.95.
0-671-22684-3.
This chronologically arranged encyclopedia has brief information for
each entry, including name of manufacturer, type of engine, horse-
power, and some additional specific information. There are some
1,300 sketches of aircraft accurately depicting each type. This is an
excellent publication for general information. For more comprehensive
information, one should consult the more expensive series published
by Jane's and available in large public and research libraries. *Grade
Level:* Grades 6–8. Grades 9–12.
ARBA, 80, n.1612; BL, 1 April 79, p.1234; WLB, June 78, p.811.

531. Album of Spaceflight.
Revised and updated. Tom McGowen. New York, NY: Checkerboard
Press; 1987 (c1983). 61p., illus. (part in color), index. $4.95pbk.
0-02-688502-7pbk.
This is an encyclopedic history of space flight, beginning with the early
rockets, satellites, and unmanned flights, including the many disap-
pointments that were encountered along the way. This is followed with
accounts of the moon exploration, study of planets, and the new
technologies of Skylab and the space shuttle. Lee Brubaker has created
some outstanding illustrations that add much to the book. The chronology of spaceflight highlights, beginning with *Sputnik* in 1957 and
ending with the *Challenger* disaster in 1986, is an especially useful
reference. Each entry in this chronology gives the spacecraft, launch
date, crew, and highlights of the flight. *Grade Level:* Grades 3–5.
Grades 6–8.
S&T, April 88, p.387; STARR, 89, n.568.

532. American Car Spotter's Guide 1966–1980.
Tad Burness. Osceola, WI: Motorbooks International; 1981. 431p.,
illus. $18.95. 0-87938-102-7.
This volume has over 3,000 illustrations of cars from 1966–1980.
Original prices, dates of introduction, engine options, and trim variations are among the points covered. It is intended to be a useful
reference work, as well as an illustrated catalog of the domestic used

cars currently for sale. Volumes previous to this one were *American Car Spotter's Guide, 1920-1939* (Motorbooks International, 1975); *American Car Spotter's Guide, 1940-1965* (Rev. ed., Motorbooks International, 1978); *American Truck Spotter's Guide, 1920-1970* (Motorbooks International, 1978); and *Imported Car Spotter's Guide* (Motorbooks International, 1980). *Grade Level:* Grades 6-8. Grades 9-12.
ARBA, 82, n.1636.

533. Complete Encyclopedia of Commercial Vehicles.
G.N. Georgano; G. Marshall Naul, eds. Iola, WI: Krause Publications; 1979. 704p., illus. (part in color). $35.00. 0-87341-024-6.
This comprehensive encyclopedia covers commercial vehicles manufactured by more than 2,500 firms. The entries are by manufacturer and then by vehicle name. The following information is given for each vehicle: country and date of manufacture, name of manufacturer, brief history of the company, and descriptions of the vehicles that were manufactured. *Grade Level:* Grades 9-12.
BL, 1 December 80, p.531.

534. Encyclopaedia of Motor-Cycle Sport.
2nd. Peter Carrick, comp. New York, NY: St Martin's Press; 1982. 240p., illus., index. $14.95. 0-312-24868-7.
This alphabetical dictionary arranged by arbitrary subject headings and proper nouns covers motorcycle racing from its inception to the heavily attended world racing events. It includes information on machines, tracks, persons, and trophies. *Grade Level:* Grades 6-8. Grades 9-12.
ARBA 84, n.635; BL, 1 October 83, p.251; LJ, 1 December 82, p.2248; WCRB, November 82, p.25.

535. Encyclopedia of American Cars 1946-1959.
James H. Moloney. Sarasota, FL: Crestline Publishing; 1980. 416p., illus. $29.95. 0-912612-16-9.
This profusely illustrated encyclopedia covers American cars for 1946-1959. There are many books of this type including another by James H. Moloney, *Encyclopedia of American Cars 1930-1942.* For another book that covers more recent cars see *American Car Spotter's Guide 1966-1980. Grade Level:* Grades 9-12.
ARBA, 79, n.1703; BL, 15 February 80, p.854.

536. The Encyclopedia of Electronic Circuits.
Revised. Rudolf F. Graf. Blue Ridge Summit, PA: TAB; 1988. 2v., illus., bibliog., index. $50.00, $29.95pbk. 0-8306-9138-3, 0-8306-3138-0pbk.
This comprehensive encyclopedia of some 1,300 schematics covers analog and digital circuits of instruments, appliances, and gadgets. The schematics have been taken from other sources. Each has the source listed. *Grade Level:* Grades 9-12.
ARBA, 86, n.1569; NewTechBks, November 85, p.310.

537. Encyclopedia of Furniture Making.
Revised and expanded. Ernest Joyce; Alan Peters. New York, NY:
Sterling; 1987. 510p., illus. (part in color), index. $29.95.
0-8069-6440-5.
This encyclopedia, first published in 1970, has become "the wood-
worker's bible." It is not an encyclopedia arranged with words "a" at
the beginning and "z" at the end. It is, instead, arranged by 10 broad
topics: basic materials of furniture making; tools and equipment of the
trade; basic techniques of joint construction; advanced construction;
metal fittings and fasteners; advanced techniques of veneering,
marquetry, inlay, lining, and curved work; running a professional
workshop; draughtsmanship and workshop geometry; furniture designs
and constructional details; and procedures for restoration, repairs, and
wood finishes. *Grade Level:* Grades 9–12.
STARR, 89, n.506.

538. The Encyclopedia of How It's Built.
Donald Clarke, ed. New York, NY: A & W Publishers; 1979. 184p.,
illus. (part in color), index. $16.95. 0-89479-047-1.
This interesting encyclopedia is divided into 27 chapters covering
everything from architecture and construction topics to machinery. It
is written for the layperson and has excellent photographs and diagrams. *Grade Level:* Grades 6–8. Grades 9–12.
ARBA, 81, n.1665; BW, 9 December 79, p.4; LJ, 15 January 80,
p.188.

539. Encyclopedia of How It's Made.
Donald Clarke, ed. New York, NY: A & W Publishers; 1978. 198p.,
illus. (part in color), index. $16.95. 0-89479-035-8.
This small but interesting encyclopedia describes how various well-
known products are manufactured. Such areas as photography, printing, and sporting goods are covered. It has excellent illustrations. For
similar book see *The Encyclopedia of How It's Built. Grade Level:*
Grades 6–8. Grades 9–12.
ARBA, 80, n.1577; LJ, 15 October 78, p.2126.

540. The Encyclopedia of Motorcycling.
George Bishop. New York, NY: Putnam; 1980. 192p., illus. (part in
color). $16.95, $8.95pbk. "A Perigee Book"; "A Bison Book."
0-399-50491-5; 0-399-12557-4pbk.
This brief encyclopedia covers international motorcycling, the riders,
and the manufacturers. Entries are included for race circuits, competitions, racing events, motorcycle associations, and special clubs. *Grade
Level:* Grades 6–8. Grades 9–12.
ARBA, 82, n.1635; BL, 1 January 81, p.604; BW, 7 December 80,
p.14; LJ, 15 November 80, p.2398; WLB, April 81, p.619.

541. Encyclopedia of Ships and Seafaring.
Peter Kemp, ed. New York, NY: Crown; 1980. 256p., illus. (part in
color), maps, index. $15.95. "A Herbert Michelman Book."
0-517-53738-9.

This is a narrative-type encyclopedia of information about the sea, navigation, diving, salvage, and biological and mineralogical resources of the sea written for the layperson. It also includes brief information about ships, men associated with shipping, and ship and boat types. *Grade Level:* Grades 9–12.

ARBA, 81, n.1701; BL, 1 January 81, p.602; Choice, February 81, p.774; WLB, January 81, p.379.

542. G.K. Hall Encyclopedia of Modern Technology.
David Blackburn; Geoffrey Holister, eds. Boston, MA: G.K. Hall; 1987. 248p., illus. (part in color). $35.00. 0-8161-9056-9.

With nearly 500 excellent, specially commissioned illustrations, this single-volume survey provides students with a basic understanding of select processes, devices, and instruments of contemporary technology. This work's visual support compensates for its brevity. Quick reference chronologies accompany descriptions of major fields of development. Illustrations include three-dimensional cut-away sections, process flow diagrams, exploded diagrams, and pictures from a variety of imaging techniques. Arrangement is by broad conceptual classes, then sub-divided by specific technologies. *Grade Level:* Grades 9–12.

ARBA, 88, n.1452; BL, 1 December 87, p.616; LJ, 1 March 88, p.33; R&RBkN, February 88, p.20; SciTech, December 87, p.30; STARR, 89, n.409; VOYA, April 88, p.52; WLB, November 87, p.93.

543. The Guinness Book of Aircraft: Records, Facts and Feats.
5th. David Mondey; Michael J.H. Taylor. New York, NY: Sterling Publishing Co./Enfield; 1988. 256p., illus. (part in color), index. $19.95. 0-85112-355-4.

This encyclopedic book is a compilation of aviation records and firsts, arranged by topic, with a chronological sub-arrangement within each chapter. It is richly illustrated, well-written in a witty style, and accurate in the accounts that are described. *Grade Level:* Grades 6–8. Grades 9–12.

544. McGraw-Hill Encyclopedia of Engineering.
Sybil P. Parker, ed. New York, NY: McGraw-Hill; 1983. 1,264p., illus., index. $72.50. 0-07-045486-8.

This spin-off of over 690 articles from the *McGraw-Hill Encyclopedia of Science and Technology* covers the engineering specialties of civil, design, electrical, industrial, mechanical, metallurgical, mining, nuclear, petroleum, and production. *Grade Level:* Grades 9–12.

ARBA, 84, n.1484; BL, 1 October 83, p.255; Choice, May 83, p.1267; LJ, 1 June 83, p.1127; SB, November 83, p.90; WLB, June 83, p.883.

545. New Encyclopedia of Motorcars: 1885 to the Present.
3rd. G.N. Georgano, ed. New York, NY: I.P. Dutton; 1982. 688p., illus. (part in color), index. $45.00. 0-525-93254-2.

Although somewhat dated, this is still a comprehensive reference source for some 4,300 different models, giving condensed histories of the manufacturers, with illustrations of the various models from the earliest production to 1982. There are many other books of this type

available but this is one of the better encyclopedias. *Grade Level:* Grades 6–8. Grades 9–12.
ARBA, 84, n.1513; BL, 1 September 84, p.44; LJ, 1 March 83, p.450.

546. Space Flight: The Records.
Tim Furniss. Enfield, Great Britain: Guinness Superlatives; Dist. by Sterling; New York; NY; 1985. 168p. illus. (part in color), index. $12.95. 0-85112-451-8.
This is another interesting Guinnes book that gives the various "firsts and bests" of anything that pertains to space flight. A description of the first 105 manned space flights is given and followed by a listing of firsts in space. There is also a section that presents the technical information about the rockets and vehicles that have been used in space flights. A biographical directory of all crew members is included. *Grade Level:* Grades 9–12.
ARBA, 86, n.1779; BL, 1 October 85, p.178.

547. The Space Program Quiz and Fact Book.
Timothy B. Benford; Brian Wilkes. New York, NY: Harper and Row; 1985. 257p., illus., bibliog., index. $15.95, $8.95pbk. 0-06-015454-3, 0-06-096005-1pbk.
This encyclopedic book is an interesting "collection of little-known details, odd facts, anecdotes, vignettes, and superlatives served up in an entertaining and educational format." Written in the form of questions and answers. *Grade Level:* Grades 6–8. Grades 9–12.
ARBA, 86, n.1777; Kliatt, Winter 86, p.59; SB, September 86, p.59; WLB, December 85, p.67.

548. This Is the Way It Works: A Collection of Machines.
Robert Gardner. Garden City, NY: Doubleday; 1980. 127p., illus., index. $9.95. 0-385-14697-3.
This interesting little volume describes the mechanics and working processes of various machines from an iron lung to a zipper to a solar heater to a steam car. It is well-written and indexed. *Grade Level:* Grades 3–5. Grades 6–8. Grades 9–12.
ASBYP, Winter 81, p.27; CBRS, Spring 80, p.117; CCB-B, September 80, p.8; CurR, September 81, p.400; SLJ, January 82, p.87; VOYA, February 81, p.43.

549. World Truck Handbook.
New. Nick Georgano. New York, NY: Jane's; 1986. 328p., illus., index. $16.95pbk. 0-7106-0366-5.
This small handbook covers the trucks currently being produced in all countries. Arrangement is by axle layout. Descriptions are concise but complete, and illustrations accompany most entries. *Grade Level:* Grades 9–12.
ARBA, 87, n.1745; R&RBkN, Fall 86, p.22.

Guides

550. Complete Guide to Reading Schematic Diagrams.
3rd. John Douglas-Young. Englewood Cliffs, NJ: Prentice Hall; 1988. 286p., illus., index. $24.95, $14.95pbk. 0-13-160334-5, 0-13-160847-9pbk.

This guide explains in detail how to read 150 electronic circuits. Basic features of each circuit are discussed and followed with a thorough analysis of every aspect. Circuits covered include voltage amplifiers, oscillators, power supplies, controls, and others. Another useful book of this type is Robert M. Brown and Paul Lawrence's *How to Read Electronic Circuit Diagrams*. *Grade Level:* Grades 9–12.
Choice, April 73, p.316.

551. The Complete Guide to Remodeling Your Home: A Step-By-Step Manual for Homeowners and Investors.
Kent Lester; Una Lamie. White Hall, VA: Betterway Publications; 1987. 272p., illus., glossary, index. $18.95pbk. 0-932620-73-6pbk.

This comprehensive guide provides essential information on house remodeling. The book is divided into two sections, planning and implementation. Planning covers all the steps that precede the remodeling work itself: legal and financial considerations, tax laws, locating the right property, evaluating remodeling potential, estimating the cost, and working with subcontractors and material suppliers. Implementation covers the remodeling work itself and provides step-by-step instructions, sample specifications, estimated completion time and cost, and a rating of various projects regarding degree of difficulty. *Grade Level:* Grades 9–12.

552. A Field Guide to Airplanes of North America.
M. R. Montgomery; Gerald L. Foster. Boston, MA: Houghton Mifflin; 1984. 212p., illus., bibliog., index. $12.45pbk. 0-395-35313-0pbk.

This guide to airplanes of North America includes 300 entries grouped by type, such as high-wing singles, twins, business jets, and military aircraft. Each plane is clearly illustrated, and the book includes a description, some history, technical data, and major distinguishing features of the planes. *Grade Level:* Grades 6–8. Grades 9–12.
ARBA, 86, n.1780; BL, 1 January 85, p.608; CSM, 7 December 84, p.B16; LJ, 1 March 85, p.42.

553. Inventing, Inventions, and Inventors: A Teaching Resource Book.
Jerry D. Flack. Englewood, CO: Teacher Ideas Press/Libraries Unlimited, Inc; 1989. 148p., illus. $21.50. Gifted Treasury Series. 0-87287-747-7.

This sourcebook for teachers gives ideas for lesson plans and background materials for curricula pertaining to inventing, inventions, and inventors. *Grade Level:* Grades 6–8. Grades 9–12. Teacher's/Librarian's Resource.

Handbooks

554. Arco's Complete Woodworking Handbook.
Revised. Jeannette T. Adams. New York, NY: Arco; 1981. 698p.,
illus., index. $19.95. 0-668-04829-8.
This well-written handbook covers all aspects of woodworking, including the use of hand and power tools, types of woods and the proper way to work with them, machinery used in heavy wood working, methods of finishing all types of woods, and construction methods used in the building industry. Previously called *Arco's New Complete Woodworking Handbook. Grade Level:* Grades 9–12.

555. ARRL Handbook for the Radio Amateur.
67th. Mark J. Wilson, ed. Newington, CT: American Radio Relay
League; 1989. 1v. various paging, illus., index. $21.00. 0-87259-166-2.
Formerly known as the *Radio Amateur's Handbook,* this volume is one of the best known radio amateur handbooks, frequently revised, covering everything that anyone would need to know to be a ham radio operator. All of the techniques, history, and know-how are included. For those wanting to obtain an amateur radio license, see the entry for *Radio Amateur's License Manual. Grade Level:* Grades 9–12.
ARBA, 78, n.1084; BL, 15 June 73, p.975, 1 May 76, p.1239; RSR,
October 79, p.32; SB, December 77, p.156.

556. Carpenters and Builders Library: Volume 1, Tools, Steel Square, Joiners; Volume 2, Builder's Math, Plans, Specifications; Volume 3, Layouts, Foundations, Framing; Volume 4, Millwork, Power Tools, Painting.
Revised. John E. Ball; Tom Philbin, eds. New York, NY: Macmillan;
1986. 4v., illus., index. $43.95set. 0-02-506450-9set.
This set of handbooks continues to give detailed information on the tools, materials, methods and related building data that would be of interest to the builder. It covers everything that a carpenter or builder would want to know, including tools, math plans, specifications, layout, foundations, framing, millwork, power tools, and painting. *Grade Level:* Grades 9–12.

557. Complete Shortwave Listener's Handbook.
3rd. Hank Bennett; Harry L. Helms; David T. Hardy. Blue Ridge
Summit, PA: TAB; 1986. 294p., illus., index. $15.95, $11.95pbk.
0-83060355-7, 0-8306-2655-7pbk.
This comprehensive handbook covering short wave radio terminology, radio receivers, antennas, frequencies, propagation, reception by general continental areas, frequency, amateur radio, citizen's band radio, FM DXing, TV DXing, utility stations, logbooks, reporting and verification, time and standard frequency stations, card swapping, radio clubs, and WDW callsigns and awards. *Grade Level:* Grades 9–12.
ARBA, 75, n.1202; RSR, January 75, p.131.

558. For Good Measure: A Complete Compendium of International Weights and Measures.
William D. Johnstone. New York, NY: Avon; 1977 (c1975). 327p., index. $2.50. 0-380-01710-5.
This is a handbook of international weights and measures, giving numerical values for a particular unit; relative size of a particular unit compared with another; how a particular unit came into being and what the unit is generally used for; ancient, obsolete, revised, and foreign units; and a conversion factor from customary to metric units. *Grade Level:* Grades 6–8. Grades 9–12.
ARBA, 76, n.1316; BL, 15 March 76, p.1002; Choice, July 76, p.646; KR, 15 December 75, p.1426; LJ, 1 December 75, p.2233, 15 April 76, p.969; WLB, April 76, p.648.

559. How to Read Electronic Circuit Diagrams.
2nd. Robert M. Brown; Paul Lawrence; James A. Whitson. Blue Ridge Summit, PA: TAB; 1988. 214p., illus., glossary, index. $20.95, $12.95pbk. TAB Hobby Electronic Series. 0-8306-0480-4, 0-8306-2880-0pbk.
This book covers the various conventions for denoting the individual electronic components and their connections in different electronic circuits. It proceeds from the basic components, such as resistors, capacitors, coils, chokes, transformers, batteries, switches, relays, fuses, and circuit breakers, to the more complex digital circuits. *Grade Level:* Grades 9–12.
STARR, 89, n.473.

560. Illustrated Handbook of Electronic Tables, Symbols, Measurements and Values.
2nd. Raymond H. Ludwig. Englewood Cliffs, NJ: Prentice Hall; 1984. 430p., illus., index. $34.95. 0-13-450494-1.
This handbook covers those tables, symbols, measurements, and values that a user would encounter in working with electronics. The emphasis is on standardization. *Grade Level:* Grades 9–12.
ARBA, 78, n.1534; RSR, October 78, p.27.

561. Machinists' Library.
4th. Thomas J. Morrisey. Indianapolis, IN: Audel; 1983. 3v., illus., index. $35.85set. 0-685-9287-1set.
These three volumes cover basic machine shop, machinery, and the toolmakers handbook. It is a well-written set for the student that details setup, operation, and care of machine shop machines, including drills, lathes, automatic screw machines, boring machines, shapers, planers, slatters, milling machines, indexing operations, and automated machine tools. *Grade Level:* Grades 9–12.
SciTech, November 87, p.36; STARR, 89, n.474.

562. Maintaining and Troubleshooting Electrical Equipment.
Roy Parks; Terry Wireman. New York, NY: Industrial Press, Inc; 1987. 179p., illus., index. $19.95. 0-8311-1164-X.

"The purpose of this book is to present the technical subject of maintaining and troubleshooting electrical equipment in as nontechnical language as possible." Successfully achieving this purpose by avoiding the use of advanced mathematics and unnecessary use of language not familiar to the beginning student, the authors present the material in a textbook fashion, with the suggestion that the beginning student should begin with chapter one and proceed through each chapter in sequence to the end. All areas of electrical equipment are included. *Grade Level:* Grades 9–12.
STARR, 89, n.475.

563. Master Handbook of 1001 More Practical Electronic Circuits.
Michael L. Fair, ed. Blue Ridge Summit, PA: TAB; 1987 (c1979). 698p., illus., index. $19.95pbk. 0-8306-7804-2pbk.
A supplement to *Master Handbook of 1001 Practical Electronic Circuits* published in 1975, this handbook has a minimum of text that merely identifies the circuit with no description of how it is used. Included are clearly printed circuit schematics for numerous circuits, including bridge circuits, detectors, battery chargers, frequency doublers, video amplifiers, test gear and metering circuits, regulators, audio amplifiers, and timers and counters. *Grade Level:* Grades 9–12.
STARR, 89, n.475.

564. Radio Amateur's Handbook.
15th. A. Frederick Colins; Robert Hertzberg. New York, NY: Harper and Row; 1983. 387p., illus., index. $14.45. 0-06-181366-4.
Although not as comprehensive as the one by the American Radio Relay League, this is still a standard work that presents the fundamental theories on amateur radio in a manner suitable for the beginner. *Grade Level:* Grades 9–12.
BL 1 April 80, p.1106, 1 September 84, p.44; SB, September 72, p.169, May 79, p.33.

565. Radio Handbook.
23rd. William I. Orr. Indianapolis, IN: Howard W. Sams; 1987. 1v. various paging, illus., index. $39.95. 0-672-77424-0.
This comprehensive handbook is considered a standard for all amateur radio operators, along with the one published by the American Radio Relay League. It covers the basic principles, operation, and use of the equipment that the operator may have at hand. *Grade Level:* Grades 9–12.
BL, 15 April 73, p.796, 1 May 73, p.853; RSR, October 79, p.32.

566. SI Metric Handbook.
John L. Feirer. New York, NY: Scribner's; 1977. 1v. various paging, illus., index. $25.00. 0-87002-908-8.
This comprehensive handbook covers metric conversion in all basic occupational areas. The first part contains a history and definition of the SI measuring system. The second part covers the metric system in design, drafting, metal working, woodworking, graphic arts, auto me-

chanics, offices, and domestic sciences. *Grade Level:* Grades 6–8. Grades 9–12.
ARBA, 78, n.1231; LJ, 15 April 77, p.936.

567. Student's Shop Reference Handbook.
Edward G. Hoffman, comp. New York, NY: Industrial Press; 1985. 531p., index. $15.00pbk. 0-8311-1161-5pbk.
This handbook is intended to "provide an affordable and dependable handbook for students in the machine shop, the tool room, and the drafting room." It covers the essential elements of machine shop practice, including gearing, screw threads, materials, machining methods, and engineering drawing. *Grade Level:* Grades 9–12.
ARBA, 87, n.1577; SciTech, November 86, p.34.

568. TAB Handbook of Hand and Power Tools.
Rudolf F. Graf; George J. Whalen. Blue Ridge Summit, PA: TAB; 1984. 501p., illus., index. $17.95pbk. 0-8306-1638-1pbk.
This handbook covers every type of hand tool and power tool that one may encounter at work, doing hobbies, in the home, or in the garden. The first part covers hand tools and the second part covers power tools and appliances. *Grade Level:* Grades 9–12.
ARBA, 86, n.1584; NewTechBks, November 85, p.316.

569. Weekend Mechanic's Handbook: Complete Guide to Do-It-Yourself Repairs.
2nd. Paul Weissler. Englewood Cliffs, NJ: Prentice Hall; 1988. 453p., illus., index. $15.95. 0-13-948100-1.
This is a well-written manual for those who want to do their own automotive repairs. It has excellent illustrations. *Grade Level:* Grades 9–12.
BL, 15 September 88, p.108.

Histories

570. American Aviation: An Illustrated History.
Joe Christy. Blue Ridge Summit, PA: TAB; 1987. 394p., illus., index. $24.60. 0-8306-2497-X.
This book provides a comprehensive history of American aviation. It contains descriptive, historical facts about people, events, and machines that have influenced the technological advances of today's civil and military aviation. The 18 chronologically arranged chapters begin with the first flying pioneers and end with the space shuttles. Special emphasis is given to the world wars and the birth of the air-mail era, which, together, led to the development of the airline industry. This book includes numerous, informative illustrations with rare photographs, plus an appendix that covers important questions and answers about American aviation. *Grade Level:* Grades 3–5. Grades 6–8. Grades 9–12.
STARR, 89, no.579.

571. Eureka!: An Illustrated History of Inventions from the Wheel to the Computer.
Edward DeBono, ed. New York, NY: Holt, Rinehart and Winston; 1979 (c1974). 248p., illus., index. $10.00. 0-03-049826-0.
This is a chronologically arranged history of important scientific discoveries from the Stone Age to the present. The inventions are divided into five major sections: man moving, man talking, man living, man working, and key devices. *Grade Level:* Grades 3-5. Grades 6-8. Grades 9-12.
ARBA, 76, n.1307; BL, 15 July 76, p.1629; CSM, 4 December 74, p.10; Choice, March 75, p.94; Kliatt, Fall 79, p.66; LJ, 15 December 74, p.3283, 1 February 75, p.278, 1 March 75, p.451, 15 April 75, p.735; RSR, July 75, p.43; SR, 17 May 75, p.28; SchLib, December 79, p.377.

572. The History of Invention.
Trevor I. Williams. New York, NY: Facts on File; 1987. 352p., illus. (part in color), bibliog., index. $35.00. 0-8160-1788-3.
This is a broad encyclopedic survey of the history of technology, with half of the text devoted to historical influences, such as "The Rise of Islam" and "The Arts of War," and half of the text focused on specific industrial developments in shipping and navigation, mining and metals, and agriculture. The biographical dictionary is especially helpful in determining the origin of particular inventions. *Grade Level:* Grades 6-8. Grades 9-12.
ASBYP, Spring 88, p.38; Choice, February 88, p.928; LJ, 1 March 88, p.33; R&RBkN, February 88, p.20; SB, May 88, p.301; SciTech, November 87, p.32; STARR, 89, n.408; VOYA, October 88, p.207; WLB, December 87, p.67.

573. History of Technology and Invention: Progress Through the Ages.
Maurice Daumas, ed. New York, NY: Crown; 1969-1978. 3v., illus., index. $30.00 per vol. 0-417-50727-7, v.1; 0-517-50728-5, v.2; 0-517-52037-0, v.3.
This is a translation of a French work covering in three volumes and in a readable style the "Origins of Technological Civilization to 1450," "First Stages of Mechanization, 1450-1725," and "Expansion of Mechanization, 1725-1860." The text is well-written for the layperson, and the illustrations are very good. *Grade Level:* Grades 9-12.
BL, 1 June 80, p. 1408; Choice, October 80, p. 270; LJ, 15 March 70, p.1041, 1 March 71, p.783; PW, 5 January 70, p.72; SB, September 70, p.150.

574. Illustrated Encyclopedia of Space Technology: A Comprehensive History of Space Exploration.
Kenneth Gatland. New York, NY: Harmony Books; 1981. 289p., illus. (part in color), index. $24.95. 0-517-54258-7.
This excellent reference book covers space history and technology. The text is authoritative, easy-to-read, and amplified by remarkable color illustrations. *Grade Level:* Grades 9-12.

ARBA, 82, n.1616; BL, 15 July 81, p.1427; Choice, December 81, p.488; LJ, August 81, p.1558; SB, March 82, p.203; SLJ, May 83, p.25; WLB, January 82, p.382.

575. Short History of Technology from the Earliest Times to A.D. 1900.
Thomas K. Derry. New York, NY: Oxford University Press; 1970 (c1960). 783p., illus., index. $29.95, $13.95pbk. 0-19-500142-7, 0-19-881231-0pbk.
Numerous general histories cover technology, but this is one of the better ones for the layperson. The text is very authoritative and easy to comprehend. *Grade Level:* Grades 6–8. Grades 9–12.
Choice, March 71, p.88.

576. Space Sciences.
Christopher Lampton. New York, NY: Franklin Watts; 1983. 93p., illus. $9.40. A Reference First Book. 0-531-04539-0.
This well-written, historical dictionary of space science for children covers space terminology and includes NASA photographs. *Grade Level:* Grades 3–5. Grades 6–8.
ARBA, 84, n.1483; ASBYP, Winter 84, p.32; CurR, October 83, p.20; SB, January 84, p.154; SLJ, April 83, p.114.

577. Space Travel: A History.
4th. Wernher Von Braun; Frederick I. Ordway, III. New York, NY: Harper & Row; 1985. 308p., illus. (part in color), bibliog., index. $29.45. 0-06-181898-4.
This authoritative history of space flight gives information about early rocket launches, flights, and the people who helped to make it all happen. There are 40 pages of plates that add to the excellent text. The previous edition was called *History of Rocketry and Space Travel*. *Grade Level:* Grades 9–12.
LJ, 1 March 86, p.51; SB, November 86, p.102; RSR, Winter 86, p.81.

578. Technology at Work.
Anthony Feldman; Bill Gunston. New York, NY: Facts on File; 1980. 336p., illus., index. $24.95. 0-87196-413-9.
This historical survey of the latest technological advances includes overland travel, marine technology, technology of flight, light and its uses, sound and its uses, energy at work, materials, military technology, communications and control, and space technology. *Grade Level:* Grades 6–8. Grades 9–12.
LJ, 15 May 80, p.1177; SB, March 81, p.205.

Indexes

579. Applied Science and Technology Index.
New York, NY: H.W. Wilson; 1913–. index. Monthly with annual cumulations. Price based on service basis. 0003-6986.
This subject index to over 200 English language periodicals covers both the theoretical sciences and engineering applications. It includes pure physics, chemistry, earth sciences, mathematics, metallurgy, and computer science, if the subjects are contained in the major scientific journals that are indexed. From 1913 to 1957, it was known as *Industrial Arts Index. Grade Level:* Grades 9–12.
ARBA, 76, n.1325, 82, n.1414, 85, n.1340; RSR, October 79, p.31, July 81, p.40, Winter 86, p.77; SerR, October 77, p.26.

580. Automotive Literature Index, 1947–1976: A Thirty-Year Guide to *Car and Driver, Motor Trend,* **and** *Road and Track.*
A. Wallace, comp. Toledo, OH: Motorbooks International; 1981. 325p. $29.95. 0-9606804-3-8.
This excellent, in-depth bibliography has a supplement for the years 1977–1981. The three magazines, *Car and Driver, Motor Trend,* and *Road and Track,* are of interest to students in high school and vocational schools. The indexing is much more detailed than that in the *Readers Guide,* thus making it easier to find more specific information for the years covered. Articles can be researched by auto make, model, and year, as well as by subject. *Grade Level:* Grades 9–12.
ARBA, 83, n.1572.

Manuals

581. Carpentry for Residential Construction.
Byron W. Maguire. Carlsbad, CA: Craftsman Book Co; 1987. 388p., illus., index. $19.95. 0-934041-21-0.
The first four chapters of this book for carpenters and builders cover the basic skills one needs to do any carpentry job—planning, drawing and specifications, estimating, and programming. The fifth chapter is a brief dictionary of carpentry and building terminology. Each of the remaining chapters covers a particular aspect of construction and building—cement work and foundations, wall framing, sheathing, roof framing, shingling, cornices, window-unit installation, door-unit installation, door installation and maintenance, siding, drywall installation, ceiling tile installation, trim, floor installation, and paneling. Step-by-step procedures for accomplishing the job are given. *Grade Level:* Grades 9–12.
STARR, 89, n.430.

582. Chilton Repair Manuals.
Chilton's Automotive Editorial Department. Radnor, PA: Chilton Book Co; 1970–. multivolume, illus., index. Price per volume varies.

This well-known publishing firm is one of the most authoritative publishing companies for automobile and other vehicle maintenance manuals. Almost every type of car, truck, and motorcycle is included. Each manual is complete and usually covers several model years. *Grade Level:* Grades 9–12.

583. Engineering Projects for Young Scientists.
Peter H. Goodwin. New York, NY: Franklin Watts; 1987. 126p., illus., bibliog., index. $11.90. Projects for Young Scientists. 0-531-10339-0.
Through a well-written text with good illustrations, this manual helps students understand the laws of physics and how they are applied to engineering. Each chapter begins with some background information on the topic, outlines preliminary investigations, and then gives some ideas for projects. All of the projects are illustrated with things one sees every day, such as cantilever-and-truss bridges, rockets, amusement park rides, musical instruments, cameras and lenses, and water waves. *Grade Level:* Grades 3–5. Grades 6–8.
BL, 15 February 88, p.990; BRpt, January 88, p.53; SB, January 88, p.166; SLJ, March 88, p.219; STARR, 89, n.413.

584. How Things Work in Your Home (and What to Do When They Don't).
Time-Life Books. New York, NY: Henry Holt and Co; 1987 (c1985). 368p., illus., bibliog., index. $12.95pbk. "An Owl Book." 0-8050-0126-3pbk.
The text of this interesting manual first describes how the machines work, then how to disassemble, replace parts, and make adjustments, and, finally, troubleshooting. The seven sections cover plumbing, electricity, small appliances, large appliances, heating, cooling, and outdoor equipment. It covers such things as repairing light fixtures, can openers, coffee makers, hair dryers, dishwashers, cooking ranges, air conditioners, lawn mowers, and chain saws. *Grade Level:* Grades 9–12.
STARR, 89, n.508.

585. How to Test Almost Everything Electronic.
2nd. Jack Darr; Delton T. Horn. Blue Ridge Summit, PA: TAB; 1988. 175p., illus., index. $15.95, $8.95pbk. TAB Hobby Electronic Series. 0-8306-7925-1, 0-8306-2925-4pbk.
This is a practical manual on "electronic tests and measurements, how to make them with all kinds of electronic test equipment, and how to interpret the results." It guides the user through the process of measuring quantity, output, and quality of electrical voltage, current, and resistance. *Grade Level:* Grades 9–12.
STARR, 89, n.487.

586. Illustrated Home Electronics Fix-It Book.
2nd. Homer L. Davidson. Blue Ridge Summit, PA: TAB; 1988. 465p., illus., index. $25.95, $16.95pbk. 0-8306-7883-2, 0-8306-2883-5pbk.

This book is easy to use with each chapter covering a specific kind of electronic apparatus. Within each chapter, various problems are highlighted and followed by an explanation of what is wrong and how the problem can be corrected. Covered apparatus include AM/FM radios, car radios, car cassette players, common portable tape players, portable cassette players and boom-boxes, cassette decks, phonographs, compact disc players, TVs, VCRs, telephone answering machines, cordless telephones, electronic games, door bells, calculators, intercoms, and battery chargers. *Grade Level:* Grades 9–12.
STARR, 89, n.481.

587. Meters and Scopes: How to Use Test Equipment.
Robert J. Traister. Blue Ridge Summit, PA: TAB; 1988. 312p., illus., index. $23.95, $14.60pbk. 0-8306-0226-7, 0-8306-2826-6pbk.
This manual is a basic introduction to electronic testing equipment. It covers specific types of instruments, including meters, transistor testers, tube testers, audio generators, and oscilloscopes. A chapter on how to build test equipment is also included. *Grade Level:* Grades 9–12.
STARR, 90, n.659.

588. Motor Auto Repair Manual.
New York, NY: Hearst; 1938–. 1st– , illus., index. Annual. $21.50 per year. 0-87851-632-8 50th ed.
This annual is an authoritative reference on mechanical repair procedures for American-made cars. Each year it includes data on tune-ups, front end specifications, service specifications, and other service and repair information for the cars that are on the market. *Grade Level:* Grades 9–12.

589. Radio Amateur's License Manual.
American Radio Relay League. Newington, CT: American Radio Relay League; 1937–. 1st– , index. Biennial. $4.00 per year.
This manual discusses the various types of amateur licensing and includes sample study questions for the various license examinations. Also included are a chart of frequency sub-bands, a list of U.S. Radio Districts, and an examination schedule. This book is a must for any amateur radio operator who expects to get an amateur radio license. *Grade Level:* Grades 9–12.

ENERGY/
ENVIRONMENT/
ECOLOGY

The topics in this chapter could just as easily have been distributed in the other chapters on Technology/Engineering, General Biology, or Chemistry. However, the areas of energy, environment, and ecology are currently of vital concern to everyone and the three topics are very much intertwined. There are few reference books for young people in these areas, but the few that are included are recommended. Future editions of this book will have many more as the nation becomes more environment-conscious.

Energy is the ability of one system to do work on another to create a by-product. Much of what is written falls into the applied science areas and reference materials in the chapter on Technology/Engineering will include such engineering materials. With the production of energy, which may be chemical, electrical, radiant, or nuclear, there are environmental concerns of pollution and its ecological effects. A whole engineering discipline is devoted to this, environmental engineering, which is concerned with the effects of humans on the environment. The study of the relationships of humans and other organisms to their environment is called ecology. These three areas generate a "cause and effect" cycle upon each other.

The 19 titles included in this chapter have been isolated because of the growing concern for our earth. To understand the detrimental effects that the production of energy can have on the environment, a majority of the 19 titles cover energy topics. A good, recent dictionary is *Dictionary of Energy* by Martin Counihan. The basic knowledge of energy and energy production does not change a great deal so books published in the early 1980s, such as *McGraw-Hill Encyclopedia of Energy* and *Energy Deskbook*, are still useful and accurate. The *Dictionary of Dangerous Pollutants, Ecology, and Environment* approaches being an encyclopedia with some of its entries. Other good environment and ecology reference works for young people include *Dictionary of the Environment, Ecology Field Glossary: A Naturalist's Vocabulary*, and *Save the Earth: An Ecology Handbook for Kids*. Finally, a very good "how-to-know" book for young people is *Energy Projects for Young Scientists*.

Dictionaries

590. Dictionary of Dangerous Pollutants, Ecology, and Environment.
David F. Tver. New York, NY: Industrial Press; 1981. 347p., illus.
$29.95. 0-8311-1060-0.
This well-written book covers air, water, and noise pollution; nuclear, geothermal, and solar energy; coal gasification; waste control biomass conversion; recycling; ecology; meteorology; and climatology. The definitions approach an encyclopedic discussion on some of the entries.
Grade Level: Grades 9–12.
ARBA, 82, n.1511, 84, n.1384; BL, 1 October 81, p.167; Choice, December 81, p.494; SB, September 82, p.8.

591. Dictionary of Energy.
Martin Counihan. Boston, MA: Routledge and Kegan Paul; 1981.
157p., illus., bibliog. $16.95. 0-7100-0847-3.
This very useful dictionary defines about 550 of the more common terms pertaining to energy for the nonspecialist. Also included are sections on units and international energy parameters, plus a good bibliography. *Grade Level:* Grades 9–12.
ARBA, 83, n.1378; Choice, June 82, p.1374; SB, September 82, p.25; SchLib, March 82, p.90.

592. Dictionary of Energy.
2nd. Malcolm Slesser, ed. New York, NY: Nichols Publishing Co; 1988. 300p., illus. $49.50. 0-89397-320-3.
According to the editor, this dictionary provides "information for intelligent people searching for concepts, ideas, definitions and explanations in areas outside that of their own expertise." An elementary definition is given first, followed, if necessary, with more detailed terminology. *Grade Level:* Grades 6–8. Grades 9–12.
ARBA, 84, p.674; BL, 15 January 84, p.730, 1 September 84, p.36; Choice, June 83, p.1432; WLB, September 83, p.65.

593. Dictionary of Petroleum Terms.
3rd. Jodie Leecraft, ed. Austin, TX: Petroleum Extension Service, University of Texas; 1983. 177p., illus. $16.00, $10.00pbk.
0-88698-000-3, 0-88698-001-1pbk.
This small dictionary contains some 4,000 terms associated with petroleum technology including, acronyms, units of measure, technologies, legal and economic terms, and slang. *Grade Level:* Grades 9–12.
ARBA, 85, n.1385.

594. Dictionary of the Environment.
2nd. Michael Allaby. New York, NY: New York University Press; 1984. 529p., illus. $60.00. 0-8147-0582-0.
This somewhat expensive but very good general dictionary covers terms associated with the environment, including those from the life and earth sciences, meteorology and climatology, and economics. The

definitions are concise and as useful to the serious researcher as to the student. The book has also been issued by Macmillan as *Macmillan's Dictionary of the Environment*. *Grade Level:* Grades 9–12.
ARBA, 85, n.1391; Choice, November 78, p.1191; SB, September 84, p.15; SciTech, March 84, p.5; WLB, October 78, p.187.

595. Ecology Field Glossary: A Naturalist's Vocabulary.
Walter H. Lewis. Westport, CT: Greenwood; 1977. 152p. $29.95.
0-8371-9547-0.
This book includes an outline of ecology, covering terrestrial, aquatic, and soil ecosystems; man's impact on all three ecosystems; and followed by a glossary that provides short, concise definitions. *Grade Level:* Grades 9–12.
ARBA, 78, n.1345; BL, 1 November 78, p.497; Choice, May 78, p.376; LJ, 1 December 77, p.2420; SB, December 78, p.161.

596. Energy Dictionary.
V. Daniel Hunt. New York, NY: Van Nostrand Reinhold; 1979.
518p., bibliog. $28.95, $16.95pbk. 0-442-27395-9, 0-442-23787-1pbk.
This dictionary contains definitions of some 4,000 terms related to the production, conservation, and environmental aspects of energy. Since the terminology of energy is not as fast changing as in some other fields, the date of this publication presents no problems. The definitions are brief. A glossary of acronyms is included. *Grade Level:* Grades 9–12.
ARBA, 80, n.1420; BL, 1 January 81, p.641; Choice, September 79, p.798; LJ, 15 April 80, p.921; SLJ, December 80, p.22; WLB, July 79, p.728.

597. Handbook of Oil Industry Terms and Phrases.
4th. R.D. Langenkamp. Tulsa, OK: PennWell Books; 1984. 347p., bibliog. $29.95. 0-87814-258-4.
The oil industry literature has many terms that need to be defined for the student and layperson. This dictionary, called a handbook, contains close to 3,200 terms that are concisely and clearly defined. *Grade Level:* Grades 9–12.
ARBA, 83, n.1468.

598. Petroleum Dictionary.
David F. Tver; Richard W. Berry. New York, NY: Van Nostrand Reinhold; 1980. 374p., illus. $18.95pbk. 0-442-28529-9pbk.
This dictionary contains about 4,000 concise and easy-to-understand definitions for terms relating to all aspects of the petroleum industry. It is not comprehensive but does include the technical, scientific, and business terms that one encounters when reading the general literature in the petroleum field. *Grade Level:* Grades 9–12.
ARBA, 81, n.1494; BL, 15 November 80, p.479, 1 September 84, p.36; LJ, 1 May 80, p.1070; SB, November 80, p.75; WLB, June 80, p.673.

599. Solar Energy Dictionary.
V. Daniel Hunt. New York, NY: Industrial Press; 1982. 411p., illus.,
bibliog. $29.95. 0-8311-1139-9.
This is a comprehensive dictionary of solar energy terms, plus related
terms from biomass, wind, and water energy. The definitions are brief
but accurate. *Grade Level:* Grades 9–12.
ARBA, 83, p.653; LJ, 1 March 82, p.538.

Encyclopedias

600. Energy Deskbook.
Samuel Glasstone. New York, NY: Van Nostrand Reinhold; 1983.
453p., illus. $31.95. 0-442-22928-3.
This is an encyclopedia of general energy information containing over
400 entries. The text is well-written and easily understood by nonpro-
fessionals and students. *Grade Level:* Grades 9–12.
ARBA, 84, n.1372; Choice, January 84, p.685.

601. McGraw-Hill Encyclopedia of Energy.
2nd. Sybil P. Parker, ed. New York, NY: McGraw-Hill; 1981. 838p.,
illus., bibliog., index. $57.50. 0-07-045268-7.
The first edition was called *Encyclopedia of Energy.* This encyclopedia
covers the field of energy through some 300 articles. All aspects of
energy, from the non-renewable to the renewable sources, are discussed. Two appendices cover "Federal Energy Legislation and Organizations" and "Energy-Related Publications." *Grade Level:* Grades 9–12.
ARBA, 82, n.1507; BL, 1 October 81, p.257; Choice, March 81, p.926;
LJ, 1 February 81, p.343; WLB, January 81, p.381.

602. World Energy Book: An A-Z Atlas and Statistical Sourcebook.
David Crabbe; Richard McBride, eds. Cambridge, MA: MIT Press;
1979 (c1978). 259p., illus. $12.50pbk. 0-262-53036-8pbk.
Energy terminology does not change as rapidly as terminology in some
other fields, so this encyclopedic dictionary of some 1,500 terms is still
useful. The definitions are very readable and nontechnical and include
many cross-references. *Grade Level:* Grades 9–12.
ARBA, 79, n.1392; BL, 15 December 80, p.592; Choice, June 79,
p.514; Kliatt, Winter 80, p.45; LJ, 15 January 79, p.180; WLB, April
79, p.589.

Guides

603. Energy Projects for Young Scientists.
Robert Gardner. New York, NY: Franklin Watts; 1987. 127p., illus.,
bibliog., index. $11.90. 0-531-10338-2.

This well-written text with good illustrations presents ideas that will help the student understand energy in its various forms. Each chapter begins with a general discussion of the topic and then presents projects that help to illustrate what has been discussed. *Grade Level:* Grades 3–5. Grades 6–8.
BL, 15 February 88, p.990; BRpt, January 88, p.53; SB, January 88, p.166; SLJ, October 87, p.143; STARR, 89, n.501; VOYA, December 87, p.248.

Handbooks

604. Energy: A Guidebook.
Janet Ramage. New York, NY: Oxford University Press; 1983. 345p., illus., bibliog., index. $13.95pbk. 0-19-289157-Xpbk.
This handbook is intended to give an overview of how energy is used and what the future outlook may be. It covers the current technologies of energy, including energy conversion, electrical, oil and gas, coal, nuclear power, water, solar, and wind. The text is detailed and descriptive. *Grade Level:* Grades 9–12.
Choice, March 84, p.998; SB, May 84, p.276.

605. Energy Factbook.
Richard C. Dorf. New York, NY: McGraw-Hill; 1981. 227p., illus., bibliog., index. $27.50, $7.95pbk. Energy Learning Systems Book. 0-07-017623-X, 0-07-017629-9pbk.
This is a small handbook of facts about energy. It explains the various forms of energy for the student and layperson, encompassing petroleum, natural gas, electric, hydroelectric, geothermal, solar, nuclear fission and fusion, and alternative sources. *Grade Level:* Grades 6–8. Grades 9–12.
ARBA, 83, n.1395; BL, 15 December 80, p.545; Choice, May 81, p.1232; LJ, 15 December 80, p.2561; SB, November 81, p.67; WLB, April 81, p.620.

606. Save the Earth!: An Ecology Handbook for Kids.
Betty Miles. New York, NY: Knopf; 1974. 91p., illus., bibliog. $8.99. 0-394-926458-7.
This handbook for children gives information on pollution and what to do about it. It lists a variety of experiments and practical ways for individuals to change their consumption habits. *Grade Level:* Grades 3–5. Grades 6–8. Grades 9–12.
BL, 1 April 74, p.877; KR, 1 February 74, p.117; LJ, 15 September 74, p.2274; Teacher, March 75, p.32.

607. Solar Energy Almanac.
Martin McPhillips, ed. New York, NY: Facts on File; 1983. 240p., illus. $15.95. 0-87196-727-8.

This collection of facts and data on solar energy covers history, passive versus active design, tax credits, solar greenhouses, careers in solar energy, building site, solar cooling, solar hot water, the underground house, movable insulation, solar cells, solar satellites, wind energy, and solar homes. *Grade Level:* Grades 6–8. Grades 9–12. ARBA, 84, n.1363; BL, 1 April 83, p.1003; LJ, 15 March 83, p.577; SB, September 83, p.26; SLJ, August 83, p.86.

Tables

608. Energy: Facts and Figures.
Robert H. Romer. Amherst, MA: Spring Street Press; 1985. 68p. $8.95pbk. 0-931691-17-6.
This is a book of tables containing pertinent information about energy. Topics covered include units and conversion factors, geometrical formulas, the solar system, solar energy, degree-days with generalized maps, energy content of fuels, fossil fuels, nuclear fission and fusion, history of energy production and consumption, consumer prices of common sources of energy, and radiation exposures in the United States. *Grade Level:* Grades 9–12.
ARBA, 86, n.1463.

MEDICAL SCIENCES

Medicine is considered an applied science and concerns itself with all aspects of healing. In order to understand medicine, one must have a strong background in the physical sciences, especially chemistry, physics, and biology. The subfields of medicine can be divided into *clinicial* and *basic.* The basic medical sciences are close to and depend upon the pure sciences. They include *anatomy*—the study of all parts of the human body; *physiology*—the study of the vital functions of the human body and how they all work together to maintain life; *psychology*—the study of human behavior as it functions biologically and with the social environment; *pharmacology*—the study of how drugs or other chemicals affect the human body; *biochemistry*—the study of all chemical processes that take place in the human body; *microbiology*—the study of microorganisms that may affect the human body; and *pathology*—the study of how diseases alter the human body. Other areas related to the physical sciences include *biophysics*—the application of physics to biology; *embryology*—the study of the early development of life; *endocrinology*—the study of the body's endocrine system; and *genetics*—the study of genes and heredity.

Clinical medicine includes many specialities. Two broad specialties are *preventive medicine*—the study of how to prevent diseases—and *public health*—the study of how to maintain and promote good health. *Surgery* concerns itself with the treating of diseases through operations; *pediatrics*—the study and treatment of health and diseases in children; *psychiatry*—the treating of problems of the mind; and *obstetrics*—the treatment of all aspects of child bearing.

The more specialized areas of clinical medicine include: *anesthesiology*—the study of anesthesia and anesthetics; *cardiology*—the study of the heart and how it functions; *dentistry*—the study of teeth and the oral cavity; *dermatology*—the study of diagnosis and treatment of skin diseases; *gastroenterology*—the study of the stomach and intestines; *geriatrics*—treating the aged; *gerontology*—the study of the chemical, biological, historical, and sociological aspects of aging; *gynecology*—study and treatment of the diseases that effect the genital tract in women; *immunology*—the study of how human organisms react to antigens; *internal medicine*—a general study of all internal parts of the human body; *neurology*—the study of the nervous system, including neurosurgery; *nursing*—that aspect of helping individuals in their promotion, maintenance, and restoration to good health; *ophthalmology*—the study of all aspects of the eye; *orthopedics*—that part of surgery that is concerned with the restoration of the functions of bones; *otorhinolarygology*—the study of medical and surgical treatment of the head and neck including ears, nose, and throat; *plastic surgery*—the restoration or changing of physical features; *radiology*—the study of the use of radioactive substances in the diagnosis and treatment of diseases; *rehabilitation*—the study of restoring individuals to normal functions or as close to normal as possible; *serology*—the study of serums and their reactions on the body; *urology*—the study of the male and female urinary tract; and *venereology*—the study of sexually transmitted diseases. There are other specialized areas.

The reference literature is voluminous in the research fields, with a full range of dictionaries, encyclopedias, manuals, textbooks, indexes, abstracts, and guides in each of the various subfields. For young children, the reference books are general, covering broad areas of medicine. There are many dictionaries in medicine, most for the medical library. They are, however, just as useful in serving young people. Included are *Black's Medical Dictionary, Dorland's Illustrated Medical Dictionary, Medical Word Finder, Melloni's Illustrated Medical Dictionary, Webster's Medical Desk Dictionary,* and *Stedman's Medical Dictionary.* There are some good general medical encyclopedias for young people, such as *Prevention's New Encyclopedia of Common Diseases, World Encyclopedia of Food, New Child Health Encyclopedia: The Complete Guide for Parents,* and *The Columbia Encyclopedia of Nutrition.* Also included in this chapter are a number of medical guides that are basically family oriented, such as *The People's Medical Manual: Everything You Need to Know About Health and Safety.*

An effort has been made within this chapter to address one of the more frightening health topics of today's society—AIDS, by including several books that pertain to AIDS or sexually transmitted diseases. Young people need more educating in this area, and the topics of AIDS, sexually transmitted diseases, and safer sex cannot be stressed and discussed enough. Those books listed are some of the better ones. However, others are available, such as the *AIDS Information Sourcebook,* which will direct readers to additional sources of information about AIDS.

Atlases—Medical

609. Human Anatomy Atlas.
Charles N. Berry; Christian A. Hovde. Maplewood, NJ: Hammond; 1960. 1v. unpaged, color illus., index. $2.95. 0-8437-9083-0.
   This small atlas for young people contains 32 full-color illustrations depicting the fundamental structure of the human body. A glossary is included. *Grade Level:* Grades 3–5. Grades 6–8.

Bibliographies

610. AIDS (Acquired Immune Deficiency Syndrome).
David A. Tyckoson. Phoenix, AZ: Oryx Press; 1985–90. 5v., index.
$21.50 per volume. 0899-9449.
This bibliography series is designed for the layperson and student. It includes citations to articles in newspapers, journals, and some monographs, most of which would be available in libraries serving these individuals. Each bibliography is arranged by topic, with the topics varying from issue to issue. Brief annotations are included. *Grade Level:* Grades 9–12.
ARBA, 87, n.1624; BL, 1 December 85, p.546; Choice, May 87, p.1383; SB, January 86, p.157; STARR, 90, n.379.

Dictionaries

611. AIDS to Zits: A "Sextionary" for Kids.
Carole S. Marsh. Bath, NC: Gallopade; 1987. 28p. $4.95pbk.
1-55609-210-5pbk.
This is by far the most interesting and well-written dictionary of sex terms for children. The definitions are frank and may offend some people, but they are written in vocabulary that a child can understand. The dictionary is more than just a dictionary; it gives advice on safe sex and what happens if one does not practice safe sex or birth control. *Grade Level:* Grades 3–5. Grades 6–8.
STARR, 89, n.365.

612. Black's Medical Dictionary.
35th. C.W.H. Havard, ed. Totowa, NJ: Barnes & Noble; 1987. 750p., illus. $36.95. 0-389-20745-4.
This excellent dictionary defines medical terms for the layperson. It is up-to-date and keeps the reader's or patient's interest in mind when defining a term. *Grade Level:* Grades 9–12.
ARBA, 89, n.1537; Choice, January 88, p.741.

613. Blakiston's Gould Medical Dictionary: A Modern Comprehensive Dictionary of the Terms Used in All Branches of Medicine and Allied Sciences.
4th. New York, NY: McGraw-Hill; 1979. 1,632p., illus. $39.00.
0-07-005700-1.
This good medical dictionary published in the United States covers all branches of medicine and contains over 75,000 terms. A smaller pocket size edition is called *Blakiston's Pocket Medical Dictionary*. *Grade Level:* Grades 9–12.
BL 1 September 84, p.38.

614. Dictionary of Drug Abuse Terms and Terminology.
Ernest L. Abel. Westport, CT: Greenwood Press; 1984. 187p., bibliog.
$35.00. 0-313-24095-7.
This dictionary contains some 3,000 terms covering drugs and drug abuse. There is emphasis on slang expressions for drugs, but the book lacks those for alcohol and tobacco abuse. *Grade Level:* Grades 9–12.
ARBA, 85, n.1578; BL, 15 June 85, p.1441; Choice, April 85, p.1135; SciTech, June 85, p.18.

615. Dorland's Illustrated Medical Dictionary.
27th. Philadelphia, PA: Saunders; 1988. 1,888p., illus. $42.00.
0-7216-3154-1.
This standard medical dictionary gives concise definitions, pronunciations, and derivations. There are two shorter versions of this work: *Dorland's Pocket Medical Dictionary* and *Dorland's Medical Dictionary: Shorter Version. Grade Level:* Grades 9–12.
ARBA, 89, n.1538; BL, 1 December 88, p.620; LJ, 1 November 88, p.46; R&RBkN, August 88, p.27.

616. Folk Name and Trade Diseases.
E.R. Plunkett. Stamford, CT: Barrett Book; 1978. 352p., illus. $17.95.
0-932684-00-9.
This delightful dictionary of diseases and afflictions that have had some reference to folk and trade history covers ailments such as academy headache, zipper trauma, and black jack disease. Each entry is defined in medically accurate terms, with reference to its first mention in the literature by its given name. *Grade Level:* Grades 9–12.
ARBA, 80, p.687.

617. Food Additives Dictionary.
Melvin A. Benarde. New York, NY: Simon and Schuster; 1981. 93p.
$4.95. A Wallaby Book. 0-671-42837-3.
This very brief dictionary of food additive terms was compiled for the layperson and student, and should not be considered as a research reference publication. Contains 158 definitions. *Grade Level:* Grades 9–12.
ARBA, 83, n.1491; BL, 15 March 82, p.933.

618. Medical Meanings: A Glossary of Word Origins.
William S. Haubrich. San Diego, CA: Harcourt Brace Jovanovich; 1984. 285p., illus., index. $9.95. 0-15-65857-3.
This is a glossary of over 1,000 medical terms, prefixes, and suffixes, giving concise, nontechnical definitions and containing etymologies and historical and mythological anecdotes. *Grade Level:* Grades 9–12.
ARBA, 85, n.1541; SB, March 85, p.206.

619. Medical Word Finder.
4th. George Willeford, Jr., comp. Englewood Cliffs, NJ: Prentice-Hall; 1983. 433p. $19.95. 0-13-947326-2.

This is a dictionary to help in spelling medical terms correctly or to locate the right medical term when needed. Syllabication is given and phonetic spellings are provided for problem words. Although not a true dictionary in the sense of supplying definitions, it has many of the other elements found in dictionaries. *Grade Level:* Grades 9–12. ARBA, 84, n.1424.

620. Melloni's Illustrated Medical Dictionary.
2nd. Ida Dox; Biagio John Melloni; Gilbert M. Eisner. Baltimore, MD: Williams and Wilkins; 1985. 533p., color illus. $24.95. 0-683-02641-0.
This is a good general medical dictionary of over 25,000 terms. The illustrations complement the definitions, which are more useful for the general reader than the researcher. It includes anatomical tables and commonly used chemical compounds and drugs. *Grade Level:* Grades 9–12.
ARBA, 80, n.1496; BL, August 82, p.1553; LJ, 15 May 81, p.1044; SLJ, December 80, p.22; WLB, January 80, p.330.

621. People's Handbook of Allergies and Allergens.
Ruth Winter. Chicago, IL: Contemporary Books; 1984. 168p. $8.95pbk. 0-8092-5391-7pbk.
This dictionary of over 500 terms relating to allergies and allergens is intended for general use by those with allergies, but health professionals will also find it useful. *Grade Level:* Grades 9–12.
ARBA, 86, n.1653; BL, 1 April 85, p.1107; LJ, 1 February 85, p.88.

622. Sex A to Z.
Robert M. Goldenson; Kenneth N. Anderson. New York, NY: World Almanac; 1989 (c1986). 314p. $9.95pbk. 0-88687-410-6pbk.
This excellent dictionary, first published in hardback as *Language of Sex from A to Z*, is comprehensive, accurate, and well-written. It includes sex terms and slang from many disciplines, including gay and lesbian. Some defined terms and phrases may embarrass some readers. *Grade Level:* Grades 9–12.

623. The Slang and Jargon of Drugs and Drink.
Richard A. Spears. Metuchen, NJ: Scarecrow; 1986. 585p. $42.50. 0-8108-1864-7.
This is a dictionary of terms that relate to drugs, alcohol, and tobacco from 1700 to the present. There are some 8,000 entries and 10,000 definitions. Each entry includes definitions, alternate spellings, parts of speech, dates, geographic origin, and source of the term. *Grade Level:* Grades 9–12.
ARBA, 87, n.1631; BL, August 86, p.1676; Choice, June 86, p.1526; WLB, May 86, p.64.

624. Stedman's Medical Dictionary.
25th. William R. Hensyl; Jacquelyn O. Oldham, eds. Baltimore, MD: Williams and Wilkins; 1989. 1,678p., illus., index. $35.95. 0-683-07916-6.

The definitions in this dictionary are grouped by category. Each term is defined for the professional. Cross-references are not found in the text but are included in an appendix. Eponymic terms are cross-referenced to diseases and syndromes. Brief biographical information is included. Special sections include instructions for use of the book, medical etymology, blood groups, a glossary of common Latin terms used in prescription writing, symbols and abbreviations, and results of laboratory analysis. *Grade Level:* Grades 9–12.
ALib, May 74, p.250; ARBA, 83, n.1445; SB, December 72, p. 257.

625. Webster's Medical Desk Dictionary.
Springfield, MA: Merriam-Webster; 1986. 790p. $18.95. 0-87779-025-6.
This excellent dictionary of contemporary usage of medical terms includes both American and British usage and spellings. Eponyms include a brief biographical sketch of the person. There are no illustrations. *Grade Level:* Grades 6–8. Grades 9–12.
ARBA, 87, n.1604; BL, 1 March 87, p.1003; SciTech, December 86, p.19, February 87, p.21.

Directories

626. AIDS Information Sourcebook.
2nd. H. Robert Malinowsky; Gerald J. Perry. Phoenix, AZ: Oryx Press; 1989. 224p., bibliog., index. $32.50. 0-89774-544-2. 1044-2138.
This sourcebook contains a chronology of AIDS events, directory of AIDS facilities, and bibliographies. It is updated on a regular basis. There are indexes to all sections, and appendices of other AIDS information. *Grade Level:* Grades 9–12. Teacher's/Librarian's Resource.
ALib, April 88, p.322; ARBA, 89, n.1560; BL, 15 June 88, p.1715; Choice, July 88, p.1671; LJ, 15 April 89, p.38; R&RBkN, June 88, p.26; SB, January 89, p.159; STARR, 90, n.532; WLB May 88, p.103.

Encyclopedias

627. Childhood Symptoms: Every Parent's Guide to Childhood Illnesses.
Edward R. Brace; John P. Pacanowski. New York, NY: Harper and Row; 1985. 322p. $10.95pbk. 0-06-181098-3pbk.
This is an alphabetically arranged encyclopedia of over 500 entries pertaining to children's health, including childhood diseases. The entries are well-written, with a minimum of medical jargon. *Grade Level:* Grades 9–12.
ARBA, 86, n.1647; KR, 15 December 84, p.1177; LJ, 1 April 85, p.134.

628. The Columbia Encyclopedia of Nutrition.
Myron Winick, ed. New York, NY: Putnam; 1988. 349p., index.
$19.95. 0-399-13298-8.
This is a good general encyclopedia covering all aspects of nutrition,
including vitamins, diet, caffeine, weight reduction, cancer and other
disease prevention, and good health habits. It contains good rec-
ommendations, many tables of information, and sample menus. *Grade
Level:* Grades 9–12.
ARBA, 89, n.1519; BL 15 September 88, p.132; LJ, 1 June 88, p.102.

629. Communicable Diseases.
Thomas H. Metos. New York, NY: Franklin Watts; 1987. 96p., illus.,
bibliog., glossary, index. $9.90. A First Book. 0-531-10380-3.
This excellent encyclopedia covers the various communicable diseases
from the common cold to the deadly AIDS virus. It is very well-written in nontechnical language for teen-agers and adults with no scientific background. The facts are presented briefly but completely and
illustrated with excellent photographs. The four pages devoted to AIDS
are particularly well-written. *Grade Level:* Grades 3–5. Grades 6–8.
ASBYP, Summer 88, p.52; BL, 1 January 88, p.779; BRpt, January 88,
p.44; SB, March 88, p.246; SLJ, March 88, p.218; STARR, 89, n.289.

**630. Encyclopedia and Dictionary of Medicine, Nursing, and Allied
Health.**
3rd. Benjamin Frank Miller; Claire Brackman Keane. Philadelphia,
PA: Saunders; 1983. 1,270p., illus. $19.95. 0-7216-6364-8.
This comprehensive encyclopedia gives definitions of a large number
of terms, with cross-references and indications of pronunciation. The
definitions are brief but adequate. Some concepts are discussed at
length. *Grade Level:* Grades 9–12.
ARBA, 79, n.1463; 1 September 84, p.38.

631. The Human Body.
Revised. Steve Parker; Alan Maryon-Davis. New York, NY: Franklin
Watts; 1989. 6v., color illus., glossary, index. $12.40 per volume.
This well-illustrated encyclopedia covers, in six volumes, touch, taste
and smell; ear and hearing; skeleton and movement; heart and blood;
lungs and breathing; and eye and seeing. Each volume contains a
glossary. *Grade Level:* Grades 3–5. Grades 6–8.

**632. New Child Health Encyclopedia: The Complete Guide for
Parents.**
Boston Children's Hospital. Frederick H. Lovejoy; David Estridge,
eds. New York, NY: Dell; 1987. 740p. $19.95pbk. 0-385-29597-9pbk.
This is a book for parents about child health from infancy to adoles-
cence. The main part of this encyclopedic reference is alphabetically
arranged by childhood disease and symptomatic indication. It provides
good, general treatment of child health and would be useful as a home
reference source. *Grade Level:* Grades 9–12.
BL, 1 December 87, p.595; LJ, 15 November 87, p.72.

633. The Nutrition and Health Encyclopedia.
2nd. David F. Tver; Percy Russell. New York, NY: Van Nostrand
Reinhold; 1989. 639p., illus., tables, charts. $39.95. 0-442-23397-3.
This alphabetically arranged encyclopedia contains a wealth of information, including body chemistry and composition, major foods,
food additives and food toxins, nutrition-related diseases, metabolic
functions, and food and drug interactions. The text is supplemented by
the use of many charts and tables. *Grade Level:* Grades 9–12.

634. Penguin Encyclopaedia of Nutrition.
John Yudkin. New York, NY: Viking; 1985. 431p., illus., index.
$7.95. 0-14-008563-7.
This excellent, inexpensive encyclopedia covers all aspects of nutrition.
It includes information on diets, vitamins and minerals, food supplies
and population, and food distribution and preservation. The text is
well-written, with a minimum of technical jargon, and intended for the
layperson. *Grade Level:* Grades 9–12.
ARBA, 86, n.1449; BL, July 85, p.1492; Choice, November 85, p.432;
LJ, July 85, p.60.

**635. The People's Medical Manual: Everything You Need to Know
About Health and Safety.**
Howard R. Lewis; Martha E. Lewis. New York, NY: Doubleday/Dial;
1986. 578p., illus. $19.95. 0-385-27649-4.
More than 500 alphabetically arranged entries cover virtually any
health-related problem in this encyclopedia, with emphasis on prevent-
ing and remedying accidents; dispelling medical myths and lay misin-
formation; and providing patients with correct information, enabling
them to ask the right questions of their physician when seeking medical treatment. It is well-written, easily understood, and intended for
the layperson and student. *Grade Level:* Grades 6–8. Grades 9–12.
ARBA, 87, n.1611; BL, 1 September 86, p.45; LJ, 15 March 86, p.74;
SciTech, June 86, p.17.

636. Prevention's New Encyclopedia of Common Diseases.
Prevention Magazine Editors. Emmaus, PA: Rodale Press; 1984.
1,048p., illus., index. $21.95. 0-87857-496-4.
Formerly called *The Encyclopedia of Common Diseases*, this book's
125 chapters cover a broad spectrum of diseases in topical fashion,
such as "Alcoholism," "Back Problems," "Cancer," "Heart Disease,"
and "Restless Legs Syndrome." Well-written and accurate, with references to journals and books given in some cases. *Grade Level:* Grades
9–12.
ARBA, 85, n.1564; BL, 15 May 84, p.1281; Choice, December 76,
p.1268; SB, September 85, p.27.

**637. The World Book Medical Encyclopedia: Your Guide to Good
Health.**
Chicago, IL: World Book, Inc; 1988. 1,040p., illus. (part in color),
tables, charts, index. $44.95. 0-7166-3195-4.

This is a general encyclopedia covering anatomy, physiology, diseases, disorders, symptoms, therapies, procedures, and the health care system. There is also coverage of exercise, nutrition, vitamins, smoking, alcoholism, drug addiction, and hygiene, as well as safety and first aid information. *Grade Level:* Grades 6–8. Grades 9–12.

638. World Encyclopedia of Food.
L. Patrick Coyle. New York, NY: Facts on File; 1982. 790p., illus. $40.00. 0-87196-417-1.
This is a good general encyclopedia on food and beverage with over 4,000 entries. For each entry identification, description, geographic location, method of consumption, and history are given. It covers all possible sources of food, including animals, fish, vegetables, fruits, grains, and prepared foods. The tables cover "Nutritive Values of the Edible Parts of Foods," "Wine and Liquor Terms," "Sodium Content of Foods," and "Cooking, Menu and Canning Terms." *Grade Level:* Grades 6–8. Grades 9–12.
ARBA, 83, n.1492; BL, 1 February 83, p.706, 15 November 83, p.485; Choice, February 83, p.807; LJ, 15 December 82, p.2329, 15 May 83, p.964; PW, 19 November 82, p.71; WLB, January 83, p.433.

Guides

639. American Medical Association Family Medical Guide.
Revised and updated. Jeffrey R.M. Kunz; Asher J. Finkel, eds. New York, NY: Random House; 1987. 832p., illus., index. $29.95. 0-394-55582-1.
Compiled and recommended by the American Medical Association, this is one of the better family guides. It is well-written with a limited amount of medical jargon. The four sections cover: "The healthy body," "Symptoms and self-diagnosis," "Diseases and other disorders and problems," and "Caring for the sick." There are many family health guides available, and new ones are being published each year, but this is one of the better ones. *Grade Level:* Grades 9–12.
ARBA, 83, n.1462; BL, 15 January 84, p.730; Choice, January 83, p.728; LJ, 15 November 82, p.2183.

640. Complete Guide to Sports Injuries: How to Treat Fractures, Bruises, Sprains, Dislocations, Head Injuries.
H. Winter Griffith. Tucson, AZ: Body Press/HP Books; 1986. 528p., illus., index. $12.95pbk. 0-89586-379-0pbk.
This nontechnical book for the sports person covers 173 of the most common sports injuries. It is alphabetically arranged in two sections, injuries and medicine. Each injury is well-described and includes a definition of the problem, the body part involved, signs and symptoms, causes, risks, preventions, complications, treatment, and advice. *Grade Level:* Grades 9–12.
ARBA, 87, n.1620; BL, July 86, p.1577; LJ 1 June 86, p.132; PW, 16 May 86, p.73.

641. "Does AIDS Hurt?": Educating Young Children About AIDS, Suggestions for Parents, Teachers and Other Care Providers of Children to Age 10.
Marcia Quackenbush; Sylvia Villarreal. Santa Cruz, CA: Network Publications; 1988. 149p., bibliog. $14.95pbk. 0-941816-52-4pbk.
This excellent book about AIDS gives facts, sometimes frankly, with much of the information in the form of questions and answers. Most of the information is aimed at parents and teachers, especially the chapter, "How to do it right," about when a school has an infected child. *Grade Level:* Grades 3–5. Grades 6–8. Grades 9–12.
STARR, 90, n.386.

642. The Good Health Book: A Guide to the Origins and Symptoms of Illness and What You Can Do to Get Well and Stay Well.
David E. Wyatt. Chicago, IL: Nelson-Hall; 1981. 490p. $27.95.
The 21 chapters of this guide cover body systems, diseases, obesity, diets, and stress. It is written for the layperson with a minimum of technical jargon. Various medical terms are defined within the text. *Grade Level:* Grades 9–12.
BL, 1 January 83, p.634.

643. Know About AIDS.
Margaret O. Hyde; Elizabeth H. Forsyth. New York, NY: Walker and Co; 1987. 68p., illus., bibliog., index. $10.95. 0-8027-6738-9.
This excellent guide covers all areas of AIDS in a factual, easy-to-read style. It does not go into great detail, but the book gives enough information to end any confusion a student might have about AIDS. *Grade Level:* Grades 3–5. Grades 6–8.
ASBYP, Fall 88, p.34; SB, May 88, p.302; SLJ, November 87, p.100; STARR, 89, n.317; WLB, March 88, p.37.

644. People's Guide to Vitamins and Minerals, From A to Zinc.
Newly revised. Dominick Bosco. Chicago, IL: Contemporary Books; 1989. 351p., bibliog., index. $11.95. 0-8092-4582-5.
This guide for the layperson and student provides information about the vitamins and minerals known to be essential for proper nutrition. In addition to discussing 16 vitamins and 16 minerals, it covers the so-called "outlaw vitamins" that have not been officially recognized by the FDA. *Grade Level:* Grades 9–12.
ARBA, 81, n.1584; BL, 15 May 89, p.1592; LJ, 1 March 81, p.518; SB, May 81, p.265.

645. Plain Words About AIDS.
3rd. William Hovey Smith, ed. Sandersville, GA: Whitehall Press-Budget Publications; 1988. 204p., illus., tables, charts, glossary, bibliog., index. $19.50pbk. 0-916565-11-4pbk.
This guide contains facts about AIDS and AIDS education. It gives historical summaries as well as current information in the form of tables and charts. An excellent glossary of terms related to AIDS is included. *Grade Level:* Grades 6–8. Grades 9–12.

646. The Pocket Medical Encyclopedia and First Aid Guide.
James Bevan. New York, NY: Simon and Schuster; 1979. 144p., illus.
(part in color). $4.95pbk. 0-671-24671-2.
This first aid guide to emergencies is divided into three parts, with the
following information about care given in each: first aid and survival;
the human body and medical problems; and safety, health, and drugs.
Grade Level: Grades 6–8. Grades 9–12.
ARBA, 80, n.1518.

**647. Safe Sex: What Everyone Should Know About Sexually
Transmitted Diseases.**
Angelo T. Scott; Thomas A. Moore. New York, NY: PaperJacks;
1987. 216p., index. $3.95pbk. 0-7701-0641-2pbk.
This is a handy guide to sexually transmitted diseases, giving facts
about symptoms, routes of transmission, affects on pregnancy, contra-
ception, gay men, drugs, and emotional aspects. Each disease is de-
scribed briefly but concisely, using as few technical terms as possible.
Grade Level: Grades 9–12.
STARR, 90, n.392.

648. Sex Care: The Complete Guide to Safe and Healthy Sex.
Timothy R. Covington; J. Frank McClendon. New York, NY: Pocket
Books/Simon & Schuster; 1987. 402p., illus., index. $8.95pbk.
0-671-52398-8pbk.
This excellent guide to safe sex practices includes information on
IUDs, condoms, creams, gels, foams, sterilization, abstinence, rhythm,
sexually transmitted diseases, AIDS, PMS, abortion, hygiene, and sex-
ual myths. It discusses all topics frankly and directly. *Grade Level:*
Grades 9–12.
ARBA, 89, n.1546; BL, 15 July 87, p.1547; LJ, July 87, p.67.

**649. Straight Talk: Answers to Questions Young People Ask About
Alcohol.**
Ralph Jones. Bradenton, FL: Human Services Institute; 1989. 88p.,
bibliog. $4.95pbk. 0-8306-9005-0pbk.
This excellent guide, in question and answer format, covers all aspects
of alcohol and alcoholism. It is intended to create an awareness within
the teenagers so they can help others or recognize their own problems.
It should be required reading for all teenagers. *Grade Level:* Grades
6–8. Grades 9–12.

650. Teaching About A.I.D.S.: A Teacher's Guide.
Danek S. Kaus; Robert D. Reed. Saratoga, CA: R&E Publishers;
1987. 75p., bibliog. $6.50pbk. 0-88247-766-8pbk.
The publishers have combined information from several of their other
publications to produce a teacher's guide for AIDS instruction in the
schools. It includes discussions and a series of questions and answers
about AIDS. This is one of the better teaching guides. *Grade Level:*
Grades 3–5. Grades 6–8. Grades 9–12. Teacher's/Librarian's Resource.
STARR, 89, n.318.

651. Teen Guide to Safe Sex.
Alan E. Nourse. New York, NY: Franklin Watts; 1988. 61p., color illus., glossary, index. $5.95. 0-531-10592-X.
This guide covers sexually transmitted diseases, how they are contacted, treated, and prevented. The discussions are brief but accurate, including information on AIDS. *Grade Level:* Grades 9–12.

652. Understanding AIDS.
Ethan A. Lerner. Minneapolis, MN: Lerner Publications; 1987. 64p., illus., glossary, index. $9.95. 0-8225-0024-8.
This well-written book for children is one of the few available providing straightforward facts about AIDS education. It covers information about AIDS, blood transfusions; hemophilia, and drug abuse. The material is presented in story form. *Grade Level:* Grades 3–5. Grades 6–8.
ASBYP, Winter 88, p.43; SB, May 88, p.311; SLJ, November 87, p.108; STARR, 89, n.320.

Handbooks

653. AIDS: What Does It Mean to You?.
Revised. Margaret O. Hyde; Elizabeth H. Forsyth. New York, NY: Walker and Co; 1987. 116p., illus., glossary, index. $12.95. 0-8027-6699-4.
This popular general information handbook is aimed primarily at audience is young adults, who may have many misconceptions about AIDS. It is written in straightforward language, covering history, possible causes, research needs, and the epidemic of fear. *Grade Level:* Grades 6–8. Grades 9–12.
BL, 15 March 87, p.1433; BRpt, November 87, p.45; SLJ, August 87, p.95, September 87, p.129; STARR, 89, n.294; WLB, March 88, p.37, April 88, p.74.

654. A.I.D.S.: Your Child and the School.
Danek S. Kaus; Robert D. Reed. Saratoga, CA: R & E Publishers; 1986. 24p., illus., bibliog. $3.00pbk. 0-88247-756-0pbk.
This small handbook is a guide for teachers and parents. It presents the facts about AIDS in a straightforward text that is accurate and easy to understand. Information included covers the definition of AIDS, symptoms, statistics, AIDS by ethnic group and gender, who is at risk, guidelines for admitting children with AIDS to schools, and some common sense and caring information. *Grade Level:* Grades 3–5. Grades 6–8. Grades 9–12. Teacher's/Librarian's Resource.
STARR, 89, n.295.

655. AMA Handbook of Poisonous and Injurious Plants.
Kenneth F. Lampe; Mary Ann McCann. Chicago, IL: American Medical Association; 1985. 432p., color illus., bibliog., index. $28.00. 0-89970-183-3.

The primary purpose of this handbook is to aid physicians in treating patients who have become ill from plants. It is also a field guide and handbook to these poisonous and injurious plants. The sections cover "Systemic plant poisoning," "Plant dermatitis," and "Mushroom poisoning." For the plants listed in the first section, trivial names, description, geographic distribution, toxic part, toxin, symptoms, management, and literature references are given. The other two sections list the needed information in the form of tables. *Grade Level:* Grades 9–12.
ARBA, 86, n.1613; BL, August 85, p.1613.

656. Barron's Sports Injuries Handbook.
J.P.R. Williams. Hauppauge, NY: Barron's; 1988. 160p., illus (part in color), index. $12.95. 0-8120-5915-8.
This good general handbook for those involved in physical fitness and sports gives information covering general fitness, general sports-related injuries, first aid, and specific sports-related injuries. *Grade Level:* Grades 9–12.
ARBA 89, n.1574.

657. Complete Book of Vitamins and Minerals.
Consumer Guide Editors. Lincolnwood, IL: Publications International; 1988. 320p., index. $3.95pbk. 0-451-15747-8pbk.
This well-written handbook advises the reader on the importance of well-balanced diets and the need for vitamins and minerals. It stresses that physicians should be consulted before taking vitamin supplements. Part of the book is an encyclopedia of "Supplement Product Profiles," where each product is described in detail. *Grade Level:* Grades 9–12.
ARBA,89, n.1587.

658. Dr. Heimlich's Home Guide to Emergency Medical Situations.
Henry J. Heimlich; Lawrence Galton. New York, NY: Simon and Schuster; 1984 (c1980). 350p., illus., index. $10.95, $5.95pbk. 0-671-24947-9, 0-671-53075-5pbk.
This well-organized handbook covers 250 medical situations. It is divided into three parts. Part one covers general information on what to do until the medical personnel arrive, including advice on bleeding, poisoning, shock, abdominal and chest pain, choking, cardiopulmonary resuscitation, burns, amputations, and coughing. Part two is a cross-reference guide to medical situations, and part three covers acute emergency reactions from drugs. *Grade Level:* Grades 9–12.
ARBA, 81, n.1592; BL, 1 June 80, p.1396; KR, 1 February 80, p.184; LJ, 1 April 80, p.869; PW, 8 February 80, p.76; SB, January 81, p.144; WLB, September 80, p.63.

659. Food Values of Portions Commonly Served.
14th. Jean A.G. Pennington; Helen Nichols Church. New York, NY: Harper and Row; 1985. 257p. $17.45. 0-06-181679-5.

For the nutritionist, dietician, student, or layperson, this handbook gives all of the food values of the portions of food that are commonly served. Each food is listed with information about its food values. *Grade Level:* Grades 9-12.
BW, 19 October 80, p.12.

660. Handbook of Poisoning: Prevention, Diagnosis and Treatment.
12th. Robert H. Dreisbach; William O. Robertson. Norwalk, CT: Appleton & Lange; 1987. 589p., illus., index. $16.50. 0-8385-3643-3.
The general considerations of prevention, diagnosis, evaluation, management, and the legal and medial aspects of poisoning are discussed in this handbook. The text is divided into six groups: agricultural, industrial, household, medicinal, animals, and plants. The clinical findings, prevention, treatment, and prognosis are given for each material. *Grade Level:* Grades 9-12.
ARBA, 81, n.1561.

661. Infections in Children: A Sourcebook for Educators and Child Care Providers.
Richard D. Andersen. Rockville, MD: Aspen; 1986. 221p., color illus., bibliog., index. $25.95. 0-87189-379-7.
This is a handbook for persons needing information on the various infectious childhood diseases. The book provides suggestions on how to prevent cross-contamination, an overview of specific infections, and the management and prevention of such infections. There is a chapter on AIDS. *Grade Level:* Grades 6-8. Grades 9-12. Teacher's/Librarian's Resource.
ARBA, 87, n.1591.

662. The Nutrition Desk Reference.
Robert H. Garrison, Jr.; Elizabeth Somer. New Canaan, CT: Keats Publishing; 1985. 245p., index. $29.95. 0-87983-328-9.
The six chapters of this handbook cover dietary factors, vitamin and mineral research, nutrition and cancer, nutrition and cardiovascular disease, dietary recommendations, and nutrition and drugs Intended for the layperson, the book is also useful to health professionals and students. *Grade Level:* Grades 9-12.
ARBA, 86, n.1452; BL, 15 January 86, p.745; Choice, October 85, p.324; LJ, 15 April 86, p.36.

663. The Sexually Transmitted Diseases.
Charles E. Rinear. Jefferson, NC: McFarland; 1986. 214p., illus., index. $19.95. 0-89950-185-0.
This handbook covers 30 sexually transmitted diseases, giving common name, incidence and prevalence, incubation period, symptoms, period of being communicable, mode of transmission, susceptibility, resistance, diagnosis, and treatment. *Grade Level:* Grades 9-12.

664. Sexually Transmitted Diseases: A Handbook of Protection, Prevention and Treatment.
C. Howard Tseng; T. Guilas Villanueva; Alvin Powell. Saratoga, CA: R&E Publishers; 1987. 154p. $9.95pbk. 0-88247-770-6pbk.
Each sexually transmitted disease is described in frank terms in this handbook through the use of questions and answers. It includes an extensive chapter on AIDS. *Grade Level:* Grades 9–12.
STARR, 90, n.400.

665. Simon and Schuster's Handbook of Anatomy and Physiology.
James Bevan. New York, NY: Simon and Schuster; 1978. 96p., illus. $8.95. 0-671-24959-2.
This well-written, small handbook is intended for the layperson and young child. It covers the cell, skeleton, joints, blood, respiration, digestion, urinary system, eye, ear, skin, hair, nails, touch, taste, smell, sex, pregnancy, children, growth, metabolism, and nutrition. In the outer margins of each chapter is a running glossary. *Grade Level:* Grades 3–5. Grades 6–8. Grades 9–12.
BL, 1 November 80, p.416; Kliatt, Winter 84, p.61.

666. Standard First Aid and Personal Safety.
2nd. American National Red Cross. New York, NY: Doubleday; 1979. 268p., illus., index. $2.50. 0-385-15736-3.
This is the handbook used in conjunction with the American Red Cross standard first aid and personal safety courses. It is intended to give all the necessary emergency information that may be needed, and is considered the standard first aid handbook. *Grade Level:* Grades 6–8. Grades 9–12.

Histories

667. AIDS: The Facts.
John Langone. Boston, MA: Little, Brown; 1988. 247p., notes. $8.95pbk. 0-316-51412-8pbk.
This thumbnail history of the AIDS virus is frank in its discussions, particularly in the area of safe sex practices and the use of condoms, a controversy in some segments of society. *Grade Level:* Grades 9–12.
BL, 1 February 88, p.895; BRpt, January 88, p.47; KR, 15 December 87, p.1225; SB, January 89, p.159; STARR, 89, n.306.

668. The AIDS Reader.
Loren K. Clarke; Malcolm Potts, eds. Boston, MA: Branden Publishing; 1988. 330p., bibliog. $14.95pbk. 0-8283-1918-9pbk.
This well-written book provides a collection of material which traces the evolution of the disease, placing it in the present perspective of what is known. It is an historical reader, with the articles representing the evolution of the disease. *Grade Level:* Grades 9–12.
PW, 22 April 88, p.76; STARR, 89, n.307.

669. Medicine: An Illustrated History.
Albert S. Lyons; R. Joseph Petrucelli, II. New York, NY: Abradale Press/Abrams; 1987 (c1978). 616p., illus., bibliog., index. $75.00. 0-8109-8080-0.
This is an expensive publication for most school and public libraries, but it is a very interestingly written history of medicine. The book is fully illustrated and is intended for the layperson and student. *Grade Level:* Grades 9–12.
Choice, May 79, p.411; LJ, 15 March 79, p.743; PW, 6 November 78, p.71.

INDEXES

TITLE INDEX

All references are to entry numbers, not page numbers.

NAME INDEX

All references are to entry numbers, not page numbers.

SUBJECT INDEX

All references are to entry numbers, not page numbers.

GRADE LEVEL INDEX

All references are to entry numbers, not page numbers.

H. ROBERT MALINOWSKY

H. Robert Malinowsky is Professor, Bibliographer of Science and Technology, at the Library of the University of Illinois, Chicago. He is the editor of *Science and Technology Annual Reference Review*, *The International Directory of Gay and Lesbian Periodicals*, and *AIDS Information Sourcebook* (with Gerald J. Perry), all published by The Oryx Press.